THE FIFTH BIENNALE OF SYDNEY
PRIVATE SYMBOL : SOCIAL METAPHOR

11 April — 17 June 1984

DIRECTOR OF THE FIFTH BIENNALE

Leon Paroissien
Former Director of the Visual Arts Board of the Australia
Council, currently Editor of *Australian Art Review*, Co-Curator of
the Power Gallery of Contemporary Art, University of Sydney,
and a Director on the Board of the Biennale of Sydney.

THE BOARD OF THE BIENNALE OF SYDNEY

Chairman: Franco Belgiorno-Nettis CBE
Chairman of the Board of the Biennale of Sydney and Chairman
of Transfield Pty Ltd.

Deputy Chairman: Elwyn Lynn AM
Editor of *Art & Australia*, former Chairman of the Visual Arts
Board of the Australia Council and former Curator, Power Gallery
of Contemporary Art, University of Sydney.

Director: Suzanne Davies
Art historian, art critic, writer; Vice President and Chairperson of
the Print Council of Australia; founding member of LIP Feminist
Arts Journal Publishing Co-operative; Lecturer, Melbourne College
of Advanced Education.

Director: Mike Parr
Australian artist, represented in the 1980 Biennale of Venice and
the Fourth Biennale of Sydney 1982, currently lecturer at the
Sydney College of the Arts.

Director: Tony Winterbotham
Executive Assistant to the Chairman of Transfield Pty Ltd.

Director: William Wright
Assistant Director (Professional) of the Art Gallery of New South
Wales, Director of the Fourth Biennale of Sydney (1982), former
Dean of Visual Arts, State University of New York at Purchase,
former Director of the New York Studio School.

Director: Robert Owen (until November 1983)
Australian artist, represented in the Biennale of Venice 1978;
member of the Board of the Fourth Biennale of Sydney 1982.

Observer: Ross Wolfe (from November 1983)
Founder and former Co-Editor of *Art Network*; from November
1983, Director of the Visual Arts Board of the Australia Council

Observer: Nick Waterlow (until November 1983)
Director of the Third Biennale of Sydney 1979, until November
1983 Director of the Visual Arts Board of the Australia Council

SECRETARIAT

Paula Latos-Valier
Assistant Director and
Head of Secretariat

Elizabeth Westwater
Exhibition assistant and
Office Administration

CONSULTANTS & PROJECT ASSISTANCE

Ambra Sancin
Visitor Co-ordinator
Jan Meek
Public Relations
David Ell
Publishing consultant

Catalogue production

Compilation: Paula Latos-Valier and
Elizabeth Westwater
Printing: Gardner Printing Co. (Vic) Pty Ltd
Typesetting: Rochester Photosetting Service
Colour and halftone reproduction: FMF Colour
Creations Pty Ltd
Editing: Leon Paroissien
Proofing: Nancy Sibtain

Poster and catalogue cover design: John
Lethbridge
Poster printing: Bloxham & Chambers

Compilers' note:

Artists participating in the Biennale of Sydney
appear in alphabetical order in this catalogue,
both in the visual and the biographical sections.

The biographies and other information in this
catalogue have been compiled from information
received from each artist or artist's
representative at the time of publication.

Biographies are selected only and have been
edited for the purposes of this publication. In
many cases, specific information regarding
biographies and works included in the
exhibition was not available at the time of
publication.

Critical and/or artists' statements preceding
biographical material were received from each
artist or artist's representative. Wherever
possible the Biennale of Sydney has ensured
that copyright clearance has been obtained.

All dimensions are for unframed works except
in instances where no other dimensions have
been available. All dimensions are in
centimetres unless otherwise indicated.
Dimensions are shown in this sequence:
height × width × depth.

Credits for photography, loans and collections,
where provided, appear on each artist's
biographical page.

Biennale of Sydney (Fifth: 1984)
  Private Symbol : Social Metaphor

  Bibliography.
  Includes index.
  ISBN 0 9596619 3 X.

  1. Arts — New South Wales — Sydney —
Exhibitions.
  I. Title

700'.74'099441

Published by the Biennale of Sydney Limited,
100 George Street, Sydney, New South Wales,
Australia.

THE FIFTH BIENNALE OF SYDNEY
PRIVATE SYMBOL : SOCIAL METAPHOR

11 April — 17 June 1984

Art Gallery of New South Wales
Art Gallery Road, Sydney

Ivan Dougherty Gallery
City Art Institute
Cnr Albion Ave & Selwyn Street
Paddington

**Aspects of Australian Figurative Painting
1942-1962**
S H Ervin Gallery
National Trust
Observatory Hill

Colin McCahon
Power Gallery of Contemporary Art
University of Sydney

Biennale Forums
13-15 April
Merewether Building, University of Sydney
Organised by the Power Institute of Fine Arts

Contents

Biennale Board and Secretariat

Acknowledgement

Chairman's Preface

Sponsors of the Fifth Biennale

Director's Introduction
Leon Paroissien

Drift
Stuart Morgan

*Latin America: Cultures of Repetition or
Cultures of Difference?*
Nelly Richard

*The German Situation, or the Other Side of
the "Wilden" Coin*
Annelie Pohlen

*Tactics and Strategies: An Abbreviated Guide
to Art in New York after the War*
Carter Ratcliff

In the Darkness
Jean-Louis Pradel
Illustrations

Satellite exhibitions
Colin McCahon
Aspects of Australian Figurative Painting
1942-1962

Artists' biographies

ACKNOWLEDGEMENTS

We are particularly grateful to the artists, their representatives, and those individuals, galleries and other institutions who have made this exhibition possible by lending works to the three exhibitions which constitute the Fifth Biennale of Sydney. They have made it possible to assemble in Sydney works from many parts of Australia and from 19 participating countries.

We are especially indebted to the trustees and the staff of the Art Gallery of New South Wales, which again is acting as host for the central contemporary section of the Fifth Biennale. The generous support and co-operation of the Director, the curators and all those departments involved in the preparation, installation and conservation of the exhibition are gratefully acknowledged.

We are also indebted to the Ivan Dougherty Gallery for providing exhibition space once again so that specially focused elements of the Biennale can be shown. The staff is warmly thanked for assistance with the installation of these works.

The two satellite exhibitions were made possible by the extraordinary efforts of a number of individuals:

The Power Gallery of Contemporary Art at the University of Sydney which has been a venue in the past, is on this occasion showing the Colin McCahon exhibition. This important survey of five decades of work by the artist was selected by Wystan Curnow. The National Art Gallery of New Zealand has generously organised the assembly and assisted with the installation. Our thanks go to the the staff of the Power Gallery for co-ordinating the showing of the exhibition.

The exhibition Aspects of Australian Figurative Painting 1942-1962 has been funded by a special exhibition grant from the Visual Arts Board of the Australia Council to the S.H. Ervin Gallery. We must thank Virginia Spate, Christine Dixon and Terry Smith, who were responsible for the selection and catalogue text of the exhibition. Thanks are also due to Dinah Dysart, Robyn Christie and Elizabeth Westwater who took responsibility for the considerable organisational burden of preparing this exhibition at such short notice.

We are especially grateful to the Department of Foreign Affairs, Canberra, and to the various Australian embassies and consulates that have given invaluable assistance in the difficult field of communication across great distances and many time zones. We are also very grateful to the embassies and consulates of participating countries for their assistance in the gathering of information and material essential for the realisation of the Biennale.

So many people in many countries and in diverse fields have supported our efforts over the two-year period of exhibition preparation. Our personal thanks go to the following:

Rini Dippel (Amsterdam); Alexa Johnston (Auckland); Bojana Peijic, Jadranka Vinterhalter (Belgrade); Elsa Fischer, Jean-Hubert Martin (Bern); Annelie Pohlen (Bonn); Malgorzata Potocka (Lodz); Brett Rogers (London); Michael McMillen (Los Angeles); Doris Olmeda (Mexico City); Flaminio Gualdoni, Tommaso Trini (Milan); John Stringer (New York); Yves Mabin (Paris); Monica Willshaw (Santiago); Russell Barker, Brigid Battersby, David Ell, Dagmar James, Felix Jones, Kerry Kinnane, Cathy Neville, Carol McFarlane, Boris Murphy, Marion Murphy, Robert Owen, Richard Pierse, Peter Rietz, Diana Smart, Connie Watkin, Joyce Weir, Evan Williams, Patsy Zeppel, Casey Zettler (Sydney); Shigeo Anzai, Ichiro Hariu, Hideo Kaido, Toshiaki Minemura, Fujiko Nakaya, Takatoshi Shinota, Bert Winther (Tokyo); David Burnett (Toronto); Dieter Ronte (Vienna); Wieslaw Borowski, Richard Boulez, Tadeusz Rolke (Warsaw); Ian Hunter, John McCormack (Wellington); Geoff Parr (Hobart). Finally special thanks are due to David Ell whose hard work and good advice helped make this publication a reality.

To name every individual who has helped with the complex organisation of the Fifth Biennale would be an impossible task. But to all those who have given freely of their advice and skills we express our deepest appreciation.

Leon Paroissien
Director

Paula Latos-Valier
Assistant Director

CHAIRMAN'S PREFACE

The Biennale of Sydney has entered its second decade. Since the first exhibition opened at the Sydney Opera House on 23 November 1973, the Biennale of Sydney has progressively reached an important place in Australia's art calendar and has won acknowledgement in many countries as a significant forum for contemporary art.

The Fifth Biennale will represent works by artists from 20 countries, the largest number of countries ever represented. It will be a more focused event with fewer artists being represented than in some previous Biennales.

Once again, I must express my gratitude to the Art Gallery of New South Wales as the main venue, the Power Gallery of Contemporary Art, and the Ivan Dougherty Gallery for providing exhibition space for the Biennale. This year another exhibition space, the S.H. Ervin Gallery, was generously made available by the National Trust of Australia.

I would like to extend a warm welcome to the 40 artists and critics from other countries who are visiting Sydney for the Fifth Biennale. I trust that for many of them this will be the first of a succession of visits to this country. Amongst these visitors are some who have attended previous Biennales and we are delighted to see them again.

On behalf of the Board of the Biennale I would like to thank the Australia Council, the New South Wales Government and the Council of the City of Sydney for their basic financial support. I would also like to thank the many funding agencies throughout the world for the support of their country's participation in the Biennale. Without this funding it would not be possible for the artists selected by the Biennale to be represented in this important exhibition. Other individuals and sponsors have made additional contributions and we are grateful for their support. Their names are listed elsewhere in this publication.

I would like also to express my deep appreciation to all those who have made the Fifth Biennale possible and hope that the Biennale of Sydney will continue to grow as a forum for contemporary art in this region of the world.

It is a great pleasure to see that Australia, having taken its place in the international arena in many fields, has now begun to be part of the international art community with a cultural focus of its own.

Franco Belgiorno-Nettis CBE
Chairman, Biennale of Sydney

SPONSORS OF THE FIFTH BIENNALE OF SYDNEY

Australia
Transfield Pty Ltd
Visual Arts Board of the Australia Council
New South Wales Government, Division of Cultural Activities
Council of the City of Sydney
Qantas Airways Limited
Trans Australia Airlines
The Flying Tiger Line Inc

Overseas
Bundesministerium für Unterricht und Kunst, Austria
Fundação Nacional de Arte, Ministério da Educaçao e Cultura, Brazil
The British Council, Britain
The Canada Council, Canada
Department of External Affairs, Canada
Komiteen for Internationale Kunstudstillinger, Denmark
Association Française d'Action Artistique, France
Ministry of Culture, Republic of Ireland
Ministero degli Affari Esteri, Italy
The Japan Foundation
Bureau Beeldende Kunst Buitenland, Netherlands
Queen Elizabeth II Arts Council, New Zealand
Ministry of Culture, Poland
Office Fédéral de la Culture, Switzerland
Institut für Auslandsbeziehungen, West Germany
Savezni Zavod Za Medunarodnu Znanstvenu, Prosvetno-Kulturnu I Tehničku Saradnju, Yugoslavia

We would like to thank the following commissioners and national co-ordinators for their assistance in assembling works and catalogue material: Peter Baum, Director, Neue Galerie der Stadt Linz (Austria); Nelly Richard, critic, Santiago, (Chile); Jean-Louis Pradel, critic, Paris (France); Noel Sheridan, Director, National School of Art and Design, Dublin (Republic of Ireland); Ida Panicelli, Curator, Galleria Nazionale d'Arte Moderna, Rome (Italy); Gijs Van Tuyl, Director, Bureau Beeldende Kunst Buitenland, Amsterdam (Netherlands); Ryszard Stanislawski, Director, Muzeum Sztuki, Lodz (Poland); Rene Block, Gallery Director, DAAD (German Academic Exchange Service), Berlin (West Germany); Marijan Susovski, Director, Galerija Grada Zagreba, Zagreb (Yugoslavia).

DIRECTOR'S INTRODUCTION

The central exhibition of the Fifth Biennale shows the work of 63 artists from 20 countries. Far from seeking to be the Olympics of art, implicit in the prize-giving tradition that lies behind such events, this exhibition brings together work by artists with a broadly-based common concern: the structuring of a personal artistic language to express an interaction with society. That interaction ranges from engagement with a private or domestic situation that has wider social ramifications, to critiques of contemporary society and its dominant cultures.

The theme for the Fifth Biennale originated in my critical response to a succession of international exhibitions I had seen in Europe. The conception of these exhibitions and the aftermath of critical debate seemed to focus on stylistic/medium categories such as Neo-expressionist painting, rather than come to terms with the complex interaction between context, form and content. The fact that work with common concerns often took on vastly different physical forms seemed to go largely unremarked, as also did work that spanned three generations, and work by artists in non-metropolitan art centres.

The Biennale of Sydney seemed to provide an ideal opportunity to juxtapose these works and to open up the possibility of new critical perspectives in an antipodean laboratory. It should be said at the outset that all artists in the exhibition, whether they come from Europe, from former European colonies, or from countries where there has been more recent economic colonisation, either work within a tradition that has been shaped by Western art or are concerned to resuscitate and reshape characteristics of regional cultures that have been swamped by Western modernism. The Biennale of non-Western art, however, must remain as a challenge for a future curator.

During two subsequent periods of travel directly concerned with the Fifth Biennale of Sydney, I developed the theme and concept of the exhibition and finalised the selection. In this process I was often working alone; at other times I worked in close consultation with a number of people credited elsewhere in this catalogue.

Meanwhile, in the early stages of work in Australia, I had discussed with Professor Virginia Spate the question of parallels and contrasts between the social themes and the resurgence of figurative art that would be evident in the central Biennale exhibition on the one hand, and aspects of the tradition of the Australian figurative painting tradition that became strongly evident from late 1930s and 1940s on the other. Believing that this comparison would provide a significant historical inflection of the Biennale, especially with regard to issues of regionalism, I invited Virginia Spate to curate a satellite exhibition for the Fifth Biennale. She agreed, but the realisation of the exhibition was a slower process than we had anticipated and she eventually had to leave for Europe before selection was finalised or the catalogue text written. At very short notice, Christine Dixon and Terry Smith accepted responsibility for the project and jointly planned an exhibition that opens up new historical dimensions in the critical role of the Biennale of Sydney.

Looking across the Tasman Sea, the idea for a second satellite exhibition was inspired by my deepening experience of the remarkable work of New Zealand artist Colin McCahon. This artist has spent decades, relatively unnoticed by the outside world, developing a unique body of work within this century's art. The Fifth Biennale provides an appropriate context in which to give McCahon's work the recognition it deserves.

The special McCahon exhibition brings another comparative vantage-point to bear on the Fifth Biennale's main theme and invites a deeper investigation of the work of one artist than is usually permitted in the context of large international exhibitions. In response to my request for a survey of Colin McCahon's work, the Queen Elizabeth II Arts Council of New Zealand commissioned Wystan Curnow to select works and write a critical introduction for such an exhibition.

There was to have been a third satellite exhibition, of the work of Mexican artist Frida Kahlo. John Stringer, Director of the Visual Arts Program of the Center for Inter-American Relations, New York, generously agreed to organise such an exhibition and did a considerable amount of preparatory work in Mexico and in the United States. To my disappointment it was not possible to raise the funding for this project. Such an exhibition would have invaluably deepened the concerns of this Biennale and I regret its absence.

As the complex elements of this Biennale are being drawn together, it is not the time for definitive analyses in advance of the event. They will come later. The exhibitions of the Fifth Biennale are intended to elucidate certain critical issues that are pertinent to the evaluation of much recent art. They are intended to provide a framework for critical debates in the presence of the works, in the presence of the 40 artists and critics who will visit Sydney for the Biennale, and in the presence of the essays and critical statements included in this catalogue.

However, some questions clearly present themselves:

1. In spite of the now substantial body of critical evidence against the notion of the practice of art being an isolated, individual creative act, artists have in the last few years asserted their freedom to observe the particular — including specific phenomena from the eddies of art history — rather than be governed by either ideologies or theories of "pure form". To what extent is this freedom illusory? Are there now proposed some new models of Romanticism that contrast with the traditional Romantic projection of the artist as an unfettered creative spirit intent on heroic deeds?

2. What is to be made of the varied forms of revived individualism in recent art? Do these tendencies suggest a new concern for imaging experience that is personally intensified? Or are they merely another aspect of colonised escapism reflected in the fabrication or revival of popular culture heroes such as Superman, the Jedi Knights or Mad Max?

3. It is currently a popular critical thesis that artists dubbed "image-scavengers" maintain a disengaged conceptual position in their plundering of elements of popular and mass culture. To what extent is this the case? To what extent does such an approach disguise or deny various forms of direct personal or social engagement by artists who employ a complex recycling of given images?

4. Is the evidence of social engagement in recent art no more than archaeological relics of the moral indignation of the late 1960s and the 1970s? Or are we currently witnessing an evolution of socially engaged art in new forms within the resurgence of figurative/narrative art?

The Biennale of Sydney would not have been possible without the generosity of the Art Gallery of New South Wales in agreeing to not only allow the use of its temporary exhibition space but to dismantle part of its permanent collection to provide adequate exhibition space that is in such short supply in Sydney. I would also like to thank the Power Gallery of Contemporary Art, the S.H. Ervin Gallery and the Ivan Dougherty Gallery for allowing their respective galleries to be used for aspects of the Fifth Biennale.

I would like to thank the members of the Biennale Board who give their time generously and are rewarded solely by having thrust on them the considerable burden of financial and artistic accountability. They provide the volatile mixture of creative freedom and entrenched debate from which a Biennale may explode. They are the guardians of the modern labours of Hercules engendered in Biennale organisation: the Hydra of seemingly insoluble problems, the elusive Erymanthian Boar of funding, and the Augean Stables of criticism.

These labours would have been intolerable if it had not been for the extraordinarily heavy burden of work very ably undertaken by the Biennale Secretariat of two (!), Paula Latos-Valier and Elizabeth Westwater. They have my sincere thanks, as does Ambra Sancin for her dedicated work in the final stages of organising the Fifth Biennale of Sydney.

Leon Paroissien
Sydney, 1984

DRIFT
Stuart Morgan

Two shapes are sketched broadly in black paint on a tarpaulin. Each is grotesque in its way — the female figure cactus-like with a blooming headpiece and cinched waist, the male a cross between a printing-press and a hammerhead shark. They stand side by side, presenting themselves ceremonially to an audience like Punch and Judy, their retinue and emblems of office behind them. And their royal stance is mimicked by a layer of superimposed cream gloss paint, daubed into parodies of human figures. Though they are silhouettes they seem to suffer, if only by feeling the effects of gravity, as the royal pair do not, with their fixed identities of tool and vegetable, the woman an ascending organic spiral which the male is designed to flatten. But titles too are part of a painting. *"JULIAN SCHNABEL"*, the label reads, *"Memory and the Stimulus for Memory."* That play of revelation and concealment recalls the way memory solidifies impressions into caricature, while continually questioning its constancy.

It may be possible to interpret a picture of this kind only by rethinking the very word "interpret", rethinking the interference the interpreter makes between it and its viewer, suspending the need to unpick simply because the artist has already indulged that urge: as might be expected of a painting about memory, it creates and uncreates as it goes, changing and editing like memory itself. Fixing the precise denotations of marks is far less important than noting the emotional resonances between layers of paint with private histories of their own. The triple curve of the left-hand cipher, on display like a sculpture on a pedestal, occupied prime position in an earlier painting *Procession (for Jean Vigo)*. It resembles a DNA molecule or a triple helix, a life force, though the regal desert plant is reminiscent of a form in Mark Rothko's *Slow Swirl by the Edge of the Sea*. While the background evokes tidal eddies, the two superimpositions, barely more than alphabet letters, are flattened, clinging on to the top and bottom edge, recalling the theme of another recent door painting, *Christ in the Bay of Naples*, in which the crucified body seems to have been crushed into the icon He became. A heiroglyph for a dangling man and a Greek "X", the symbol for Christ, have been added to complement the central figures, all the stranger because of the air of judgement it brings to a painting which began life as a kind of epithalamion.

"Began life"? A work of art begins life when the viewer catches sight of it. Since catching sight of this picture, its constituent parts have assumed now one, now another relationship, resisting solution in the mind. Samuel Beckett said that Joyce's writing was not *about* anything; it *was* that thing. This painting *is* that thing and is *about* that thing too, and like the superimposed flow of housepaint another duality is offered if the viewer wants to make the connection: between present and past, sound and echo. It rings in the mind like a remark you thought you had forgotten.

And, of course, it quotes as it shifts in the mind. While Salle, with his ready stock of images, is praised for the aptness of his quotation, Schnabel is blamed for the same reason. If Rothko *is* present somewhere in the painting in question no more appropriate reminiscence could be imagined; *Slow Swirl*, sometimes described as a wedding portrait[1] of the artist and his wife, is indebted to textbook diagrams of cell development[2]. Schnabel's weird tree hints that his couple are Adam and Eve. Rothko was determined to take the story back to blobs of protoplasmic slime. But Schnabel is interpreting Rothko — translating him. (There was a time when the two words meant the same.) Perhaps he is even measuring himself against a great artist — or at least a great painting — and seeking to overthrow by misreading, letting the mind wander. Freud used the word *Bedeutungswandel*[3], "wandering signification". Bringing the two together in his own theory of creative misreading, Harold Bloom has rethought terms such as "influence" and suggested that what poets and critics do with a poem is exactly the same.

A tradition-minded modernist would object that Schnabel was simply situating himself historically; who you quote is what you want to be. T.S. Eliot knew what culture was: a row of books on a shelf, in chronological order. These days the "canon" is out of fashion. More use to us is Walter Benjamin's habit of arranging *his* book collection by means of impossible taxonomies: large next to small, and so on. Systems collapse, and a man who so enjoyed getting lost or drugged must have known this better than most. The late writings of Barthes describe such a state of collapse. In *The Pleasure of the Text* he remembered a night when, half asleep in a bar, he tried to count all the languages he could hear and in doing so became "an exemplary site", a public square in Tangiers[4] through which fragments passed without congealing into a sentence. The experience of the here and now, the "performative" tense, would occupy him more than once in his last writings[5]. And he had a word for that state of mind in which no sentence formed. "Drifting", he wrote, "occurs whenever *I do not respect the whole*"[6]. For him it was also present in writing and desire.

Writing is an act, while desire is a state of mind. Barthes may have disagreed. "Drift", an intransitive verb, may be a state of mind, but to begin to drift involves consenting to passivity, allowing will-power to fall into abeyance. Certainly this may be exciting but it is a private sort of excitement. Sensitive, secretive men, both Barthes and Benjamin — in most of their writing, at least — seem far removed from that declaration which activity presumes. Their pleasures entail loneliness and childlike selfishness. If not entirely capable of being *willed*, pleasure is always *wilful*. Little wonder that the word "drift" enters the vocabulary of Achille Bonito Oliva as a way of appreciating the skittish poetry of Italian figuration[7]. And little wonder that a habit of distraction, an involuntary unfocusing, should be so prized when models of culture itself have changed. Culture, Abraham Moles remarks in his book *La Sociodynamique de la Culture*, is a table of magazines in a dentist's waiting-room[8].

Drifting, by definition, is aimless. Plural, paradoxical, pleasurable and provocative, the ideal text proposed by French poststructuralists like the late Barthes was also aimless; its direction was not "here" or "there"

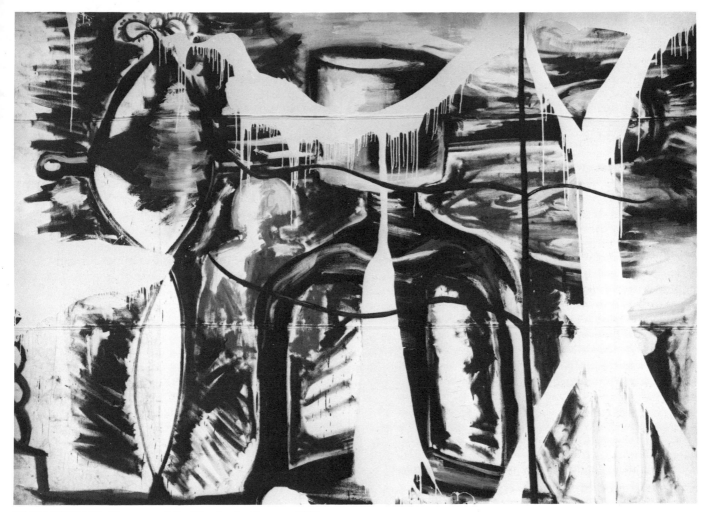

JULIAN SCHNABEL, Memory and the Stimulus for Memory, 1983
Oil, fibre glass, canvas, 290 × 400
Photograph André Morain, Paris

but "between", as his definition of intertextuality demonstrated[9].

> "Any text is a new tissue of past citations.
> Bits of codes, formulae, rhythmic models,
> fragments of social languages etc. all pass
> into the text and are redistributed within it,
> for there is always language before or around
> the text. Intertextuality, the condition of any
> text whatsoever, cannot of course be reduced
> to a problem of sources or influences; the
> intertext is a general field of anonymous
> formulae whose origin can scarcely ever be
> located: of unconscious or automatic
> quotation, given without question marks."

By 1980 it seemed that intertextuality was such a main asumption of art practice that it had become the pivot of entire works, such as Laurie Anderson's *United States*, which deliberately dramatised what Barthes saw as a universal condition. Anderson perfected a way of allowing media to ricochet off each other, the complete antithesis of traditional notions of *Gesamtkunstwerk* or synaesthesia. It could serve equally well as a worked example of other poststructuralist conventions: the shift from "work" to "text", for instance, or the "death of the author"[10]. Anderson's functional, *Neue Sachlichkeit* disguise, deliberately asexual and ironic, stressed a rift between creator and creation. It was one of the most perfect of many experiments with the self in eighties

art: Clemente's chameleonism, Sherman's identikit females, Borofsky's dream refractions, Kiefer's representative German...

Though the death of the author was a major assumption of literary theorists the conclusions to be drawn from it were debated. Foucault urged[11] that it was crucial to reverse the traditional role of the author in literature, imagined as a genius from whom meaning proliferates precisely because we fear that proliferation, using the concept "author" as the image of the creator as a roly-poly Santa Claus who is great because he is good, or vice versa. In suppressing the male stereotype Father-God-Author relationship to their own production artists, as Foucault would see it, are attacking a mode of discourse intimately connected with property and power. His thesis may be borne out by the evidence of power as a dominant preoccupation in recent art. Or perhaps not.

For every period there exists an accepted apology for the relationship of art to politics. Clement Greenberg looked at the time when artists who had previously been WPA members retired to their garrets to paint Abstract Expressionist pictures and decided that their new-found Bohemianism[12] was "heroic". Michael Fried explained[13] that for artists technical decision-making both paralleled and subsumed decision-making in the moral sphere. The contemporary art critic who tries to find "the" answer for 1980s art will have to ask first how compromised a reputedly avant-garde art is by pricing, the gallery-system and most of all by the sheer power of the dominant "official" culture to remove its sting. One solution, in the practice of Hans Haacke or the theory of Thomas Lawson, would be to challenge the system from within. Their opponents in this — and to oppose their theoretical solutions is not necessarily to disagre with their diagnosis of the problem — would reply that such single-mindedness is needed for the fight that to oppose the system is *all* that their art is able to do. As artists they might choose to address themselves to more individual matters. Indeed, a return to the studio has been remarked by commentators, basing their findings, perhaps, on the resurgence of interest in painting. Yet the studio provides a good hideout for the *agent provocateur*.

An ideal site for a painting, said Sandro Chia, is the outside wall of a building, facing the street. Certainly a main structural model for recent art is a wall of graffiti, the visual equivalent of that Moroccan square or a mind in the process of wandering. Anonymous underground figures hovering between public and private domains, graffitists are fresh kids who scrawl what they wish. Gradually what they do hides, then transforms the building, or makes a mobile painting out of a subway train. Neither Bohemians nor business gents, 1980s artists often seek such a cultural interface, translating, interpreting, then leaving their work drifting in a condition of *cultural* intertextuality. So the political statement they make will be putative at best; even though they might be writing their name over and over again, graffitists really *say* nothing on walls. They perform a therapeutic activity, allowing aesthetic decisions to be made in an improvisatory way. Name has become image. But that image is camouflage, concealing and transforming as it pretends to "express". There is only one way to signal the impotence of the artist in such a situation: to engage with images that are beyond hope of control — not images we understand, as David Salle has said, but images that understand *us*.

There is certainly a danger of being misunderstood by making such choices, and a related danger of being unable to fight the chosen images. Charles Jencks pictured postmodern architects as switchboard operators plugging and unplugging a set of wires, each with a label and textbook signification[14]. Sometimes the board jams. Commenting on "Fascist" elements in Aldo Rossi's architecture, he decides that these are not yet sufficiently neutral to be used, but that given time they will be. (Did Fascist references in Philip Johnson escape comment simply because of his flippant manner?) After years of posing as eccentrics Gilbert and George adopt the stance of average Englishmen in photocollages which juxtapose studies of racial minorities, self-portraits of the artists and obscenities scrawled on London walls. The large split photographs naturally take their place within the private odyssey the artists have pursued for so long, a return to the streets after the crisis of *Dark Shadow* but a disorienting one in which stability is promised only by emblems of patriotism — union jacks, bronze warriors on statues, the stuff of Falklands wartalk as well as National Front aggression pursued by precisely those skinheads who figure as objects of

desire for two besuited middle-aged bachelors. Outside the terms that any artist's "world" seems to create for its parts, the picture of Whitechapel promulgated by these works is so loaded that it is hardly surprising if British critics attacked them on moral grounds. Yet Gilbert and George are after all engaging with images that fascinate them, like Anderson or Longo, and pushing the equivocation inherent in their working method to a limit.

Any answer to the question of possible political engagement in art should bear in mind first the assumptions that art makes, isolated here as a cluster of ideas from French poststructuralist thought. It should also take account of three paradoxes. First, that neo-Expressionism, the myth of the liberated brushstroke, is locked in a deadly embrace with that of the artist as image processor. Second, that just as French poststructuralism itself has been regarded as a reaction to the failure of the 1968 student revolution[15], a tacit decision that henceforth subversion would be carried out on paper by a process of continual analysis of language itself, the return to the studio could be interpreted either as a resurgence of interest in the methods and lost causes of late sixties conceptualism or an admission of defeat. Thirdly, that Barthes and Benjamin may have been performing a service by forcing us to see that what had been regarded as an interiorised activity has great public significance, that in the condition of "drifting" lies the possibility of subversion. Arising from thoughts of the collapse of the systems, it treats that collapse as a permanent, above all enjoyable, state in which creative alteration can take place.

Notes:
(1) Diane Waldman, *Mark Rothko 1903-1970: A Retrospective*, p45, Guggenheim Museum, New York 1978;
Robert Rosenblum, *Mark Rothko: The Surrealist Years*, p8, Pace Gallery, New York 1981
(2) Stephen Polcari, "The Intellectual Roots of Abstract Expressionism: Mark Rothko", *Arts*, pp124-134, September 1979
(3) Harold Bloom, *A Map of Misreading*, p89, Oxford University Press, New York 1980
(4) Roland Barthes, *The Pleasure of the Text*, p49, translated R. Miller, Hill & Wang, New York 1975
(5) Roland Barthes, *Empire of Signs*, p6, translated R. Howard, Cape, London 1983;
"The Dream: To know a foreign (alien) language yet not to understand it . . .", cf. Elias Canetti in *The Voices of Marrakesh*, Marion Boyars, London 1982 ("*A Dream: A man who unlearns the world's languages until nowhere on earth does he understand what people are saying.*")
(6) Roland Barthes, *The Pleasure of the Text*, p18
(7) Achille Bonito Oliva, *La Transavangarde Italienne*, Politi, Milan 1980
(8) Edgar Morin, *New Trends of Study of Mass Communications*, University of Birmingham Centre for Contemporary Cultural Studies (occasional paper), n.d.
(9) Roland Barthes, "Text, Discourse, Ideology", in R. Young (ed.), *Untying the Text*, p39, Routledge, Boston London 1981
(10) Roland Barthes, "From Work to Text", and "The Death of the Author", in Image-Music-Text, translated

S. Heath, Fontana, London 1977

(11) Michel Foucault, "What is an Author?", in *Textual Strategies*,pp141-160, J.V.Harari (Ed.), Methuen, London 1980

(12) Clement Greenberg, *Art and Culture*, p230, Thames & Hudson, London 1973 ("Some day it will have to be told how *anti-Stalinism*, which started out more or less as *Trotskyism*, turned into art for art's sake and thereby cleared the way, heroically, for what was to come.")

(13) Michael Fried, *Three American Painters*, pp9-10, Fogg Art Museum, Harvard 1965 ("This means that while modernist painting has increasingly divorced itself from the concerns of the society in which it precariously flourishes, the actual dialectic by which it is made has taken on more and more of the denseness, structure and complexity of moral experience — that is, of life itself, but life as few are inclined to live it: in a state of continual intellectual and moral alertness. The formal critic of modernist painting, then, is also a moral critic: not because all art is at bottom a criticism of life but because modernist painting is at least a criticism of itself.")

(14) Charles Jencks, *The Language of Post-Modern Architecture*, Studio, London 1977

(15) E.G. Terry Eagleton, *Literary Theory*, p142, Blackwell, Oxford 1983

LATIN AMERICA: CULTURES OF REPETITION OR CULTURES OF DIFFERENCE?

Nelly Richard

I FORMS OF REPRODUCTION

1. For works that come from peripheral regions to appear in an international setting means giving up a part of their own motivation as works: to show these works in another continent involves risking renunciation of the past because the new context ignores and denies all that precedes them; it means risking mutilation of their present by suppressing every linkage to what defined their *milieu*. By cutting themselves off from the social whole of which they are part (and which is also a part of them), and by severing the web of their relationships — interproductive relationships — to other activities, the works even run the risk of appearing incomprehensible. In any case, they must sacrifice a part of their historical and cultural meaning.

The wall — gallery wall, museum wall, international exhibition wall — that displays the fate of these works as cut off from their whole, becomes the support of transference. It erases any reference that is not museological; inevitably it neutralises the living impulses that gave the work a social potency.

Coming from peripheral regions to appear in international events therefore involves bearing the cost of this transference; but it also gives the work an opportunity of confronting other circumstances, to new cross-roads of experience, thus reactivating their original meaning while putting it to the test of such a contradiction. For these works to be presented elsewhere comes to mean the certainty that they are not foreclosed, and this is all the more important as those works are frequently deprived of breathing space.

2. For those of us in Latin American countries, appearing in an international context means a challenge; it signifies for us fighting for our own legitimacy within a framework that tends to subordinate any secondary (marginal, peripheral) activity to the forms promoted as models by the international power centres. Fatally, the products of our cultures are condemned to the role of duplications; any one of our forms then appears as dependent on other forms, internationalised by metropolitan cultures — as plain repetition or copy, imitation, replica or image similar to one belonging to an international stock. The dictatorial international perspective tends to look for the whole. It encompasses within that whole all relevant works (even if they come from contradictory or different historical processes) and places them with a uniform historical sequence. It does not take into account the different processes that specify each history as the history of a minority — as a form of dissidence in respect to the international dogma of modernism.

Our forms, then, are deprived of the spaces in which they are validated by national histories. The circumstances in which they have appeared are forgotten. The specific social and cultural conditions determining their manifestation are obliterated.

3. Peripheral cultures find it very hard to reverse the process that mutilates their ability to engage in dialogue and condemns them to being merely the recipients of messages of others.

These cultures of ours, deprived of the capacity of exchange, are seen as purely passive, acquiescing or ratifying what has already been expressed; the one-sidedness of international communication imposes upon them the condition of subscribers to forms perceived as dominant.

In our cultures, our lack is not only the product of quantitatively limited information, but also of a relationship to information that is qualitatively limited. The dominant cultures force us to relate to information as to a monopoly.

4. Our cultures have formed themselves within a historical and geographical lag, and are thus identified not by the production of forms but by their reproduction. Historically it has always been their fate to have belated contact with international models through copies. A work is then, for us, nothing but the trace of itself: a delayed signal of something that has already happened, and whose value as an event has been cancelled through repetition.

This art situation that excludes us as actors and even as witnesses, shows itself to us always after the fact (in a moment that is no longer there) and through some form of translation, and thus turns our cultures into the cultures of dubbing.

Our cultures are also those of pruning: the works we see are fragmented by photographic selection of the image and thus severed from their situation.

5. A country in the process of being colonised, or one that has been colonised, shows itself by its patchwork, by the remnant character of its tradition. Its memory of the past is made up of remainders of other histories, a memory formed by hybrid traces in different layers and by the residues of petrified forms of language.

The international mechanism of imposing signs does not take into account the national specificity of productive complexes into which those signs will be inserted. Therefore, our production appears as irregular, our references heterogeneous. Our histories feign a certain succession, a certain continuity. Our histories are fakes; they are travesties of social correlation. As the doubles of something else, they are alienated and relate to culture through substitution.

II PRODUCTION OF FORMS

1. However, it is possible to consider the validity of works which, even if they have been built on a foreign stock of pre-existing images, are able to re-elaborate those images critically, in relation to previous conditions of existence and functioning. It is possible to force those pre-existing images (through the pressures of a different context) to signify in Latin America what they had never the chance to signify before. Those forms detach themselves, here, from the security of their own past and have to venture into a present unknown to them; they disengage here from a tradition whose weight neutralised their strength and served as a buffer for their impact,

depriving them of their vehemence and their aggression. Here, unprotected, those forms expose themselves at last to the strength of a conflict, in the enormity of the act of stumbling upon our facts, our reality appears extreme in relation to theirs.

International forms, in moving both geographically and historically into a context of deprivation such as ours, have to reset the perspective in which they initially appeared. The urgency with which they are confronted strengthens their signification, no longer in relation to a past (as in the case of a history continuous in relation to itself or to its memory) but in relation, now, to a future exceeding, for us, the notion of history itself.

International forms, in each case, turn back on themselves and thus modify their own origin; even if they come from another tradition, no forms can save themselves from the shock of their transit through our history — a history constructed of abject poverty or repression.

We are, in consequence, prepared to consider as valid the activity of "building our own phrases through a vocabulary and a syntax received from others"(1), and to see in it a very important strategy of criticism, as it subverts an order in which we appear as secondary, as it modifies the meaning attributed to us from outside: we are prepared to consider as valid the creative handling of international techniques, seen as a way of using (misusing, reusing, recycling, harming) them for the purpose of building our own historical signification.

2. Even though we have to fight against what, in an international sphere, forces upon us alien forms of conscience, and even though we have to fight againt hegemonic pressures from Europe or the United States, we do not have to give up the chance of profiting from the information coming from those countries, information that we might process for our own ends.

Colonisation is alienating. Equally alienating (in the sense of myth-making) is the wish to see "authentic" Latin America only in the remains of its pre-colonial past.

The mythologising of the Latin American identity (based on the primitive), in forms of art aspiring to be aboriginal, caricatures that identity. The exotic (the myth of the savage as a return to nature, the myth of native culture as a legendary spring, as folkloric memory) and the picturesque lead Latin American culture into a regression of identity. The origins (the pre-cultural) may be the only legitimate way of deciphering a history abbreviated to the memory of its past, a history unable to participate in the real dynamics of the present.

Even though myth, in our continent, is a sub-stratum feeding its own forms of culture, to yearn for the virginal, pure indigenous forms of culture, free from all foreign participation, means to subtract Latin American culture from the dialectics of history. In erasing the traces of conflict amongst different cultural pressures that have clashed during the diverse processes of colonisation, the possibility of a Latin American form of conscience open to a process of self criticism regarding its own contradictory

condition (that of several histories interacting, contradicting one another) is denied.

3. The non-coincidence of international and Latin American forms, the non-synchrony of relation to international standards of contemporaneity; the difficulty, for example, in seeing the point of aesthetics such as that of the "trans avant-garde" in regions as marginal as ours denotes but separates the traumatic consciousness that we have of our history (failed, incomplete) and the satisfied consciousness of Europe that leads Europeans to relate to the past in terms of over-abundance of art historical references. This leads European art to smother itself in its own references. In the case of Europe, any innovation appears in the form of a quote, since each form has necessarily been anticipated by a predecessor, absorbing the new form into continuity. The accumulation of references and proliferation of quotations leads European cultures to constitute themselves in a web of presuppositions and reminiscences.

In the case of Latin American practices, born of deprivation (from non-belonging and from residues, the leftovers from satiated cultures), tradition can hardly be considered as a heritage, since it is based on a series of acts of dispossession; the game of quoting, here, would only be a parody of history, disinherited by the numerous ways of expropriating life.

4. Refusing annexation, in the form of becoming the cultural territory of someone else, does not mean shutting ourselves off from foreign contributions in the name of so-called authentic local consciousness. It means working on forms of critical consciousness that will make us capable of evaluating such contributions in accordance with our own historical convenience, and of discriminating amongst such contributions in accordance with our own standards. It means designing a fighting strategy through which we might profit from what is imposed on us, by distorting its original frame of reference.

The same heterogeneity of references that formed our own pruned identity, this historical fragmentation and disparity of our productive web, this discontinuity of our processes of cultural reference, demand that our practices have to be such as to render (and make productive) their own peripheralisation, to produce their own shift in processes.

For instance, our practices try to render, through their own processes, the technological inequality between imposing signs and the local structures receiving those signs. Our practices present the social stratification that results from the incompatibility of different modes of working that are anachronistic in their processes.

The more recent Latin American practices take as their theme (and even dramatise) their conditions of production, generating a dynamic of signification capable of rendering the destiny of a work in so far as it is divided among cultural processes antagonistic to each other.

5. The Latin American signs that are in revolt (rebelling against their origin) emerge in the interior of our language. The language moves signs from one

zone to another, bringing by means of their underlying conflictual charges a clash between the different levels of culturisation to which our histories have been submitted. In the interior of sign the different levels of social historicity enter into conflict.

Within each one of our histories, two opposing forces face each other: the one from outside imposes signification in conformity with standard international norms; the one from inside assumes the defence of what is our own (not that which is native), rising up against that external frame of imposition.

The regime of censorship that reigns in many Latin American countries and affects our cultures takes a double form. It proceeds from the imperialism of international cultural forces that peripheralise our production with respect to the metropolitan webs of artistic signification. It proceeds also from the authoritarianism of the political regimes that subject the countries to the officialism of their models of repression. A double silencing, a double law of censorship that we have the responsibility to fight in all modes of language — the only field of action and the only place where we can imprint the gesture of our disobedience.

The language with which we work in our practices is in itself this battlefield, a zone of emergence of signification that intends to subvert the regimes of dominance imposed upon it.

The underlying tactics of resistance and of combat against what is proscribed is being developed as a subculture occupying the hidden face of the codes. This activity works with clandestine references, disguising itself through processes of travesty of signification, parodying the order and metaphorising the law.

Only an archaeology of our languages can reveal the stratification of the obverse of dominance and exhume that which lies buried under so many graves.

(1) Michel De Certeau: *L'Invention du Quotidien*

Santiago, Chile
August 1983
Translation: Adriana Valdes

THE GERMAN SITUATION, OR THE OTHER SIDE OF THE *WILDEN* COIN.

Annelie Pohlen

The future won't be found in the immediate past or on the rubbish heap.

Time contains its own magic. Contrary to any reading of history one measures its passing in decades and centuries as if reality, actual or imagined, ever bothered about such distinctions. Man needs to impose order on confusion and so he puts everythng away into the simplest compartments.

In Germany, or anywhere else for that matter, the art scene is no exception. The latest trend is the "duel" between the art of the 1970s and that of the 1980s. While one group tends to emphasise the enormous differences between what was produced during the two decades, the other will painstakingly seek out the similarities. With the passage of time it is natural, of course, that there should be changes and developments in the material as well as spiritual conditions of human societies. These are neither linear, as the staunch believers in progress would have it, nor as easily measured as by those who neatly divide time into decades and centuries to obtain a clearer overview. From all these revolutionary, reactionary and contradictory directions, clarity of thought has to be somehow distilled. In the current German socio-political situation (more accurately in the West German one) this leads to the *Wende* (reaction — new political order) and from an international cultural viewpoint to a declaration of the victory of post-modernism over modernism.

Even if cultural and political ideals have never had much in common, *Wendepolitiker* (reactionary politicians) and post-modernists do share one preoccupation: their need to reform the immediate past — a shameful retreat into the arsenal of historical values. These are restored to life, uncritically and unashamedly by politicans while post-modernists, showing little concern for their previously held position and current context in time, adapt it to a socially irresponsible, idealistically anarchic scenario. The progressive positivists of the immediate post-war era, as well as the critical revolutionaries and those advocates of humanist Utopias from the late 1960s, are in their attempts to visualise the future all accused of delusion. They talk as if the artists of 1968 had not already, in their revolution against internationalist *rigor mortis*, fought for the ideal of a humanity rooted in the historical process as a basis for future vision. The creative products of a whole decade are reduced to a formalist and intellectualised spectacular of innovation while the worthlessness of the Utopias is measured by the failure of political and social reform.

The more the reactionary politicians try to denigrate the last social Romantics of modernism (well supported as they are by *petit-bourgeois* desires to retain material possessions), the more certain young cultural militants indulge in proclaiming the end of social responsibility in the arts. Overnight the *Neuen Wilden* (new wild ones) as they were hastily tagged, at least by their promoters and probably also by themselves, emerged from that post 1960s movement which so carefully nurtured the responsibility of art to create a humanistic future. From here on a total subjectivism reigns and anything from the grab-bag of history is available for use in the production of art works: an anarchic outpouring of the subsconscious without any communicable social relevance. From the supermarket of culture only the technical media were eliminated as these were regarded as the impotent tools of a beleaguered technocratic age. "No future" became the logical catch-cry. "All Quiet on the Western Front" was the somewhat more refined version[1].

Two cities in West Germany became centres for the new attitude: Berlin, fixated for a long time in an inbred critical realism, hurled itself back into the centre of cultural world awareness with the help of the young *heftigen* (tough) painters. The *Wilden* (wild ones) of the *Mühlheimer Freiheit* originated in Cologne from where they went on to conquer the entire Western art scene. It was only fair that their predecessors, the painters Baselitz, Lüpertz, Immendorff, Kiefer and Penck, left out in the cold all through the 1970s, were thus thrust into the long awaited international limelight. If one were to take the reactions in foreign publications to these international triumphs seriously, then it would be impossible not to come to the following conclusion: despite the world wide profusion of the "new painting", it is the expressive stance of a few German artists, nurtured by a trivialised mythic mood, that continues to call forth an effusion of amazed comment on the continuation of an unbroken Nordic tradition. The quite obvious differences between individual artists go unnoticed and they only see German pathos, surging dark mythology, wild excitability, raw monumentality and a world stage with Wagner and Nietzsche calling the tune. The mythological chaos of the German soul conquers the world.

Now, slowly perhaps, the trench warriors of the 1970s and 1980s are getting tired. We are becoming curious to see if there are not other creative attitudes to be discovered among the supposedly socially disinterested young painters and sculptors of today. Even the indiscriminate appraisal of the so called *Wilden* or German expressive painters and their closely aligned sculptor compatriots is coming ever more under review.

In order to simply kill off modernism its critics have conveniently turned on the creative potential of their fathers from the at least German Bauhaus and concentrated their attack on the terrorist, technocratic and inhuman functionalism instigated by the inheritors of the Bauhaus ideal. But the "Modernists" in the development of German art are in no way all unimaginative rationalists, any more than the Post-Modernist, Neo-Expressionists of the 1970s and 1980s are all obsessively emotional anarcho-subjectivists. The relationship between the generations in their use of media and means of expression, as well as in their attitude towards the function of art in a social context, is considerably more complex and also more involved than the successful reductionists of the general as well as the specifically German art scene would have us believe[2]. Just as there is little to be found in common among such representatives of the older generation of German artists, so often mentioned in one breath, like Baselitz, Immendorff, Lüpertz and Penck, there is also much common ground to be found among the representatives of different generations and styles, such as Beuys and Felix Droese, Polke and Christa Näher, Penck and Oppermann or Gerhard Richter, Hanne Darboven, Dieter Rot among the older, and Klaus Mettig, Astrid Klein, Charly Banana/Ralf Johannes among the younger ones. Despite the clamour created by the political swing to the right (*Wende*) and the advent of Post-Modernism, a remarkably lively art scene continues to flourish in Germany, existing as it does in its many branches between the big movements of resigned "no future" anarchy and a stubbornly committed art which ignores the mood of *fin de siècle* resignation.

Astrid Klein
Photograph Lothar Schnepf, Cologne

The refusal to become fixated on one attitude seems in the German art-scene to be of as much importance as its widely discussed raw, mythic expressiveness. We can be grateful that the existence of an extraordinarily large number of public and private galleries has assured that we would not be completely snowed under by the current *Wilden* boom. So we will not be too surprised with what we find when our curiosity leads us to look at the work of the "other" young artists. Looked at in this way, the question raised by the Biennale of transmitting "Private Symbols" in "Social Metaphors" is thus

adressed in a rather more limited context by this quantitatively comprehensive German contribution. Despite the priority of painting, it certainly demonstrates the multiplicity of directions in current German art.

The change from a post-war internationalism to a currently progressive autonimisation of the regional/national should, at closer examination, be seen as a problem of communication rather than one of the nature of artistic production — at least from the German point of view. Just as the Italian *Arte Povera* movement was not hampered by the mainstream of international conceptualist art, neither can Polke's work be compared to American Pop Art or Gerhard Richter's with American Photo Realism. Were one to take such superficial similarities seriously one would have to regard the new *Inhaltsmalerei* (content painting) as the most decisive product of the Internationalist school of thought.

It is a conscious simplification of the truth to maintain that art in West Germany after the war, especially after the 1960s, was anti-doctrinal, trendless in its most positive sense and highly individualistic in its exploitation of internationally represented artistic endeavours. The search for an appropriate rationale necessarily implies some speculation. Within this speculation, the special historical and political situation of West Germany has to be taken into consideration. The so called "zero hour" after the terror regime of the Nazis and the lost war; the succeeding firm ties to the USA as the front line state of the Western powers, which is only in most recent times being reflected upon critically right across the German social spectrum and, since the War, the constant confrontation with the other, the communist German state, has caused disruption and distortion in attitudes towards life in West Germany.

A thorough going reflection on the past had as little chance of contributing to any self-analysis as a doctrinaire fixated one (capitalist based, liberal democratic, communist based totalitarian) had of providing an objective overview of the present. In order to hold on to that lofty contention of being the nation of poets and thinkers there was a propensity to refer back to the tradition of Goethe and Kant, while consciously excluding that of Nietzsche and Wagner, so eternally discredited by the Nazi regime. Shielded by the materialist progress boom, the social awareness of the status quo in the Federal Republic of Germany was seriously preoccupied with overcoming its own historical past, as well as trying to come to terms with its current American satellite state status. From this developed an essentially multi-faceted, anti-status-quo creativity which grew up between the cultural mainstreams and the individual regional attitudes. Obliging heroes make room for ever changing muses. The individualised grammar and the suitably serious minded persons become central to creative, social analysis. Artists like Beuys and Darboven, Polke and Immendorff, Oppermann and Sieverding, Rebecca Horn and Ulrike Rosenbach, Penck and Buthe, are certainly more closely aligned in this general attitude than the formal appearance or the specific content or aims of their work would at first suggest. A symbolic grammar arises from individual and subjective experiences which are translated into an appropriate social image — fertile ground for a, in the best sense, Romantic uprising leading towards a society fit for real human individuals. In this sense the literary references to the German situation in Immendorff's pictures are as pertinent as the historical myths in Anselm Kiefer's work are to an identifiably German ethos. Here we see, growing up in the everyday life of Germany today, consumer clichés elevated to quasi-mythical cult objects, like in the work of Polke, or a conceptual heightening of the subject by Anna Oppermann in her obsessive analysis of fragments of reality as they experience constant opposition and imaginative leaps, approximations and bridges, one step forward, one step back, ideas and facts, all as a pathology of the present and as a potential Utopian ideal for coming to terms with the future.

The visual langue of A.R. Penck is based decidedly on his own experiences of a specifically German blockade of human understanding that has an essentially social significance in a specifically German situation, as much as in a world wide alienation of the human individual through the pressures of the economic system.

The art of the immediate past in Germany is carried along by a Romantic-revolutionary impetus which in all its variety remains undoubtedly recognisable. In its social context this art is clamorous and optimistic with regard to its effectiveness. It is supported by an analytical consciousness as well as by a spirit of Romantic anarchism against the stifling of the individual by the forces of the status quo. At the same time this optimism is increasingly accompanied by an aggressive attitude towards the obvious hardening of socio-cultural developments.

Like an avalanche of hope, Joseph Beuys hurls real rocks at prevailing "end of the world" perceptions. In Jörg Immendorff's trivially expressive pictures we see the last standard bearers of cultural and spiritual liberation fighting an increasingly aggressive battle against the encroaching Ice Age; allegories of totalitarian attitudes in the East and West; a pointedly ghastly spectacular of the comic triviality of the international daily scene and the bombastic mythology of the past and future from which the exemplary artist and his fellow travellers attempt to escape. Anselm Kiefer hurls a repressed history with its burnt symbols, like its still unconquered heroic myths, into the landscape of painting above which the painter's palette hovers, visible or invisible, like a manically nagging question about the development of art and culture. Sigmar Polke who, long before the world-wide mania for graffiti, created a sheet full of written abuse, and who filled his sketchbook with mentally and visually disorienting intertwined figures and distortions long before the advent of the young *Inhaltsmaler* (content painters); a clowning anarchic revolt against the clichéd dictates of the norms of western civilisation; carries the painterly game of disorientation between triviality and mythical genius to the extreme. Amongst trivial fragmens of reality Penck, with the help of an unbroken ritual system, searches for the instruments of understanding in which prehistoric cave painting and present day street graffiti melt into an Utopian code. Anna Oppermann's assemblages carry an analysis derived

Klaus Mettig
CHINA, 1978
Installation
Photograph Walter Klein, Gerresheim

Charly Banana/Ralf Johannes
KENIA — BUMM BUMM, 1981
90 × 120
Courtesy the artist

from subjective reactions ever deeper into a realm obsessively occupied by a system of continuities and contradictions, associations and imaginative leaps — a problem solving exercise for the appropriately serious artist. Anna Oppermann's subjective reaction is the germ-cell and the manifestation of a socio-cultural urgency in a world which is threatening to suffocate from its loss of intuition and a thoughtlessness in its relationship to reality: a world in which the essential connection between nature, man and culture could soon become finally severed.

The leading representatives of the 1968 generation have by no means relinquished their claim to prominence in the 1980s. Driven by an intuitive obsession they have stepped up the pace and, contrary to all expectations, have found among the younger artists of an apolitical art for art's sake and "no future" generation, a surprising number with whom a creative dialogue is possible.

The subjective experiential dimension — affected as it is by an historical, political and "civilised" reality, tied into a system which is threatening by its emphasis on production and consumerism and by its moral and spiritual dishonesty to stifle the last gasps of individual and social life, forces its way triumphantly wavering between analysis and mania, towards an increasingly obsessive, while at the same time pathetic and ironic trivialising of the scope of the visual arts. However, especially among the young German artists the predominance of traditional media like painting and sculpture remains undiminished. Photography and video also claim an acknowledged place through the work of outstanding young artists like Klaus Mettig, Astrid Klein, Klaus vom Bruch and Marcel Odenbach for example. The video works of Oldenbach and vom Bruch, for example, reveal themselves as obsessively loaded metaphors of the subject, entangled in the quasi-mythical "cults" of the technocratic age, which are no less present for German civilised society than are the irrational myths of the past. Astrid Klein's monumental photographic works evoke in their threateningly dark symbolism in artistically transformed human silhouettes borrowed from modern communications systems, intertwined with timeless archaic symbols, a last gasp of the mortally wounded human subject. Traumatic visions of the timeless duel between life and death, sexual power and erotic liberation, between the illusion of reality and the mighty presence of multi-layered symbolism, these signals, from the churning morass of the unconscious.

No less obsessive is the transformation of subjective experiences into a social "image" as it appears in the work of Klaus Mettig, which combines media images of mundane reality with those photographed by the artist himself in monumental, space filling works comprised of still-photos and slides. The suposedly analytical character of these quasi-documentary transfers from politics, entertainment and advertising, interspersed with barely noticeable references to natural phenomena and everyday happenings and the seamlessly interwoven comments on the threatening nature of the Western and Eastern systems of government, liberate the powers of the intuitive, creative individual from the terrorism of the false images created by manipulating technocrats. It seems necessary to refer to these remarkable young photographic artists on the German scene in order to avoid the dangerous one-sidedness with which it is so often regarded.

It is certainly not restricted to an expressionistic, mythical, cult-like and irrational painting scene. When we do find a mysterious symbolism appearing in paintings and sculpture, this does not necessarily point to an apolitical, mythic-irrational and anarchic hot-house culture. In the area of painting, but especially in sculpture, a great number of different developments can be found. The group "Normal" (centred on Milan Kunc, Peter Angermann and Jan Knap) creates through its ironical combining of "high art" mythologies with the comic strip imagery of the consumer society a pointedly poster-like imagery to be used as a weapon by the average person in his struggle against social alienation.

Charly Banana/Ralf Johannes takes to extremes the conflict created by erotic consumerism and its dire consequences in his horribly kitsch and mythologically trivial images (a mixture of painting and collage). Alongside this, particularly in the field of sculpture, we find a committed language developing, stamped as it is by an anarchic sense of design, which commands an irridescent position somewhere between archaic cult objects and pithy science-fiction visions. Bogomir Ecker, Harald

Bogomir Ecker
LADEN-LAGER, ADMIRALITÄTSCH
Hamburg 1983
Courtesy the artist

Klingelholler, Reinhard Mucha and Thomas Schutte are representative of a school of three dimensional thought which sets up an open ended store of symbolism against the anonymous powers of the status quo. From this only cursory description the varied contribution of the younger German artists to the Biennale can be appreciated without falling into the trap of referring to clichés about the irrational, raw and myth-prone German soul.

There are obsessive painters like Christa Näher, who produces threateningly excessive pictures in her rage at the exploitation of life, at the authoritarianism of mankind and at the suppression of the primal strengths of animal life: erotic-aggressive duels between the naked, helplessly comic self depiction of the artist and the mythically powerful animal which appears to be threatening revenge. As if driven by instinct the animal rages or lurks, persistenlty striking dangerous poses as a metaphor for the power of life which mankind is depriving itself of through an increasing accommodation to a fictitious normality and a static order. Their expressive-dynamic painting style reaches back to that specifically German tradition in painting where the content is existentially interconnected with the form.

It is from this connection of form and content that the work of Felix Droese, independent of media and stylistic categories, gains its oppressive energy. Monumental scissor cuts, small format drawings and coarse symbol-like objects from the refuse of industrial society as well as strangely cult-like installations combine a reaching back for traditional art techniques with a painfully limited symbolic

Holger Bunk
EUROPA 79
Courtesy Galerie Handschin, Basel

language. The cutting and slashing, the use of broken glass and rusty metals, cheap paper and ceremonial cloths, imply the gaping wounds of the social slaughterhouse. Here rage is at work: be it at the destruction and damage wreaked on the human imagination or at the victory of sheer exploitation and dishonesty, the means with which the powerful wage war with horrible success on the last vestiges of a "great dream". In Droese's work a bitter struggle takes place in the form of symbols and suggestions between the timeless symbols of hope and the mighty powers of destruction in the arena of suggestive reductions and a pithy archaic cult-like monumentality.

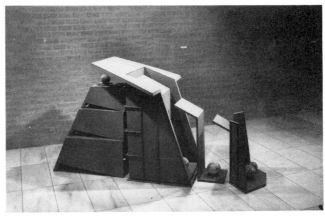

Harald Klingelhöller
VIER ENTWÜRFE FÜR EIN REDNERPULT UND EIN UNBEKANNTER PLANET
150 × 280 × 130
Courtesy Galerie Schmela, Düsseldorf

Just as in Näher's and Droese's work the content is not style but an expression of creative insurrection and belligerent vision, so it is in Olaf Metzel's inherently artistic paintings and sculptures in which all categories and connections are negated. The artist opposes the daily experienced aggression towards the right to humanity to the aggressiveness inherent in his own work of sculptural destruction. In places which have become destined for demolition, due to their complete economic exploitation, he sets the symbols of moral destruction against those of the physical environment through the use of the materials of capitalist society (e.g. concrete) and their brutal instruments (e.g. circular saw, crowbar). These pseudo idylls of holidays on Italian beaches, in a concrete landscape on the floor and walls of a workshop, the swastika scrawled on the walls of a deserted flat once inhabited by Turks and then wrecked by the artist, the red concrete headless man and those brutally agressive paintings. Aggression is the game, not a retreat into the realm of the private.

When artists translate the subjectively experienced destruction ritual of their everyday environment into an obsessive symbolism, they maintain a provocative distance from an unequivocal, worn out mythology as well as from any all-too-vague promised solutions. The raw, expressive method of production, the ragged impoverishment of both commonly known and commonly experienced circumstances and their simultaneous removal from the known and accepted order of things, as well as an overheated atmosphere of impending disaster, do not originate in dark private mythologies. As the specific experiences of the artist they are hurled out in a passionate display of the potential for social resistance. These are not blueprints for action but the bacilli of hope, there where the field is not handed over without a fight to the exploiters by the arts retreating into the ivory tower of aesthetic self-congratulation or into a nostalgic-reactionary museum culture.

(1) Travelling Exhibition of Berlin Artists (Luzern, Genf, Aachen 1981-2)

(2) The discriminating conception of German Art "Art Allemagne Aujourd'hui" in ARC, Paris, 1981. Graubner, Laib, Darboven as German contribution to the Venice Biennale 1982.

Translation by Michael Schlieper

TACTICS AND STRATEGIES: AN ABBREVIATED GUIDE TO ART IN NEW YORK AFTER THE WAR

Carter Ratcliff

Jackson Pollock, Barnett Newman and their colleagues joined Parisian modernism with local, jerry-built myths of cultural origins to open up a complex and boundless terrain of possibilities. Wandering there, Pollock and his generation devised the allover field. For young New York artists like Barbara Kruger, Cindy Sherman and Robert Longo, the zones pertinent to art are mapped by the images of the news, of advertising, of entertainment — in short, the media. Their vision saturated by media-currents, they produce art that looks very different from a Pollock drip painting or a Newmanesque expanse of colour. Not that these newcomers have dismissed the precedents set by the first generation of the New York School, so-called. That is far from the case. And yet if we focus too narrowly on methods of "image-appropriation", we will see none of the links between New York's past and its present.

"Image-appropriation", "image-scavenging" and all the rest of it is a matter of tactics, which is to say a matter of style. Stylistically, most of these new arrivals look like Pop artists with consciences. They pay for their media appropriations with the effort it takes to supply these borrowed bits of rhetoric with a critical edge. But such critiques are legible only under conditions provided by galleries, museums and art magazines, not in the arenas of consumerism and mundane politics. For Barbara Kruger, Jenny Holzer and others who make political use of ready-made images, acceptance in the art world appears to be at least as important as addressing a general public. They want to be a part of New York School history. To understand this desire and the way they go about realising it, we must step up from tactics to larger scale strategy.

The allover field, which first appeared in Jackson Pollock's drip paintings of 1947, provides local artists with their measure of seriousness. Suggesting unbounded immensity, those paintings reduced the edges of the canvas to arbitrariness. No longer did the frame enclose the familiar harmonies of an orderly composition, nor even the compositional fragments that Cubists, Constructivists, de Stijl and so many other styles preserved. Allover painting was a response to the unstructured nature of American life. This was a new kind of painting, a pictorial strategy that broke through stylistic lines to new territory. As so often happens with an innovative strategy, this one has often been reduced to a formal exercise. For Pollock and those who followed him into the uncertainties of alloverness, this way of making images produces emblems of a self cast by its own efforts into the farthest reaches of ambiguity and doubt.

There is unbounded space to be seen in landscpe painting of earlier centuries. But there is no reason to suppose that any of the first generation figures paid the least bit of attention to these Dutch, British and 19th century American developments, all of which were peripheral to the main currents of Western art. So the allover field strikes the New York art world as primordial, a realm of beginnings absolutely new and absolutely American. Pollock, in particular, looms on the scene like a Titan, myths clinging like clouds to his craggy eminence. Every ambitious young American artist of the last three decades has attempted to match his achievement — that is, to plunge into a limitless field and take possession of it.

Success consists of stamping chaos with a presence undeniably one's own. As might be expected, ambition's feints and ploys are largely unconscious. In New York, as elsewhere, most talk about art focuses on the politics of style. Nonetheless, all the major styles of post-war American Art — from Pop to the medley called Neo-expressionism — are veils stretched in front of the unseemly (because parricidal) desire to surpass the achievements of Jackson Pollock. In recent seasons, such veils have sometimes looked a bit diaphanous. Julian Schnabel, for instance, is so anxious to equal Pollock's mastery of the void that he has driven himself to an on-going burlesque of alloverness. Most New Yorkers are subtler, which is to say that they have learned to take their cues from Jasper Johns.

Johns cooled down the Action Painter's passion. His allover surfaces are icy and contemplative, not hot and desperate (like Pollock's) or filled with an ecstatic yearning for the sublime (Barnett Newman). Johns's fields are infinitely less to the eye than to the mind, for which he demonstrates the peculiar truth that an image — say, an American flag — induced to match its edges to those of the canvas is an image deprived of all scale. That flag could be, and for speculation is, any size at all, including infinitely large. Thus is alloverness brought under the sway of a dandified will. Johns's wilfulness (which is to say the finesse with which he rescued New York art from the inconvenience of passion) has been his most important legacy to later generations. Pop artists, Minimalists, even certain Conceptualists and earth artists have all accepted Johns as a mediator between themselves and Pollock's Titanic generation.

Andy Warhol occupies the field with the blankness of a soup-can grid, while Robert Ryman's blankness is more literally empty — an all white emblem of unboundedness, an expanse of white held flat to the canvas only by the mundane evidence of facture. Warhol the Pop artist and Ryman the Minimalist have nothing in common save their attempts, each in its own way successful, to invent a recognisable variant on first generation alloverness. Pattern painters offer more variants still, as do narrative Conceptualists, New Image painters, and so on. And on. It's easy to get the feeling that New York artists have reduced their heritage to a play of thoroughly aesthetic options. If the allover field began as a vast, ungraspable image of some American enigma, all that mystery appears to have drained away as competition with Pollock's example becomes a frenzied struggle for pre-eminence in Manhattan's style wars.

I have mentioned Julian Schnabel's success in reducing the struggle with Pollock to parody. David

Salle is less a parodist than a proponent of genteel farce. He begins with an allover field in the form of a Minimalist monochrome, then fills it with bits and pieces of imagery, some of them emotionally charged, others not. As New York usage demands, the final results refuse to cohere. Though Salle violates the integrity of the field with figurative images, this overlay is so vapid that Minimalist alloverness survives intact or, if not intact, not seriously threatened. As hints of compositional order and narrative import fade, Salle puts in his claim to a place in the history of American painting after Pollock. His is field painting of an eclectic, art school variety. Johns's iciness hinted that first generation strategies could be reduced to academic routine. Salle has realised this possibility. Like Schnabel, he makes the allover field safe for the exercise of fashionable taste.

Generated from a sense of risk, the earliest of the allover fields presented the imagination with a wide-open, dangerous place. Graffiti artists — or "writers" — who work in the subways of New York have found a way to convert the imagination's danger to an actuality. In pursuit of their art, they are subject to arrest and the physical abuse that often goes with it. As the work of the graffiti "writers" spread over the surface of subway cars, critics began to claim that these untaught artists had found a way to rescue the allover field from the academic futility, not to mention the marketable shallowness, which has afflicted this New York School innovation in so many of its recent forms. But the images of the graffitists are unfocused, naive, repetitious. Though dangers to the body must be braved in order to "write" these gigantic logos, this sort of art requires nothing of the self to be put at risk. Nor does the pseudo-graffiti of such gallery artists as Keith Haring, originally a subway "writer".

Jonathan Borofsky, by contrast, exposes the very texture of his inward self. Having appropriated the energies of graffiti, he channels them into a rcdcfinition of the installation art that developed in the late 1960s from Minimalist literalism. Minimalism tried to endow the material aspects of form with absolute clarity. The early installation artists (who included certain Minimalists — Robert Morris, for instance) wanted to extend that clarity to the space in which form appeared. The gallery became the allover field, rendered pure by a minimalist emptiness. Borofsky retains that version of the field while rejecting its dubious purity. As the scrawling, compulsive, graffiti-like notations of his dreams and reveries fill the walls, as three-dimensional images make an attempt to capture space, Borofsky charges the environment with his own obsessions, transforming space into a field of private emotions — the alloverness of dream.

Performance art was another of Minimalism's offshoots. In its earliest form, it tried to treat the body like a Minimalist object — see Vito Acconci's work of the late 1960s and early 1970s. Soon Scott Burton had augmented the body's presence with a "Minimalised" repertoire of gestures. Other artists, among them Laurie Anderson, began to load performance with an astonishing array of options. In Anderson's case these ranged from violin solos to electronic synthesizers, all of them injected, so to speak, with Minimalism's icy numbness. Since these developments often had a narrative thrust, Minimalist frigidity gave way to an attitude of a different sort — the ironic detachment of the story-teller whose story is not to be taken at face value. In Anderson's mature work, the Minimalist void has become an unbounded field of knowing scepticism — or a field of scepticism unbounded.

Now that Anderson's performances have come to resemble rock concerts complete with light shows, her field has taken palpable shape in the immense screen where she projects her visual motifs. Faced with the image-barrage of the media, Anderson is inclusive. Barbara Kruger is the opposite. Blending current images with the cloud of out-dated words and pictures floating in our imaginations, Kruger confines herself to a graphic designer's version of the picture plane. With a sharply disciplined play of dubious photo fragments and language shards, she opens her work to the flow and counterflow of political and marketplace manipulation. Thus she raises a sceptical mirror to the chaos of the moment's ideological field.

Though Jenny Holzer has collaborated with painters and other producers of pictures, she is at her best when she focuses on her brilliant burlesques of contemporary polemics — right wing, left wing or so demented its position cannot be charted. Deprived of visual imagery, her art draws on the physical environment where it appears. This might be a gallery, a collector's house or a street in midtown Manhattan. Holzer's bursts of language aesthetise these places, turning them into potentially limitless fields of meaning. Though the Minimalists provide the bitter edge of her irony with no precedents, her use of space recalls theirs and that of the installation artists who expanded the reach of the Minimalist look. And, by way of Minimalism, Holzer's urban field finds a link with the alloverness of New York's first generation painters.

Those who insist that such connections must be stylistic have difficulty in seeing how Holzer, Kruger and Anderson have anything to do with Jackson Pollock. Yet these young artists have everything to do with him, for they sustain the energies of post-war American art on the only legitimate terms — their own. Cindy Sherman's terms are those of a deep understanding of the way the media's image-field has submerged women in exploitive roles. At first her photographic self-portraits referred with pinpoint accuracy to movie *clichés*. Later she began to give her art a nebulous fervour, almost Expressionist in its intensity. Over the last few seasons, she has assigned herself a range of roles sufficiently wide to evoke the entire web of social usage in which women — and men — are caught.

Mimicking the image-barrage, Sherman appears to reject its premises even while accepting them. Like so many of the best artists who have appeared in the 1980s, she is an ironist. Robert Longo is not. Stepping beyond the familiar perspectives of irony he has seen that, beneath its flickering surface, our public imagery is static. For him the image-field is composed of monuments, not fast-moving flashes. His over-sized figure drawings, Deco-style blocks of statuary and relief sculptures all evoke this oppressive stasis in a spirit of acceptance. He hints at the way the grandiose, usually hidden impulses of the self seek derisory Lascaux. The artist shuffles the cards which would define the instruments as moments of the "creation", delighting in sowing seeds of trouble in the very means of our perception: the work is never where one expects it. It is like a ghost or perhaps a myth.

Annette Messager, using a completely different imbrication of painting and photography, gives form to the chimera unfurling on the wall, fragile and monstrous, coloured and yet black, strange and cruel. These ample figures spring from a cascade of exacerbating antagonisms convoked by some sort of bizzare angel for a frenetic sabbath. Faced with this fodder of human morsels, the eye is lost in seeing too much: first of all, eyes of all kinds and sizes, a crowd of indiscrete anatomical fragments and then dancing monsters, stars, and spiders ... a gigantic masked ball of figures which appear and disappear at the whim of our perceptions, seeming by turns to be all encompassing and focused, where the tree is finally prisoner of a dream forest.

Annick Nozati, using voice and gesture, blends her own fantasies with women's shared memories. Her improvisations are demonic jugglings where the truth of the moment is continuously confronted by a catalogue of received ideas. In this game of being and appearing, she also shuffles the deck through vocal performance, the range of which brings together the classical singer and the popular singer, as well as all the innovations of jazz. It is opera, but the essence of an opera lived in a dream life.

The four artists have set off on paths that lead to the deepest parts of the self, overthrowing accepted codes. Their manipulations, more than dandyism in a cynical world, are as many challenges of that incurable state of things where Owell's *Nineteen Eighty-Four* meets the pitiless punctuality of the calendar. From the black contours of François Boisrond to the spotlights of Annick Nozati, traversing Georges Rousse's demolished sites or Annette Messager's hallucinations, there is the same desire to tear apart the darkness where no sound is heard except a chorus of those taking up the phrase with which Aragon chose to end his last novel:

> *Je n'attends rien de la vie*
> *qu'un bruit brisé de charrettes.*

Paris, December 1983
Translation Paula Latos-Valier
and Leon Paroissien

PARTICIPATING COUNTRIES

Australia
Austria
Brazil
Britain
Canada
Chile
Colombia
Denmark
France
Hong Kong
Republic of Ireland
Italy
Japan
Netherlands
New Zealand
Poland
Switzerland
United States
West Germany
Yugoslavia

PARTICIPATING ARTISTS:

Davida Allen
Armando
Art & Language
Terry Atkinson
Breda Beban
Joseph Beuys
Tony Bevan
Annette Bezor
Francois Boisrond
Peter Booth
Tomasz Ciecierski
Tony Cragg
Juan Davila
Antonio Dias
Gonzalo Díaz
Eugenio Dittborn
Felix Droese
Marlene Dumas
Edward Dwurnik
Mimmo Germana
Gilbert & George
Mike Glier
Hans Haacke
Jenny Holzer
Ralph Hotere
Jörg Immendorff
Berit Jensen
Birgit Jürgenssen
Mike Kelley
Peter Kennedy
Anselm Kiefer
Karen Knorr
Barbara Kruger
Robert Longo
Colin McCahon
Syoko Maemoto
Sandra Meigs
Cildo Meireles
Gianni Melotti
Marisa Merz
Annette Messager
Olaf Metzel
Sara Modiano
Michael Mulcahy
Josef Felix Müller
Christa Näher
Annick Nozati
Anna Oppermann
Andy Patton
A.R. Penck
Robert Randall & Frank Bendinelli
Jytte Rex
Georges Rousse
Klaudia Schifferle
Hubert Schmalix
Cindy Sherman
Vincent Tangredi
Peter Taylor
Dragoljub Raša Todosijević
Vicki Varvaressos
Jenny Watson
Michiko Yano
Eva Man-Wah Yuen

Artists appear in the above order for both the
illustration and biographical pages.

DAVIDA ALLEN

JOSEPHINE AND SELF BY THE FIRE II, 1983, oil on canvas, 154 × 140

JOSEPHINE AND SELF BY THE FIRE I, 1983, oil on canvas, 154 × 140

ARMANDO

WALDRAND, installation view, Stedelijk Museum , 1981

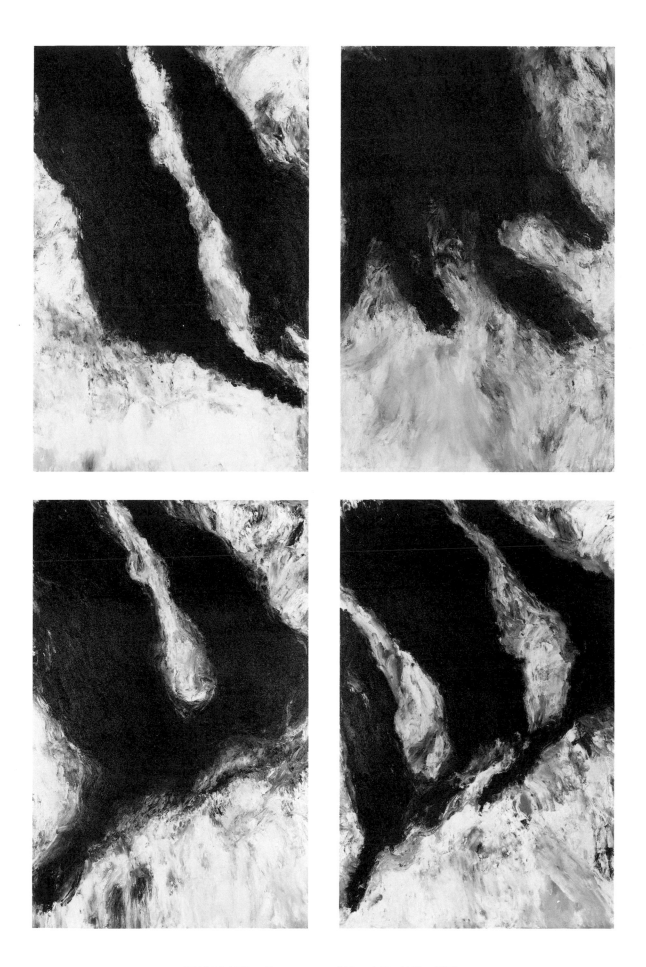

WALDRAND, oil on canvas, 210 × 145, 1982−1983

INDEX: THE STUDIO AT 3 WESLEY PLACE PAINTED BY MOUTH. 1982,
ink and crayon on paper, 343 × 727.5

TERRY ATKINSON

COMIC-MAP MADE BY BOTH TROTSKY IN HEAVEN AND TROTSKY IN HELL — A REALLY DIALECTICAL
CONDITION . . . , 1982/83, acrylic on canvas, 146 × 91

PICTURE WITH BOTCHED-UP DRAWING DEPICTING BRITISH PROLETARIANS ATTACKING GERMAN
PROLETARIANS, BOTH SETS OF PROLETARIANS DEFENDING THE INTERESTS OF THEIR RESPECTIVE
CAPITALISMS, 1981, Conte crayon and gouache on paper, 104 × 94

BREDA BEBAN

TRISTAN AND ISOLDA, 1983, acrylic on canvas, 135 × 175

LITTLE DEATH, 1982, acrylic on canvas, 250 × 290

JOSEPH BEUYS

ACTION 7000 OAKS, DOCUMENTA 7, KASSEL, 1982, tree-planting

ACTION 7000 OAKS, DOCUMENTA 7, KASSEL, 1982, stones in front of the Fridericianum

TONY BEVAN

NATURAL MYSTIC, 1983, pigment on canvas, 274.3 × 182.9

THE PROPHET, 1982, dry pigment on canvas, 452.2 × 335.3

VENUS EMERGING, 1983, oil on canvas, 200 × 190

A BEDROOM PIECE I, 1983, oil on linen, 192.5 × 203.5

FRANCOIS BOISROND

UNTITLED, 1982, acrylic on canvas, triptych, 270 × 350

UNTITLED, 1982, acrylic on canvas, 3 panels, 120 × 215

PETER BOOTH

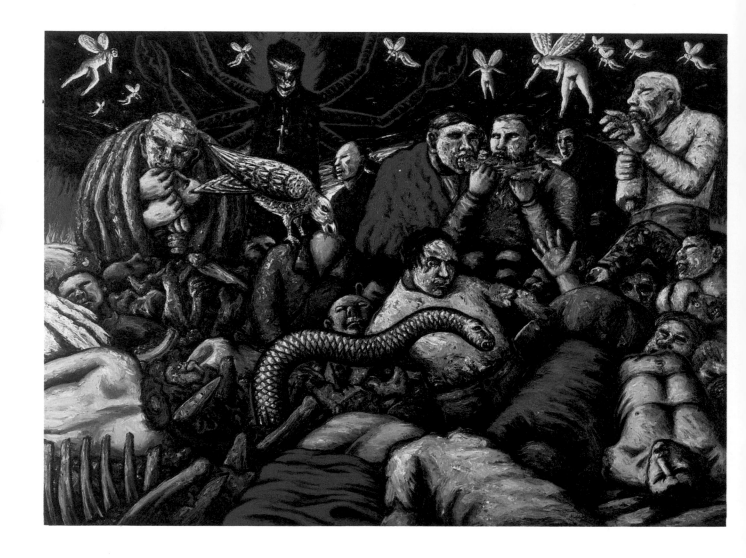

PAINTING 1982, 1982, oil on canvas, 197.7 × 274

PAINTING, 1982, oil on canvas, 170 × 260

TOMASZ CIECIERSKI

DOGS, 1983, oil on canvas 190 × 360

KNOT (WEZEL), 1983-84, oil on canvas, 190 × 360

TONY CRAGG

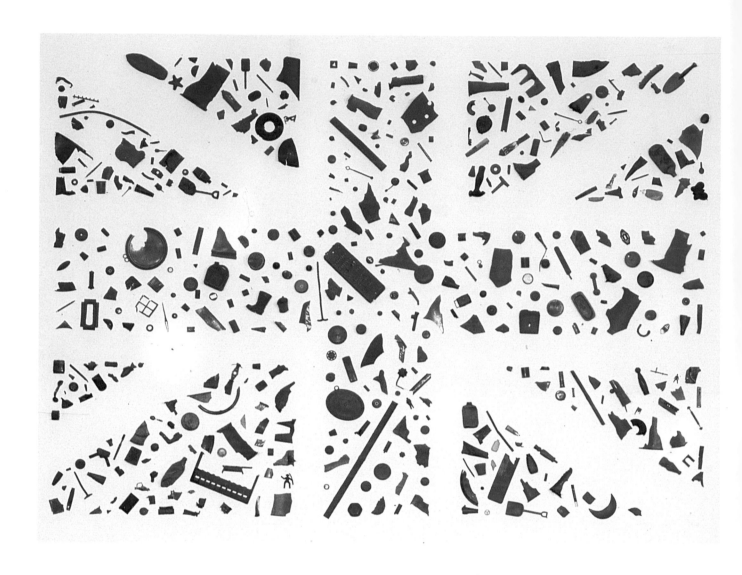

POSTCARD UNION JACK, 1981, plastic fragments, 250 × 400

BRITAIN SEEN FROM THE NORTH, 1981, mixed material, 91 × 124

JUAN DAVILA

GULF, 1983, oil on canvas, 274.3 × 274.3

NEO-POP, 1983, oil on canvas, 274.3 × 274.3

ANTONIO DIAS

WATER AND SALT/DAILY, 1983, iron oxide, graphite, gold and bronze paint on newspaper on canvas, 55 × 120

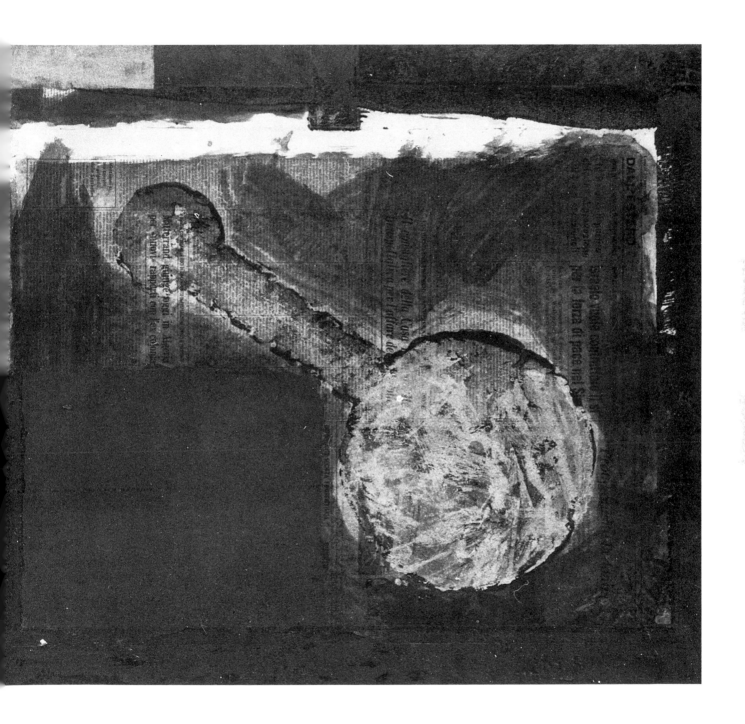

GONZALO DÍAZ

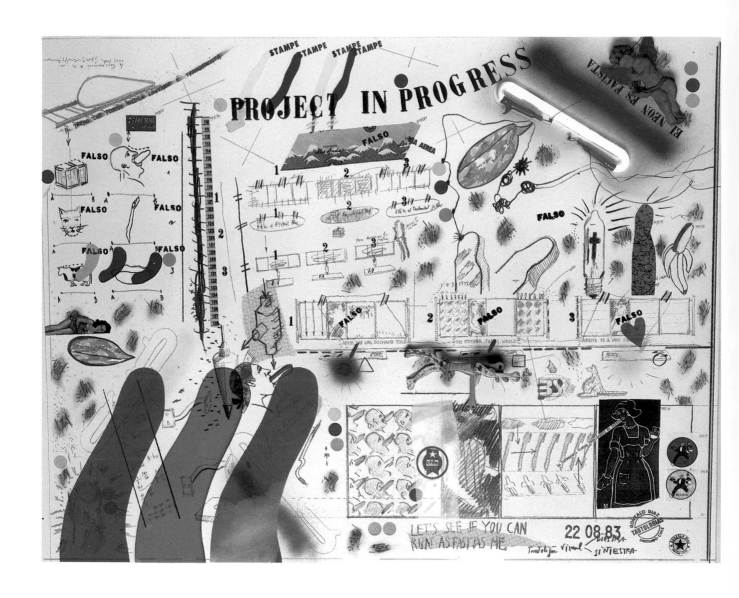

PROJECT IN PROGRESS, graphite, enamel, enamel spray, coloured plastic transparencies,
neon and objects on cotton paper, 77 × 98

LET'S SEE IF YOU CAN RUN AS FAST AS ME, 1983, photo serigraphy and stencil on polytoile
with green neon and object, 270 × 400

EUGENIO DITTBORN

A WHOLE DAY OF MY LIFE, 1983, photo silkscreen and painting on acrylic, cotton and masonite,
each panel 240 × 77.6

PIETA, 1983, work in progress, Vinilplus and photo silkscreen on P.V.C., 160 × 170

FELIX DROESE

Detail from "DORT" (THERE), 1981-3, I-XIII, timber

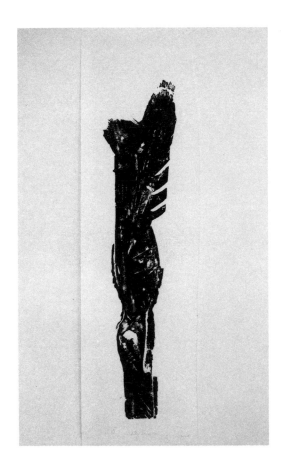 

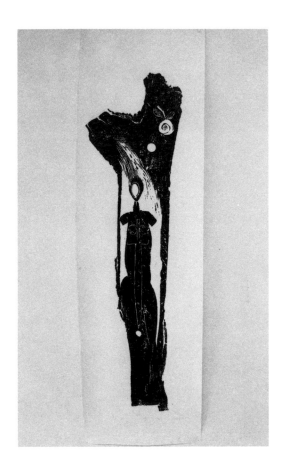

Detail from "DORT" (THERE), 1981-3, I-XIII, prints on paper

MARLENE DUMAS

DE DRIE KRONEN VAN HET EXPRESSIONISME (THE THREE CROWNS OF EXPRESSIONISM),
1983, oil on canvas and photograph, 2 parts, 250 × 120

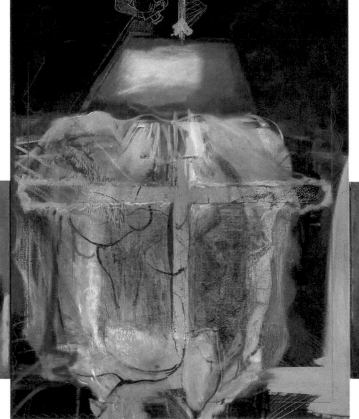

THE FUTILITY OF ARTISTIC CONFESSION, 1983, triptych, oil on canvas, 160 × 240

NIEDZIELNA MSZA, (SUNDAY MASS),1983, oil on canvas, 146 × 114

PO TRENINGU (AFTER TRAINING), 1972, oil on canvas, 146 × 114

MIMMO GERMANA

LA CASA SULL'ISOLA, 1983, oil on canvas, 205 × 300

IMMAGINE CIRCOLARE, 1983, oil on canvas, 240 × 420

GILBERT & GEORGE

YOUTH ATTACK, 1982, photo-piece, 302.5 × 606

MIKE GLIER

KIKI, 1983, oil on canvas, 162.6 × 218.4

NUCLEAR ACCOUNTABILITY: I, BLAST ME, 1983, wall installation
Whitney Museum of American Art, chalk and latex, approximately 548.6 × 914.4

HANS HAACKE

REAGANOMICS, 1982-83, colour transparency, fluorescent lights, 182.9 × 124.5

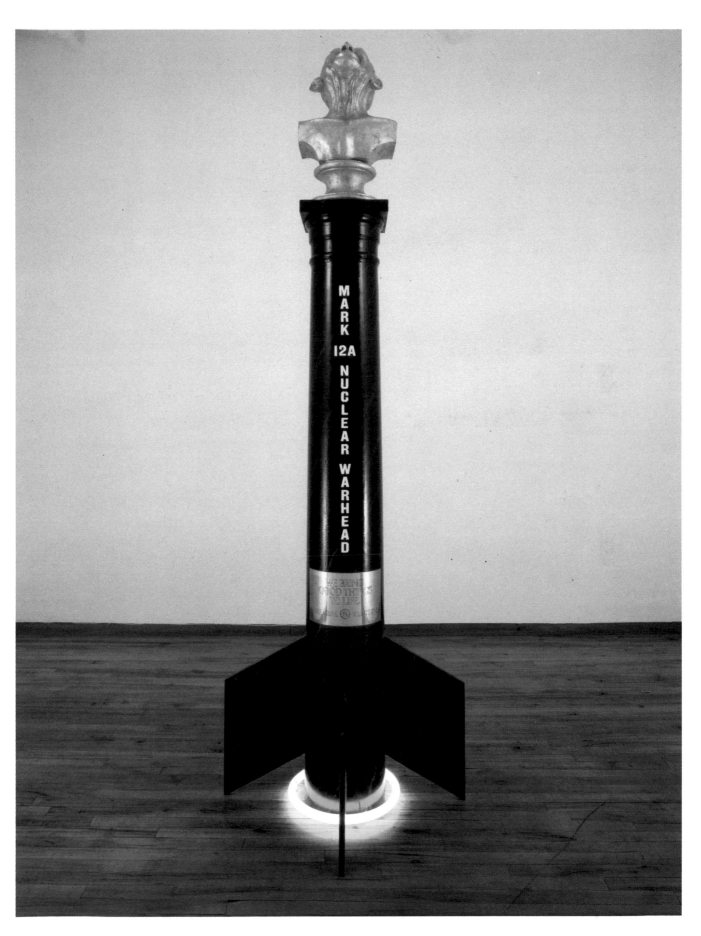

WE BRING GOOD THINGS TO LIFE, 1983, installation John Weber Gallery, marbled wood pillar with fins,
copper plate, gold leafed plaster bust and circular fluorescent tube, 279.4 × 88.9

JENNY HOLZER

INFLAMMATORY ESSAYS, 1979-83, colour offset posters, each 43.2 × 43.2

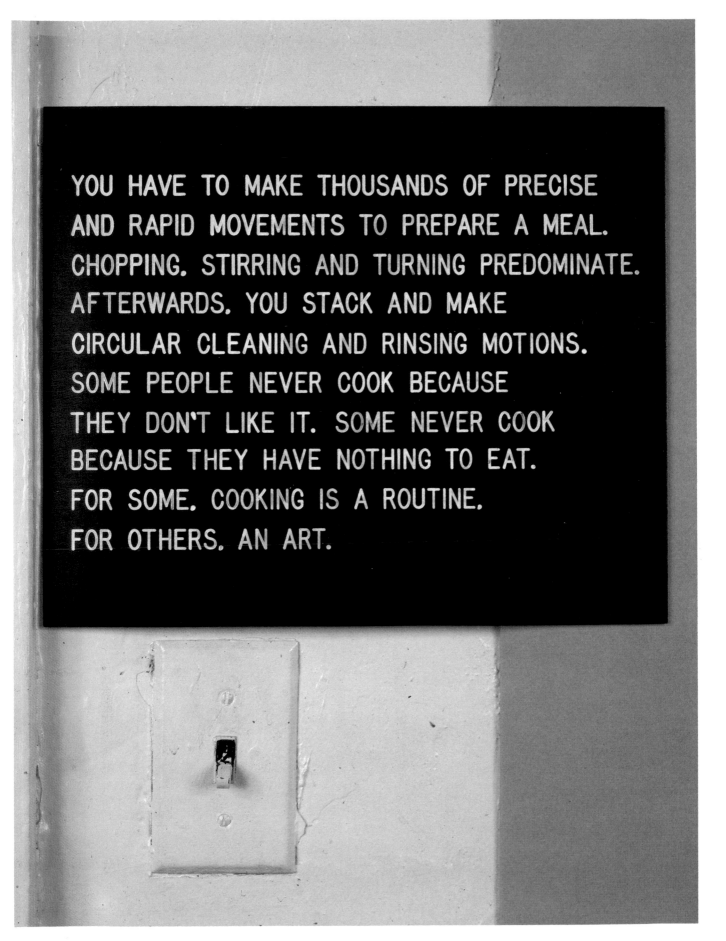

YOU HAVE TO MAKE THOUSANDS OF PRECISE
AND RAPID MOVEMENTS TO PREPARE A MEAL.
CHOPPING, STIRRING AND TURNING PREDOMINATE.
AFTERWARDS, YOU STACK AND MAKE
CIRCULAR CLEANING AND RINSING MOTIONS.
SOME PEOPLE NEVER COOK BECAUSE
THEY DON'T LIKE IT. SOME NEVER COOK
BECAUSE THEY HAVE NOTHING TO EAT.
FOR SOME, COOKING IS A ROUTINE,
FOR OTHERS, AN ART.

Black enamel plaque from THE LIVING SERIES, installation view

RALPH HOTERE

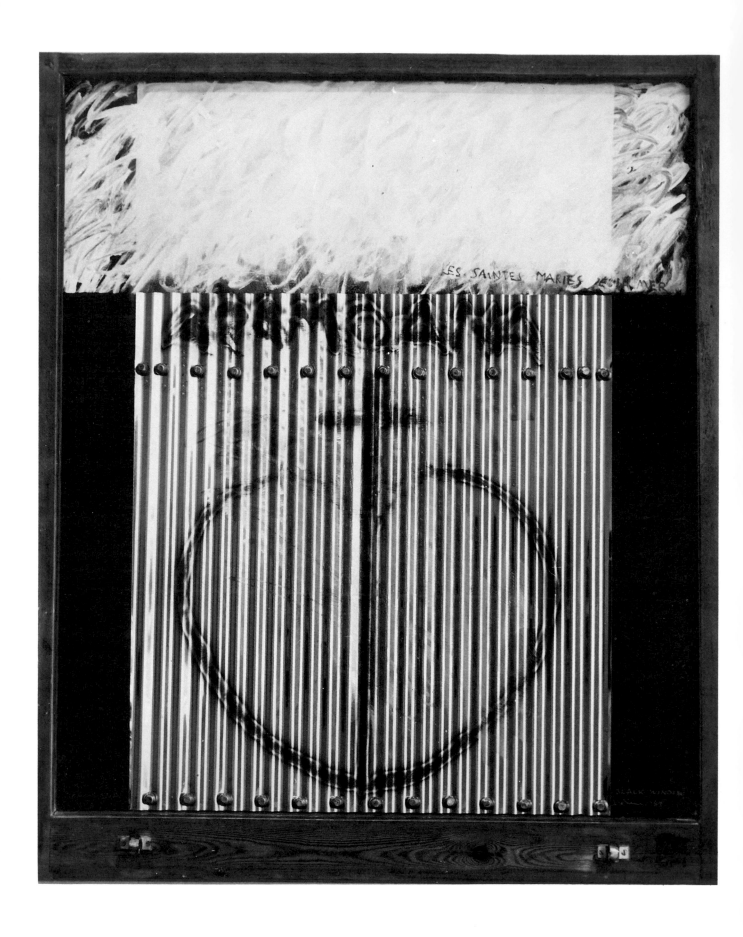

BLACK WINDOW, 1983, burnt corrugated stainless steel and acrylic on hardboard, 121.9 × 96.5

BLACK WINDOW TOWARDS ARAMOANA, 1982, acrylic and lacquer on board, 121.9 × 121.9

JÖRG IMMENDORFF

REICHSSACHE, 1983, oil on canvas, 250 × 250

C.D.-ZEITSCHWEISS, 1983, oil on canvas, 150 × 200

BERIT JENSEN

RUSSELL'S AMUSEMENTS 1-10, NO. 3, 1983, dispersion on canvas, 188 × 200

RUSSELL'S AMUSEMENTS 1-10, NO. 1, 1983, dispersion on canvas, 188 × 200

BIRGIT JÜRGENSSEN

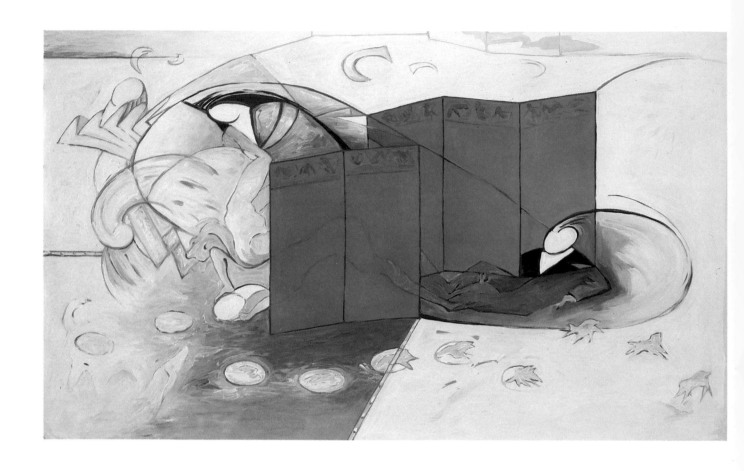

GRENZERZIEHUNG, 1983, oil on paper, 150.5 × 245

DER VERFUHRTE NARZISS, 1983, oil on paper, 150.5 × 227.5

MIKE KELLEY

MONKEY ISLAND, 1983, installation Rosamund Felsen Gallery

THE BELLS, 1982-83, from MONKEY ISLAND, acrylic on paper, 59.7 × 196.9

THE POOR FARM WET AND DRY, 1982-83, from MONKEY ISLAND, acrylic on paper, 91.4 × 133.4

PETER KENNEDY

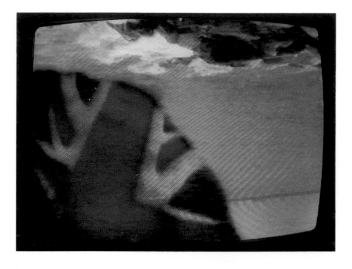

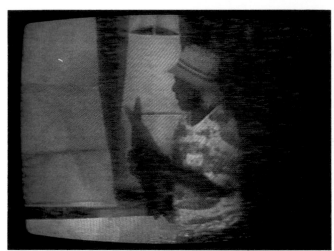

ON SACRED LAND, 1983-84, video stills, Peter Kennedy with John Hughes

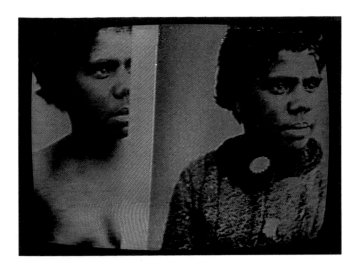

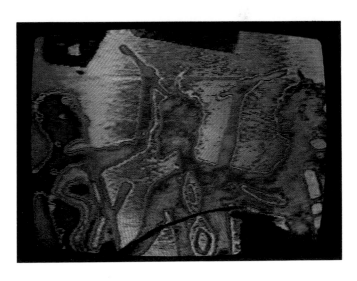

ANSELM KIEFER

WEGE DER WELT WEISHEIT: DIE HERMANSCHLACHT, 1978-80, woodcut on paper, oil on canvas, 290 × 390

DER RHEIN, 1982 woodcut on paper on canvas, 380 × 280

KAREN KNORR

Whatever a Man's
Social origin,
once he has been elected
he is looked upon
as an Equal by his
Fellow-Members.

GENTLEMEN, 1981-83, photography image/text bromide black and white mounted on museum board, 58.4 × 45

How he longed
desperately
for the halcyon Days
of his Youth
when an Englishman
could satisfy his own Honour.
No questions asked.

GENTLEMEN, 1981-83, photography image/text bromide black and white mounted on museum board, 58.4 × 45

BARBARA KRUGER

UNTITLED, 1983, black and white photograph, 182.9 × 121.9

You substantiate our

UNTITLED, 1983, black and white photograph, 304.8 × 243.8

ROBERT LONGO

PURPLE KIDS (HEAT), 1983, charcoal, graphite, acrylic on dyed paper, 243.8 × 121.9

PURPLE KIDS (SOUND), 1983, charcoal, graphite, acrylic on dyed paper, 243.8 × 121.9

COLIN McCAHON

VICTORY OVER DEATH 2, 1970, synthetic polymer paint on canvas, 207.5 × 597.7

WATER IN MY MIND, 1981, mixed media

SOSHU YAKYOKU, 1983, mixed media installation

SANDRA MEIGS

SEMI WIND-UP BOUT, 1982, installation, 30 Conte crayon drawings framed, audio loop, sculpture/film loop, printed cards, drawings each 50.8 × 66

Up against the ropes. Relentless

SEMI WIND-UP BOUT, 1982, detail drawing, 50.8 × 66

Round 6. He was just about to think.

"I don't know"

SEMI WIND-UP BOUT, 1982, detail drawings, each 50.8 × 66

GIANNI MELOTTI

UCCELLO IN ANAMORFOSI, 1983, acrylic on canvas, 200 × 300

SOLIDI, 1983, acrylic, various dimensions

MARISA MERZ

PARTICOLARE DELLA MOSTRA DA SALVATORE ALA, MILANO, 1977, cup with wax

QUANDO L'OCCHIO I ALLA MONTAGNA, 1980, iron chair, nylon filament, wax, 75 × 50 × 50

ANNETTE MESSAGER

CHIMERES, 1982-83, installation view, photographs and paint

ANNETTE MESSAGER

CHIMERES, 1982, photographs and paint, 100 × 200

OLAF METZEL

TURKENWOHNUNG, ABSTAND 12.000 DM (VB), installation

TANKSTELLE, LANDSBERGERSTRASSE 193 (BZ), installation

SARA MODIANO

THE DISAPPEARANCE OF A CULTURE, 1983, Cibachrome photographs

MICHAEL MULCAHY

SIGNPOST, 1983, acrylic on canvas, 161 × 204

AT WAR, 1983, acrylic on canvas, 267 × 379

JOSEF FELIX MÜLLER

ARSCH, 1983, dispersion on packing paper, 290 × 400

TISCH, 1983, dispersion on packing paper, 290 × 400

CHRISTA NÄHER

UNTITLED, 1983, dispersion on canvas, 250 × 200

UNTITLED, 1983, dispersion on canvas, 250 × 200

ANNICK NOZATI

THE ARTIST IN PERFORMANCE

ANNA OPPERMANN

ENSEMBLE ON THE ECONOMIC ASPECT, 1978-81, installation Serpentine Gallery London 1981, detail

ENSEMBLE ON THE ECONOMIC ASPECT, 1978-81, installation Serpentine Gallery London 1981, 300 × 600 × 900, partial view

ANDY PATTON

UNFURL, 1983, oil on canvas, 152.4 × 198.1

THE STRUGGLE FOR PRIVACY, 1983, oil on canvas, 152.4 × 213.4

A.R. PENCK

WIRD ZEICHEN REALITAT?3, 1982, acrylic on canvas, 200 × 300

LORSFELD, 1983, acrylic on canvas, 200 × 300

ROBERT RANDALL &
FRANK BENDINELLI

BLIND DATE from LOVE STORIES — TOWARDS A VIDEO NARRATIVE, 1982-84

**ROBERT RANDALL &
FRANK BENDINELLI**

LOVE FEVER from LOVE STORIES — TOWARDS A VIDEO NARRATIVE, 1982-84

SPEAR, 1983, one of nine drawings, indian ink and chalk, each 64 × 45

SPEAR, 1983, one of nine drawings, indian ink and chalk, each 64 × 45

GEORGES ROUSSE

UNTITLED, 1983, Ektachrome photograph of installation, 127 × 157

UNTITLED, 1983, Kodachrome colour photograph of installation, 127 × 156

KLAUDIA SCHIFFERLE

3 WUNSCHE (3 WISHES), 1983, lacquer on canvas, 210 × 297

SELBSTPORTRAIT (SELF-PORTRAIT), 1983, lacquer on canvas, diameter 200

HUBERT SCHMALIX

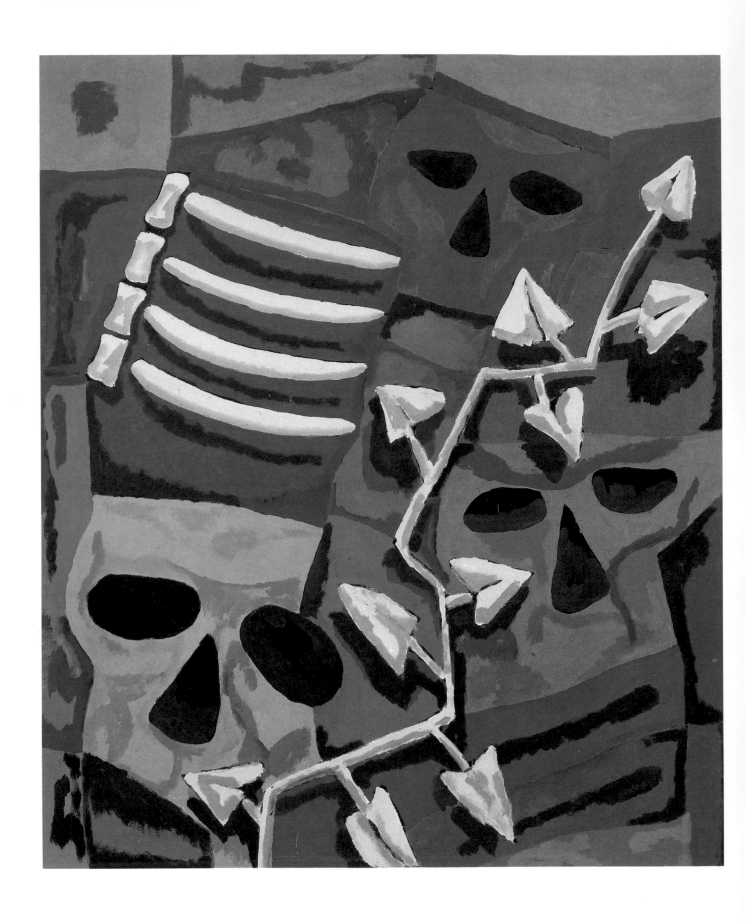

LEBEN UND STERBEN (LIVE AND DIE), 1983, tempera on canvas, 240 × 200

LEBEN UND STERBEN (LIVE AND DIE), 1983, tempera on canvas, 240 × 200

UNTITLED, 1983, colour photograph, 87.6 × 57.2

UNTITLED, 1983, colour photograph, 88.3 × 41.91

VINCENT TANGREDI

THREE LIVING — THREE DEAD, 1983, fresco on canvas, 213.4 × 182.9

THE DEVIL'S PIG, 1983, fresco on canvas, 213.4 × 182.9

PETER TAYLOR

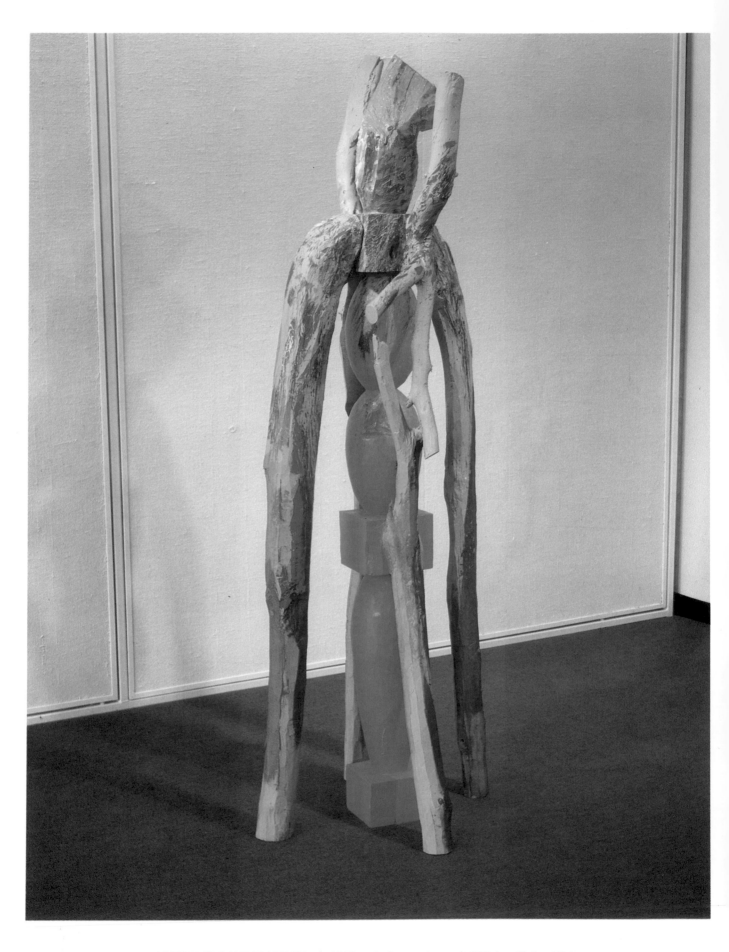

FIGURE IN LANDSCAPE NO. 1, 1983, polychromed wood, 203.4 × 50.8 × 50.8

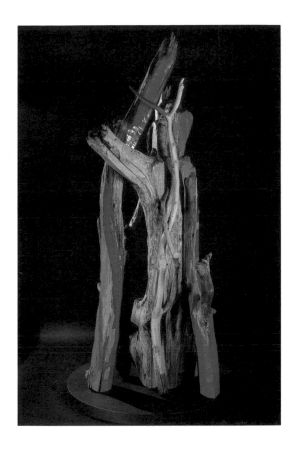

FIGURE IN LANDSCAPE NO. 2, 1983, polychromed wood, 222.7 × 91.4 × 91.4

DRAGOLJUB RAŠA TODOSIJEVIĆ

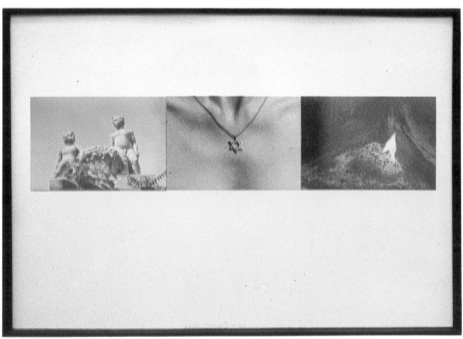

SCHLAFFLAGE (from the series SCHLAFFLAGE), 1981, installation view, Gallery of Museum of Contemporary Art, Belgrade, 1982

Motifs from Phaidon
My name is Pablo Ruiz Picasso. I am painter, but many claim that I am also gifted draftsman. The "Picasso" is after my mother.
I know, there are not many Picassos in the Balkans. In Belgrade? I doubt it, I am not certain, I wouldn't know. There may
be some Pikasovitchs or Pikasitchs, yes, but the surname Picasso is a rarity. The sly sniggering about my personality leaves
me indifferent. I am proud of my name. It is true that I am not of Spanish origin. That is a complete misconception. I am
one hundred percent Slav, South Slav if you insist on knowing the details. You say that my mother's maiden name was
Ruzhitch and my father ws Pikachevitch?! Well, that's a family matter. Does it lessen my greatness, hombre? No, on the
contrary!

MY NAME IS PABLO PICASSO, 1981-83, drawing on paper and text, 24.5 × 19

VICKI VARVARESSOS

I CAN'T EXACTLY . . ., 1983, acrylic on canvas, 127 × 154

CLAIRE EXPLAINS . . ., 1983, acrylic on canvas, 154 × 142

JENNY WATSON

TRANSPORT, 1983, acrylic, oil, ink, charcoal, pastel and cord on hessian, 274.3 × 304.8

THE HORSE HOSPITAL, 1983, oil, acrylic, pastel, charcoal and glass beads on cotton duck, 274.3 × 304.8

MICHIKO YANO

JUKO, TABLE BLUE — KILLZY, 1982, bronze, wood, clay, acrylic, lacquer, 600 × 350 × 240

THE THIRD FACE, 1983-4, work in progress, paper heads, 20.3

THE THIRD FACE, 1983-4, work in progress, paper heads, 20.3

Colin McCahon

For some time now, Colin McCahon has been thought of in New Zealand as that country's greatest painter. In fact, he is an extraordinary artist by anybody's standards. The exhibition for the Fifth Biennale of Sydney at the Power Gallery of Contemporary Art is the first substantial showing of his work outside New Zealand, so visitors to it will be quite unprepared for the power and originality of the art they encounter there.

Modernism came late to New Zealand, as it did to other provincial places, like the United States. At the end of the Second World War, a small group of painters including McCahon began the task of bringing New Zealand art into the twentieth century. It was a hard task and the loudest of the "kicking and screaming" was reserved for McCahon's.

In provinces like Australia and New Zealand, modernism's advance was complicated and in many respects blunted by a regionalist and/or nationalist agenda. On the other hand, it can be argued that painting's present revival has had something to do with the persistence on the periphery of painters like McCahon who kept their distance, and that regionalist ideas permitted them to keep it with conviction. These are painters who never were converts to "formalism", Greenbergian modernism, and who were unmoved by stories of painting's decline and fall. 1970, the year of the "dematerialisation of the art object", was the year of Colin McCahon's mammoth 27 foot *Practical Religion* — a painter's vote of confidence in his medium if ever there was one.

> There are those who want a text (an art, a painting) without a shadow, without the "dominant ideology"; but this is to want a text without fecundity, without productivity, a sterile text ... The text needs its shadow: this shadow is *a bit* of ideology, *a bit* of representation, a *bit* of subject: ghosts, pockets, traces, necessary clouds: subversion must produce its own chiaruscuro.
>
> Roland Barthes, *The Pleasure of the Text* (1973)

Although it is retrospective (works from the last five decades are included) the exhibition does not pretend to represent the full range of McCahon's production. Instead it aims to give the viewer a good idea of McCahon's longstanding interest in

THE VALLEY OF DRY BONES, 1947
Oil on canvas
93.4 × 90.2
Courtesy National Art Gallery, Wellington

re-presenting texts and numbers. The twenty or so works include 1940s figurative paintings which contain comic book style conversation bubbles, "allover" word paintings of 1969 and 1970, 1-10 number series of the 1960s and examples of the 1-14 *Stations of the Cross* series of the 1970s. They exemplify the constant disintegrating and integrating of word, image and number, which process characterises McCahon's *oeuvre* as a whole.

> It isn't in any significant way a question of staging a Holy Communion service or a Sun Dance but of re-establishing the conditions of "communion" as a most general proposition about all our work. The problem, after all, is largely Western, because in the West there was this historical consignment of great areas of human experience to the domain of something called the secular — like dance, like comedy, like the natural world itself to take a really major instance.
>
> Jerome Rothenberg (interviewed by Dick Higgins, 1977)

McCahon's use of text and number is inseparable from his religiosity. Painting becomes an occasion for translation, reading, ritual contemplation and meditation. For story-telling. Neither figurative nor abstract modes are as suitable, although McCahon's position is an inclusive one and he will use both. That is because, as he continues to canvas the possibilities of painting, his work continues to approach and retreat from the condition of language.

Wystan Curnow
New Zealand, 1983

**Power Gallery of Contemporary Art
University of Sydney**

Aspects of Australian Figurative Painting 1942-1962

Dreams, Fears and Desires.

S.H. Ervin Gallery
National Trust
Observatory Hill

The recent worldwide return to figurative painting has generated great interest in the already popular period of Australian painting from the 1940s to the 1960s.

The renewed concern with issues surrounding Australian figurative painting of this period, and especially with aspects of expressionism, has generated the assembly of this exhibition for showing at the S.H. Ervin Gallery, Sydney. When shown in the context of a major exhibition of international contemporary art such as the Fifth Biennale of Sydney, these works from an earlier period take on new meaning and in turn sharpen our perception of present art forms.

The different approaches taken by artists to similar subject matter during this major period of Australian art are examined and re-interpreted, the period being one that has been largely neglected by critics, art historians and the public over the last fifteen years.

The paintings selected are striking, expressive and surprising, and have strong visual and social impact. The exhibition itself is divided into seven sections:
Rebellions and Rehearsal, an introduction showing the stylistic sources of the late thirties and early forties; and six thematic sections: *Marks of Violence I: A World of Wars, II: The Wounding of Women; Myths of Place I: Still Life in the City, II: Empty Centre and Anti-Hero; Signs of the Other I: Constructions of Childhood, II: White on Black.*

A major theme is alienation, both personal and social. The exhibition challenges the orthodox view of the 1950s that sees the period as comfortable, increasingly wealthy and secure. Artists showing the darker side — the threat of the Bomb, psychological insecurities and sexual tensions, the ambivalent relationship of Australians with the bush, their view of the cities, the position of the Aborigines — are represented, as well as those presenting a rosier picture of Australian society.

Conceived by: Profesor Virginia Spate
Curated by: Christine Dixon with Terry Smith
Organising gallery: S.H. Ervin Gallery, Director: Dinah Dysart

This exhibition has been made possible by a generous grant from the Visual Arts Board of the Australia Council.

Artists:

Charles Blackman
Herbert Badham
Jean Bellette
Josl (Yosel) Bergner
Arthur Boyd
David Boyd
John Brack
Noel Counihan
Ray Crooke
William Dargie
Robert Dickerson
William Dobell
Russell Drysdale
Adrian Feint
Donald Friend
Sam Fullbrook
James Gleeson
Pro Hart
Weaver Hawkins ("Raokin")
Ivor Hele
Sali Herman
Joy Hester
Jacqueline Hick
Francis Lymburner
Jon Molvig
Mirka Mora
Albert Namatjira
Sidney Nolan
John Olsen
John Perceval
Margaret Preston
Clifton Pugh
Jeffrey Smart
Grace Cossington Smith
David Strachan
Albert Tucker
Danila Vassilieff
Brett Whiteley
James Wigley

Catalogue of works

Measurements are in centimetres; height precedes width.

Rebellions & Rehearsals

1. Danila Vassilieff (1897-1958)
   Street Scene, Surry Hills, 1936
   54.6 × 50.3
   Oil on canvas
   Private collection, Melbourne

2. Danila Vassilieff
   Street scene with graffiti, 1938
   45.5 × 61.1
   Oil on plywood
   Private collection, Melbourne

3. Josl (Yosel) Bergner (b.1920)
   Two Women, 1942
   48.7 × 60.6
   Oil on hardboard
   Presented by Mr I. Engelhard, 1979
   Collection of National Gallery of Victoria, Melbourne

4. William Dobell (1899-1970)
   Knocking Off Time at an aerodrome — Bankstown, 1943
   39.9 × 50.1
   Oil on hardboard
   Collection of Australian War Memorial, Canberra

5. William Dobell
   Night Recreation at C.C.C. Camp, 1944
   25.9 × 31.1
   Oil on cardboard
   Collection of Australian War Memorial, Canberra

6. James Gleeson (b.1915)
   The Sower, 1944
   76.2 × 50.8
   Oil on canvas
   Collection of Art Gallery of New South Wales, Sydney

7. Albert Tucker (b.1914)
   Image of Modern Evil (Night Image) #14, 1944-45
   70.9 × 66
   Oil on composition board
   Gift of the artist, 1981
   Collection of Australian National Gallery, Canberra

8. Herbert Badham (1899-1961)
   Snack Bar, 1944
   41.5 × 50
   Oil on pulpboard
   Collection of Mrs M.E.K. Adams, Sydney

9. Sidney Nolan (b.1917)
   Boy in township, 1943
   61 × 72.5
   Ripolin on cardboard mounted on hardboard
   Collection of Art Gallery of New South Wales, Sydney

10. John Perceval (b.1923)
    Recollection of the artist as a small boy (riding a goat), 1942-43
    75 × 95
    Oil on hardboard
    Landau collection, Sydney
    On loan to Macquarie University, Sydney

11. Arthur Boyd (b.1920)
    The Seasons, 1943-44
    Suite of 4 paintings:
    The beach, 1944
    Oil on cotton gauze on composition board;
    The orchard, 1943
    Oil on cotton gauze on cardboard;
    The cemetry I, 1944
    Oil on cardboard;
    The hammock, 1944
    Oil on cardboard

    127.8 × 152.3 overall

    The Arthur Boyd Gift
    Collection of Australian National Gallery, Canberra

12. Arthur Boyd
    The Hunter II (The Flood), 1944-45
    99.6 × 91.5
    Oil on canvas on wood
    Gift of Arthur Boyd and the Museum of Modern Art of Australia, 1972
    Collection of Art Gallery of New South Wales, Sydney

13. Noel Counihan (b.1913)
    In the Waiting Room, 1943
    62 × 43.5
    Oil on hardboard
    Collection of Art Gallery of New South Wales, Sydney

14. Adrian Feint (1894-1971)
    The Jetties, Palm Beach, 1942
    50.7 × 45.7
    Oil on canvas
    Gift of Howard Hinton, 1942
    Collection of New England Regional Art Museum, Armidale

15. Margaret Preston (1875-1963)
    Grey Day in the Ranges, 1942
    51 × 50.7
    Oil on masonite
    Collection of Art Gallery of New South Wales, Sydney

Marks of Violence I: A World of Wars

16. Arthur Boyd
    The Mockers, 1945
    84.5 × 102.9
    Oil on canvas
    Collection of Art Gallery of New South Wales, Sydney

17. Donald Friend (b.1915)
    Demolitions, 1945
    35.5 × 38.1
    Pen and coloured ink, coloured wash and Chinese white
    Collection of Australian War Memorial, Canberra

Danila Vassilieff
Street scene with graffiti, 1983
45.5 × 61.1
Oil on plywood
Private collection, Melbourne
Photography Terence Bogue, Melbourne

18. Albert Tucker
    Hiroshima, 1947
    26.7 × 35.6
    Watercolour, gouache, pen and ink
    Collection of Australian National Gallery, Canberra

19. Weaver Hawkins ("Raokin")
    (1893-1977)
    Atomic Power, 1947
    61 × 78.5
    Oil on masonite
    Collection of Art Gallery of New South Wales, Sydney

20. Ivor Hele (b.1912)
    Taking Wounded from Korea to Japan — Medical Air Evacuation, 1953
    96.3 × 202.1
    Oil on hardboard
    Collection of Australian War Memorial, Canberra

21. Sidney Nolan
    Shellburst Soldiers I, 1962
    52.2 × 63.8
    Textile dye on card
    Collection of Australian War Memorial, Canberra

22. Sidney Nolan
    Swimmers at Gallipoli, 1958
    30.4 × 25.4
    Oil crayon and acrylic on card
    Collection of Australian War Memorial, Canberra

23. Sidney Nolan
    Drowned Soldier, c.1958
    25.4 × 30.4

    Acrylic on card
    Collection of Australian War Memorial, Canberra

Marks of Violence II: The Wounding of Women

24. Danila Vassilieff
    Alec and Jean, 1944
    47.3 × 39.5
    Oil on plywood
    Collection of Heide Park and Art Gallery, Melbourne

25. Sidney Nolan
    Gippsland Incident, 1945
    91.5 × 122
    Ripolin on hardboard
    Gift of Sidney and Cynthia Nolan, 1974
    Collection of Art Gallery of South Australia, Adelaide

26. Donald Friend
    Showers in a Ruin, 1945
    77.4 × 57.1
    Pen and coloured ink, coloured wash and gouache
    Collection of Australian War Memorial, Canberra

27. David Strachan (1919-1970)
    The Lovers, 1946
    43.2 × 53.5
    Oil on pulpboard
    Collection of S.H. Ervin Gallery, Sydney
    National Trust of Australia (New South Wales)

28. Joy Hester (1920-1960)
Drawing from the Love Series, c.1949
75.3 × 55.5
Brush and ink on paper
Collection of Australian National
Gallery, Canberra

29. Joy Hester
Two figures, c.1957
50.5 × 63.7
Brush and ink on paper
Collection of Australian National
Gallery, Canberra

30. John Perceval
The Expulsion, 1948
38.3 × 48
Pencil on paper
Gift of the artist, 1977
Collection of Australian National
Gallery, Canberra

31. Margaret Preston
Expulsion, 1952
64.1 × 59.9
Gouache, stencil and overpainting on
black paper
Gift of Mr W.G. Preston, 1967
Collection of Art Gallery of New
South Wales, Sydney

32. Jon Molvig (1923-1970)
The Lovers, 1955
210 × 119
Oil on composition board
On loan to the Australian National
Gallery, Canberra from the Mertz
Collection of Australian Art,
Archer M. Huntington Art Gallery,
University of Texas at Austin

33. Arthur Boyd
Lovers with a Stockman, 1961-62
159.5 × 182.6
Oil on composition board
The Arthur Boyd Gift, 1975
Collection of Australian National
Gallery, Canberra

34. Arthur Boyd
*Figure in Landscape, (Nude Washing
in a Creek III)*, 1961
159.4 × 182.9
Oil and tempera on Swedish wallboard
Collection of Art Gallery of New
South Wales, Sydney

35. John Brack (b.1920)
*Wedding Series: The bride and
groom*, 1960
97 × 130
Oil on canvas
Collection of Australian National
Gallery, Canberra

36. Clifton Pugh (b.1924)
The Descent, 1962
92 × 137.5
Oil on hardboard
Collection of Mr A.D. Christensen
Art Gallery of Wesern Australia,
Perth

Margaret Preston
Grey Day in the Ranges, 1942
51 × 50.7
Oil on masonite
Collection Art Gallery of New South Wales,
Sydney

Myths of Place I: Still Life in the City

37. Albert Tucker
*Tram Stop (Image of Modern Evil
[Night Image] #26)*, 1945-46
80 × 120
Oil on hardboard
Collection of ICI Australia Limited,
Melbourne

38. Charles Blackman (b.1928)
Dreaming in the Street, 1960
122.2 × 183.2
Oil on composition board
Collection of the National Gallery of
Victoria, Melbourne

39. John Brack
Study for Collins Street 5 p.m., 1955
88.9 × 38.1
Oil
Collection of National Gallery of
Victoria, Melbourne

40. Robert Dickerson (b.1924)
The Tired Man, 1957
137.1 × 152.7
Synthetic enamel on hardboard
Collection of National Gallery of
Victoria, Melbourne

41. Jacqueline Hick (b.1924)
Late Shift Workers, 1945
51 × 61
Oil on canvas
Collection of Art Gallery of New
South Wales, Sydney

42. Noel Counihan
Aboriginal in Fitzroy, 1958
30.5 × 53
Oil on canvas
Collection of Sam and Rosa
Goldbloom, Melbourne

43. Noel Counihan
Two Youths, 1963
101.6 × 76.1
Oil on hardboard
Acquired with funds from the Nanny

Barker Bequest, 1964
Collection of Art Gallery of Western
Australia, Perth

44. Brett Whiteley (b.1939)
The Soup Kitchen, 1958
101 × 76
Oil on canvas
Collection of the artist, Sydney

45. Herbert Badham
The Cinema, 1958
37.8 × 30.4
Oil on board
Private collection, Sydney

46. Francis Lymburner (1916-1972)
Circular Quay, n.d.
54.5 × 87.6
Oil on canvas on composition board
Collection of Australian National
Gallery, Canberra

47. Sali Herman (b.1898)
Reconstruction, 1950
40.5 × 60.5
Oil on canvas
Collection of Art Gallery of South
Australia, Adelaide

48. Jeffrey Smart (b.1921)
Cahill Expressway, 1962
81.2 × 111.7
Oil on plywood
Collection of National Gallery of
Victoria, Melbourne

49. Grace Cossington Smith (b.1892)
The Open Door, 1960
60 × 90
Oil on masonite
Collection of Bathurst Regional Art
Gallery, Bathurst

50. Danila Vassilieff
Mildura Wedding, 1954-55
91 × 122
Oil on composition board
Collection of Heide Park and Art
Gallery, Melbourne

51. John Olsen (b.1928)
*Entrance to the Siren City of the Rat
Race*, 1963
121.9 × 182.9
Private collection, Melbourne
On loan to Macquarie University,
Sydney

Myths of Place II: Empty Centre & Anti-Hero

52. Sidney Nolan
Kelly, 1946
63.5 × 76.1
Ripolin on strawboard
Collection of Nolan Gallery,
Canberra

53. Russell Drysdale (1912-1981)
Walls of China, Gol Gol, 1945
76.2 × 101.6
Oil on hardboard
Collection of Art Gallery of New
South Wales, Sydney

54. Jean Bellette (b.1909)
    Jason and Medea, c.1947
    45.5 × 60.7 Oil on cardboard
    Collection of Australian National
    Gallery, Canberra

55. Charles Blackman
    The Trip (Thumbalina), 1951
    75 × 100.3
    Synthetic polymer paint on
    hardboard
    A.M. & A.R. Ragless Bequest Fund,
    1976
    Collection of Art Gallery of South
    Australia, Adelaide

56. Sidney Nolan
    Durack Range, 1950
    91.5 × 121.9
    Oil on composition board
    Collection of National Gallery of
    Victoria, Melbourne

57. Russell Drysdale
    Desert Landscape, 1952
    102.9 × 128.3
    Oil on canvas
    Acquired with funds from the A.H.
    Smith Bequest, 1959
    Collection of Art Gallery of New
    South Wales, Sydney

58. Sidney Nolan
    Carcass, 1953
    90.8 × 121.3
    Ripolin on board
    Collection of Nolan Gallery,
    Canberra

59. John Brack
    The Car, 1955
    41 × 101.8
    Oil on canvas
    Collection of National Gallery of
    Victoria, Melbourne

60. Clifton Pugh
    Swamp Form, 1958
    69 × 96
    Oil on hardboard
    On loan from the Christensen Fund
    Art Gallery of Western Australia,
    Perth

61. Albert Namatjira (1902-1959)
    *Ghost Gums and Mountain Range
    No. 2*, 1950s
    26.6 × 36.8
    Watercolour over pencil on smooth
    woven paper
    Collection of Queensland Art
    Gallery, Brisbane

62. Jon Molvig
    Ballad of a Dead Stockman, No. 2,
    1959
    122 × 198.7
    Oil on hardboard
    Collection of Art Gallery of New
    South Wales, Sydney

63. Albert Tucker
    Antipodean Head, 1958
    122 × 87.5
    Synthetic polymer paint and sand on

Sidney Nolan
Gippsland Incident, 1945
91.5 × 122
Ripolin on hardboard
Collection Art Gallery of South Australia, Adelaide

Albert Tucker
Tram Stop (Image of Modern Evil [Night Image] #26), 1945-46
80 × 120
Oil on hardboard
Collection of ICI Australia Limited, Melbourne
Photography Terence Bogue, Melbourne

composition board
Collection of Australian National
Gallery, Canberra

64. Pro Hart (b.1928)
    *Miner waiting for his work clothes to
    dry*, 1963
    62 × 72
    Oil on hardboard
    Collection of North Broken Hill
    Limited, Broken Hill

Signs of the Other I: Constructions of Childhood

65. Danila Vassilieff
    Four faces of the street, 1949
    45.4 × 43.1
    Oil on composition board
    Private collection, Melbourne

66. Charles Blackman
The shadow, 1953
59.2 × 75.4
Tempera on composition board
Collection of Heide Park and Art
Gallery, Melbourne

67. Robert Dickerson
Boy in Street, 1956
91.4 × 122
Oil on masonite
Collection of Mrs J. Bellew,
Melbourne

68. Joy Hester
(Baby Boy),
38.2 × 30.6
Brush and ink on grey paper
Gift of Mrs Robert Dulieu, 1981
Collection of Australian National
Gallery, Canberra

69. Joy Hester
Girl with Hen, 1956
75.6 × 55.3
Brush and ink on paper on
paperboard
Collection of Australian National
Gallery, Canberra

70. Clifton Pugh
The World of Shane and Dailan,
1957
91.4 × 137.1
Oil on hardboard
Maude Vizard-Wholohan Art Prize
Purchase Award, 1958
Collection of Art Gallery of South
Australia, Adelaide

71. Mirka Mora (b.1928)
The Sky is Full with Stars, 1958
91.5 × 60.8
Enamel on composition board
Collection of Heide Park and Art
Gallery, Melbourne

72. Charles Blackman
Alice in the Garden, 1957
91.4 × 121.9
Oil on board
Collection of Geoffrey Hassall,
Sydney

Signs of the Other II: White on Black

73. Russell Drysdale
Station Blacks, Cape York, 1953
60.3 × 72.4
Oil on masonite
Collection of National Gallery of
Victoria, Melbourne

74. James Wigley (b.1918)
The Half Caste, 1958
60 × 45
Oil on board
The Boxer Collection, Canberra

75. David Boyd (b.1924)
Trucaninny's Dream of Childhood,
1964
183 × 121.8
Oil on composition board

Robert Dickerson
The Tired Man, 1957
137.1 × 152.7
Synthetic enamel on hardboard
Collection National Gallery of Victoria, Melbourne

Collection of Australian National
Gallery, Canberra

76. Russell Drysdale
Mangula, 1961
183 × 122
Oil on canvas
Collection of Art Gallery of New
South Wales, Sydney

77. Ray Crooke (b.1922)
The School Bell, Thursday Island,
1958
119.5 × 147
Oil on hardboard
Collection of ICI Australia Limited,
Melbourne

78. William Dargie (b.1912)
Portrait of Albert Namatjira, 1956
102.1 × 76.4
Oil on canvas
Collection of Queensland Art
Gallery, Brisbane

79. Noel Counihan
Albert Namatjira, 1959
51.3 × 23.4
Linocut
Collection of Art Gallery of New
South Wales, Sydney

80. Sam Fullbrook (b.1922)
Death in the Afternoon, 1961
63.7 × 76.6
Oil on canvas
Collection of Queensland Art
Gallery, Brisbane

81. Noel Counihan
Family, Swan Hill, 1960
86.2 × 91.3
Oil on hardboard
Collection of Art Gallery of Western
Australia, Perth

DAVIDA ALLEN

Born 1951 in Charleville, Queensland
Lives at Purga Creek, near Brisbane,
Queensland

Davida Allen has not so much been
recruited by the new spirit of
expressive painting as she has had
her attitudes reinforced by it. Her
line and paint are not fluid, but thick,
snared, and frantic. When she moves
towards elated colour she will tame
it, smother it with forbidding greys,
blacks and sullied whites. Surface
speeds are halted by ruffling. One
feels that her figures are rebelling
with furious paint against the
confinement of houses, hands, birds
and all manner of harmless objects
that may, in special circumstances
arouse *angst*. And more than most
Neo-Expressionists her figures seem
in rebellion against the constrictions
of the frame, so that the canvas is
not an area for happy pursuits or a
stage for tableaux.

However, in her series of drawings
and some of her paintings on the
death of her father she began to
isolate shapes whether of the dying
man, his second last refuge, the arm-
chair, or his ultimate refuge, the
coffin. These began to float in the
threatening void without her habitual
tone of defiance. In fact, her present
uniqueness lies in the fact that she
has become an expressionist of
acceptance evoking all the intensity
of feeling that such acceptance
entails. In fact, she does what
innumerable painters have done; she
transforms life into painting, but she
makes of the transformation a
personal ritual with the audience as
observers rather than participants.

Elwyn Lynn
September-October 1982
Modified from *Art International*

Studied

1965-69 Stuartholme Convent,
Brisbane
1970-72 Central Technical College,
Brisbane

Selected Individual Exhibitions

1973 Ray Hughes Gallery,
Brisbane
1975 Ray Hughes Gallery,
Brisbane
1978 Ray Hughes Gallery,
Brisbane
1979 Ray Hughes Gallery,
Brisbane
1981 Ray Hughes Gallery,
Brisbane

Selected Group Exhibitions

1979 *Roy Churcher, Ian Smith
and Davida Allen* , Solander
Gallery, Canberra
1981 *Ray Hughes at Pinacotheca*,
Pinacotheca, Melbourne
Australian Perspecta 1981,
Art Gallery of New South
Wales, Sydney
Nine Queensland Artists,
Perc Tucker Regional
Gallery, Townsville
1982 *Fourth Biennale of Sydney,
Vision in Disbelief*, Art
Gallery of New South Wales,
Sydney
Big Drawings, Ray Hughes
Gallery, Brisbane
Five Painters, Fine Arts
Gallery, University of
Tasmania, Hobart (touring
exhibition)
1983 *Against the Wall*, Works of
the Michell Endowment
Collection of the National
Gallery of Victoria,
Melbourne University
Gallery, Melbourne
*Recent Australian Painting
— A Survey of the Seventies
and Eighties*, Art Gallery of
South Australia, Adelaide
*D'un Autre Continent:
l'Australie. Le Rêve et Le
Réel*, ARC, Musée d'Art
Moderne de la Ville de
Paris, Paris

Selected Bibliography

Sue Webster, "Six Brisbane Artists",
Art and Australia, Vol 18 No 4,
Sydney 1981
Bernice Murphy, *Australian Perspecta
1981*, catalogue, Art Gallery of New
South Wales, Sydney 1981
Janine Burke, "Art for the End of the
World", *Meanjin*, Vol 40 No 3,
Melbourne, October 1981
Bernice Murphy, "Painting",
Australian Art Review, Sydney 1982
Sue Webster, "Visitors Add Vitality:
Current Trends in Contemporary Art
in Queensland", *Australian Art
Review*, Sydney 1982
Elwyn Lynn, "Letter from Australia",
Art International, Vol 25 Nos 3/4,
Lugano, Switzerland, 1982
Bernice Murphy, "Recent Painting in
Australia", *Flash Art*, No 110, Milan,
January 1983
Leon Paroissien, "Report from
Sydney: The Fourth Biennale", *Art in
America*, New York, February 1983
Davida Allen, "Russell Drysdale: Man
Feeding his Dogs — Artist's Choice
No.14", *Art and Australia*, Vol 20
No 4, Sydney 1983

MY LIFE NOW, 1-20, 1984
Oil on canvas
Each 100 × 120 or 120 × 100
Courtesy Ray Hughes Gallery,
Brisbane

Photography Ian Poole, Brisbane

ARMANDO

Born 1929 in Amsterdam
Since 1979 has lived and worked in
West Berlin

. . .The subject *Waldrand* has to do
with my experiences during the war:
"the enemy and his victims under
the watchful eye of a completely
indifferent nature".

Letter from Armando
1 November 1983

. . .Armando thinks mainly in events.
For him every observation evokes
the past.

. . .this is not an antiquarian interest.
It has no academic pretentions to
objectivity and checkability, but it is
not the opposite either, a subjective
mythomania that distorts the
historical reality. Armando's passion
for the past extends to those
moments or events that possess a
personal and suprapersonal value at
one and the same time. They do not
have to be events in which he
himself has participated, but they do
have to link up with his own
memories if they are to acquire
significance for him.

The second world war occupies a
crucial place in Armando's
experience. The period of the
German occupation, which he lived
through as a boy of eleven to
sixteen, a stone's throw from the
transit camp at Amersfoort, has
imprinted itself indelibly on his
memory as an extreme situation in
which human nature showed itself in
the raw, in which life was more real.
Behaviour, actions, thoughts,
emotions, nothing was free from
constraint; everything had direct
implications, moral ones too. It was
this experience that determined
Armando's view of life and whatever
persons, events and developments
come to his notice in the past or in
the present, they are related to and
measured against that piece of
history that he himself witnessed.

Over the course of the years
Armando's creative work has been
directed ever more stubbornly at
keeping that past alive, in images
and in languages.

Carel Blotkamp
"Speak memory, recent work of
Armando"
Translated by Patricia Wardle

Studied art-history in Amsterdam

1954	*Peintures Criminelles* (first one man exhibition) *Espaces Criminels* (black and red monochromes)
1958	Co-founder Nederlandse Informele Groep (Dutch Informal Group)
1959	*Paysages Criminels*
1960	Co-founder Nederlandse Nulgroep (Dutch Zerogroup)

Selected individual exhibitions

1974	Retrospective, Stedelijk Museum, Amsterdam
1975	Gallery Art & Project, Amsterdam
1977	Centraal Museum, Utrecht
1979	Van Abbemuseum, Eindhoven Akademie der Kunste, Berlin
1980	Gallery Collection d'Art, Amsterdam
1981	Gallery Springer, Berlin Studio Carlo Grossetti, Milan Stedelijk Museum, Amsterdam
1982	Van Abbemuseum, Eindhoven
1983	Gallery Springer, Berlin Gallery Nouvelles Images, The Hague
1984	Nationalgalerie, Berlin Westfälischer Kunstverein, Münster Städtisches Museum, Mönchengladbach

Selected group exhibitions

1962	*Nul*, Stedelijk Museum, Amsterdam
1964	Project *Black Water*, Haags Gemeentemuseum, The Hague
1981	*Schwarz*, Kunsthalle, Dusseldorf
1982	*60-80*, Stedelijk Museum, Amsterdam *documenta*, Kassel
1983	*Modern Dutch Painting*, National Gallery, Athens

WALDRAND (EDGE OF WOODS),
1983
Oil on canvas
210 × 145

WALDRAND (EDGE OF WOODS),
1983
Oil on canvas
210 × 145

WALDRAND (EDGE OF WOODS),
1983
Oil on canvas
210 × 145

Courtesy of the artist

Photography Angelika Weidling,
Berlin

ART & LANGUAGE

Michael Baldwin
Born Chipping Norton, Oxfordshire,
1945
Lives Middleton Cheney,
Northamptonshire

Mel Ramsden
Born Ilkeston, Derbyshire, 1944
Lives Middleton Cheney,
Northamptonshire

Art & Language assumed from way back that the universalising claims were all out. The job was to address the contingent and to treat the production of art or a second-order discourse as contingent. Always. And in producing paintings from 1977 onwards, Art & Language were addressing the contingent, learning how to make critiques of paintings of expression, of expression claims. It was addressing the aesthetic and artistic margins of what in more innocent days would have been called "the contradictions of the present". *Flânerie* without traditionally identifiable materials, without the contradictions or the aesthetics. Some of the remainder of the materials were what appeared to be taken seriously in the galleries. Almost. Art & Language produced paintings which could be seen as providing, or enabling, some kind of critical discourse and redescription about those things and a discourse which would remainder their universalising claims by eventually bombarding and illuminating them with their own reflected contingency.

Fred Orton
University of Leeds
August 1983

Studied

Michael Baldwin
1964-67 Coventry College of Art

Mel Ramsden
1962-63 Nottingham College of Art

Selected individual exhibitions

1967 *Hardware Show*,
Architectural Association,
London
1971 Galeria Sperone, Turin
Tape Show: exhibition of Lectures, Dain Gallery, New York
1972 *The Art & Language Institute*, Galerie Daniel Templon, Paris
1973 Lisson Gallery, London
Index III, John Weber Gallery, New York
1974 Galerie Bischofberger, Zurich
1975 MTL, Brussels
Art & Language 1966-1975, Museum of Modern Art, Oxford
Art Gallery of New South Wales, Sydney
National Gallery of Victoria, Melbourne
1976 *Music-Language*, Galerie Eric Fabre, Paris
1977 *Illustrations for Art-Language*, Robert Self Gallery, London
1978 *Flags for Organisations*, Cultureel Informatief Centrum, Ghent
1979 *Ils Donnent leur Sang; Donnez Votre Travail*, Galerie Eric Fabre, Paris
1980 *Portraits of V.I.Lenin in the Style of Jackson Pollock*, Lisson Gallery, London and Van Abbemuseum, Eindhoven
1981 *Gustave Courbet's Burial at Ornans Expressing . . .*, Galerie Eric Fabre, Paris
1982 *Index: Studio at 3 Wesley Place Painted by Mouth*, De Vleeshal, Middleburg
1983 *Index: Studio at 3 Wesley Place*, Gewad, Ghent
Los Angeles Institute of Contemporary Art

Selected group exhibitions

1968 *Language II*, Dwan Gallery, New York
1969 *March*, catalogue show, Seth Sieglaub, New York
Language III, Dwan Gallery, New York
557,087, Seattle, Washington
1970 *Conceptual Art and Conceptual Aspects*, New York Cultural Center
Information, Museum of Modern Art, New York
1971 *The British Avant-Garde*, New York Cultural Center
1972 *documenta 5*, Kassel
The New Art, Hayward Gallery, London
1973 *Contemporanea*, Rome
1974 *Projekt '74*, Cologne
Kunst uber Kunst, Cologne
1976 *Drawing Now*, Museum of Modern Art, New York
Biennale of Venice
1977 *Lisson Gallery*, Fine Arts Building, New York
1978 *Poster Work*, Belgrade Museum, Belgrade
1980 *Kunst in Europe na '68*, Museum Van Hedendaagse Kunst, Ghent
1982 *documenta 7*, Kassel
1983 *New Art*, Tate Gallery, London

Selected bibliography

Selected books and pamphlets
Frameworks — Air Conditioning, Art & Language Press, Coventry 1967
22 Sequences: The French Army, Art & Language Press, Coventry 1968
Art & Language 1966-1975, selected essays, Museum of Modern Art, Oxford 1975
Collected Slogans, 21 songs written and produced by Art & Language,
Music-Language, New York/Banbury 1976
Art & Language 1975-1978, selected essays by Art & Language (French-English edition), Eric Fabre, Paris 1978
Kangaroo?, LP, Art & Language with The Red Crayola, Rough Trade Records (Rough 19), 1981
Art & Language, selected essays 1966-1980, Van Abbemuseum, Eindhoven 1980
Art & Language, Los Angeles Institute of Contemporary Art, Los Angeles 1983

Selected articles by Art & Language
"Status and Priority", *Studio International*, January 1970
"Us, Us and Away", *Data*, February-March 1977
"Nous ne donnons pas notre Travail", *Newcastle Writings*, Robert Self Publications, London, November 1977
"Art for Society?", *Art Monthly*, October 1978
"Portrait of V.I. Lenin in the Style of Jackson Pollock", *Artforum*, February 1980
"Art History, Art Criticism and Explanation", *Art History*, Vol 4 No 4, December 1981
"Art & Language Paints a Picture", *Gewad Informatief*, Ghent, March 1983

Selected books and articles
L. Lippard, *Changing: essays in art criticism*, Dutton, New York 1971
G. Celant, "The Book as Art Work", *Data*, No 1, September 1971
L. Lippard, *Six Years : The Dematerialisation of the Art Object*, Preager, New York 1973
T. Smith, "Art and Art & Language", *Artforum*, February 1974
C. Philpot, "Art Magazines and Magazine Art", *Artforum*, February 1980
C. Harrison and F. Orton, *A Provisional History of Art & Language*, editions Eric Fabre, Paris 1982
S. Morgan, review of Art & Language Work at documenta 7, *Artforum*, September 1982
C. Harrison, "The Orders of Discourse: The Artist's Studio", in *Art & Language*, catalogue for exhibition at Ikon Gallery Birmingham, May 1983

INDEX: THE STUDIO AT 3 WESLEY PLACE, PAINTED BY MOUTH, 1982
Ink on paper
343 × 727.5
Private collection, Paris

PAUL SIGNAC. LE PROFOND REVE DE L'AVENIR, 1983
Oil on canvas
300 × 480
Courtesy the artists

Photography Wim Niemens fotograaf nvf, Middleburg NL

TERRY ATKINSON

Born 1939 in Thurnscoe, near Barnsley, Yorkshire

In the broadest sense, Terry Atkinson's project can be seen as a reading "against the grain", taking as its subject those invisible relations that exist between cultural hegemony, on the one hand, and economic, state and military power on the other. The works assume a confrontational mode through a fragmentation and disjunction of image and text, a Brechtian de-familiarisation of the aesthetic and the political.

For Atkinson, not only is the significance of the image critically surveilled, but its existence as an effect of specific processes of signification — mark, gesture, expressive skill — is also seen as a particular kind of production. This is not to suggest that these uncomfortable works simply continue the Modernist tradition of interrogation of the object, although this is an aspect of their historical frame of reference, but that their status as *cultural* objects can, perhaps, be re-conceptualised as a "field of forces" intersecting with the social categories from which they draw their meanings. Consequently the relation of text to image is crucial, not only in signifying the pathways that a reading of the work might follow, but in also asserting the presence of the linguistic in our experience of the visual.

Despite the intellectual pessimism of these works, their uncompromising engagement with the forms of social and economic power represents an attempt to reveal those necessarily hidden relations of dominance and oppression that determine the lived reality of both individual subjects and subject peoples.

Jon Bird
1983

Studied

1959-60 Barnsley School of Art
1960-64 Slade School of Art, London

Activities and selected exhibitions

1962 Exhibited "Dead Cat on a Runway" at the *Young Contemporaries* exhibition.
1963 Exhibited "Postcard from Ypres" at the *Young Contemporaries* exhibition
1964 Formed a group called *Fine Artz* with John Bowstead, Roger Jeffs and Bernard Jennings. They collaborated on the production of *Action Chair*

1965-67 Taught part-time at Birmingham College of Art
1966 Fine Artz present projection/sound show *Miss Misty and the Tri-Cool Data*, Birmingham Polytechnic
Began teaching at Coventry College of Art where he met Michael Baldwin. They began to collaborate, producing in this year *Print (Two Sections A & B)*
1967 Began meeting regularly with Michael Baldwin, David Bainbridge and Harold Hurrell
Visited New York for the first time and met Sol LeWitt and Robert Smithson, who subsequently arranged for publication of Baldwin's *Remarks on Air Conditioning: An Extravaganza of Blandness* in *Arts* magazine, November issue.
Atkinson and Baldwin together produce a number of prints, broadsheets, pamphlets and texts, including *Air Conditioning Show, Air Show, Frameworks* and *Hot/Cold* which were published by Art & Language Press in the following year. Others were subsequently published in 1974 by Editions Bruno Bischofberger, Zurich. The letterpress prints were produced in small editions at Coventry College of Art.
1968 *22 Sentences: The French Army* published by Precinct Publications, Coventry and shown later that year at *Language II*, Dwan Gallery New York.
May — Art & Language Press founded.
June — Atkinson exhibited a "lecture" on Duchamp's *Bottle Rack* at *VAT 68*, Herbert Art Gallery, Coventry.
Dematerialisation Show, Ikon Gallery, Birmingham.
1969 May — first issue of *Art-Language*, vol 1 no 1, published in May, including the unattributed Introduction written by Atkinson.
Went to New York in July and met Ian Burn, Mel Ramsden and Joseph Kosuth.
1970 Art & Language participated in: *Information*, Museum of Modern Art, New York
Conceptual Art and Conceptual Aspects, New York Cultural Center
Idea Structures, Camden Arts Centre, London
1972 Art & Language exhibit in *documenta 5*, Kassel

1973 Atkinson resigned teaching post at Lanchester Polytechnic. For the next two years he and Michael Baldwin were financially reliant on sales of Art & Language work, showing regularly at the Lisson Gallery, London; Paul Maenz, Cologne; Daniel Templon, Paris; Gian Enzo Sperone, Rome; as well as in large survey exhibitions, including *Contemporanea*. From this period attributions of individual or joint authorship of published and exhibited work were subsumed under the Art & Language name.
1974 Art & Language exhibit in *Projekt '74*
1975 After leaving Art and Language, Atkinson took up a Gulbenkian Foundation Fellowship, working at Sidney Stringer School in Coventry on the Community Education Video Project.
1976 Exhibition of Atkinson's work since leaving Art & Language organised by Lynda Morris for the Midland Group, Nottingham, and at the Robert Self Galleries, London and Newcastle.
1977 On completion of the Gulbenkian project, took up a post of Lecturer in Fine Art at Leeds University
1979 *Art for Society*, Whitechapel Art Gallery, London, and Leeds City Art Gallery
1980 Selected a work by Jasper Johns for *Pictures for an Exhibition*, Whitechapel Art Gallery, London
1982 *Hayward Annual 1982: British Drawing*
1983 Open University Art History program on Duchamp (25 minute film)
Whitechapel Gallery, London
Ikon Gallery, Birmingham
Orchard Gallery, Derry
City Art Gallery, Leeds
1984 Van Abbemuseum, Eindhoven

Selected bibliography

Art & Language
"Status and Priority", *Studio International*, London 1970
"From an Art & Language Point of View", *Art-Language* vol 1 no 2, February 1970
"Lecher System", *Studio International*, July/August Exhibition Book, London 1970
Theories of Ethics, New York Cultural Center in association with Art & Language Press, 1971
"De Legibus Naturae", *Studio International*, London, May 1971

"Some Post-War American Work and Art-Language: Ideological Responsiveness", *Studio International*, London, April 1972
"The Index" in *The New Art*, catalogue, Hayward Gallery, Arts Council of Great Britain, 1972

Publications by the artist:
"Looking Back, Going On", Parts 1 and 2, *The Fox*, Nos 1 and 2, New York 1975
"Reply to Joseph Kosuth's Uber eine Anthropologisierte Kunst", *Extra*, No 3, Cologne 1975
"Notes: Communities, Artists, Modernism", *Studio International*, London, March/April 1976
Notes, catalogue, Midland Group, Nottingham 1976
"Some remarks which may contribute something", in *What do you expect from a radical gallery?*, Paul Maenz, Cologne 1977
"Images of People", *Studio International*, London, February 1978
"Materialism, by Jove!", *Block*, Middlesex Polytechnic, 1979

BURIAL AT BECOURT WOOD 1916.
SECOND AUSTRALIAN DIVISION, 1976
Conté on paper
243.8 × 119.8

COMIC-MAP MADE BY BOTH
TROTSKY IN HEAVEN AND
TROTSKY IN HELL —
A REAL DIALECTICAL CONDITION.
TROTSKY, ENTERING ON LEFT
FROM LIMBO,
ONE FINDS THE SAME CHRISTIAN
SKIN COMPLAINTS IN BOTH
PLACES.
THIS IS THE FINAL DIALECTICAL
SITUATION —
A CONTRADICITION, EH!
NEVERTHELESS THERE'S A
STANDARD ISSUE
OF ELECTROPLASTS IN BOTH
PLACES WHICH CLEANSE THE SKIN
AND ANNIHILATE FALLOUT-
EFFECT.
ONE OF THE MOST TEDIOUS JOBS
HERE
IS THAT OF INTERMINABLY
CARTING MARSYAS' SKIN
BACK AND FORTH BETWEEN THE
TWO PLACES.
THIS IS DONE ON A SHIFT-WORK
BASIS OF COURSE,
SINCE HEAVEN ABOLISHED
SLAVERY IN HELL IN 1866.
THE SKIN IS CARRIED ON A
PERSONNEL CARRIER.
CAPITALIST AND STALINIST TANK-
CREWS ALTERNATE — THE
SCHEME IS THAT CAPITALIST
CREWS TAKE THE HEAVEN-TO-
HELL JOURNEY.
SINCE THE JOURNEY HAS BEEN
GOING ON SINCE 1928
THERE ARE SO MANY STALINIST
CREWS IN HEAVEN
AND CAPITALIST CREWS IN HELL

IT GETS HARD TO TELL WHICH
PLACE BELONGS TO WHICH CAMP.
ORIGINALLY, IT WAS CLEAR!
HEAVEN WAS CAPITALIST, HELL
WAS STALINIST!
A FILM CREW ACCOMPANIES THE
TANK CREW ON EACH JOURNEY.
THE IMF FUND THE ENTIRE
OPERATION, INCIDENTALLY,
FOR ALL THE ART LOVERS: WHAT
PRICE THE DIALECTIC
OF PAINT?
Acrylic on canvas
231 × 370

PICTURE WITH BOTCHED-UP
DRAWING DEPICTING BRITISH
PROLETARIANS ATTACKING
GERMAN PROLETARIANS, BOTH
SETS
OF PROLETARIANS DEFENDING
THE INTERESTS OF THEIR
RESPECTIVE CAPITALISMS.
Conté and gouache on paper
239 × 264

Courtesy of the artist

BREDA BEBAN

Born 1952 in Novi Sad, Yugoslavia

As a painter, Breda Beban comes from conceptual art, in which, as she herself puts it, she has "accepted the shifting of aesthetics to the level of self-analysis, i.e. of cognition and ethics". But she could never find complete satisfaction in that kind of work; she felt the need for a more direct contact with the medium and visual thinking and for the release of energy which takes place in the process of painting. She turned to painting in order to satisfy her need for ethics and painting — the need to assimilate various things and images and to build them into her own world. She adopted a way of painting which enables her to be true to her principles of action and consistency of artistic procedure. In the process of painting every theme provokes her in its own way. Breda Beban allows the spontaneous automatism of emotions and its images to determine the sign repertoire and the message of her paintings. Good and evil, male and female, positive and negative are expressed through the symbols of angel and devil, day and night, the symbols of geometric figures and the iconography of myths and legends from medieval frescoes. She transposes subtle emotions into pictures that may seem breezy and decorative but are in fact gloomy and hard. She tries to define the forces that run her life and registers the undefined presence of "shadowy beings", which she cannot define as good or evil. The fear of death and of cruelty gives rise to melancholy — the interspace between life and death.

The figures, symbols and meanings which come from the artist's private world and are presented in dark colours and swirling surfaces, express her search for cathartic relief from the traumatic situations of conflict which she feels. What pleasure is there in sowing death, what is the "killer's pleasure"? Breda Beban finds the answer in Novalis:

"It is strange that the link between pleasure, religion and cruelty should not have long ago drawn people's attention to the close kinship and the common tendency in these phenomena. It is strange that the real source of cruelty is pleasure."

Marijan Susovski
Zagreb 1983

Studied
1972-76 Academy of Visual Arts, Zagreb

Selected individual exhibitions
1981   Gallery PM, Zagreb
1982   Studio, Gallery of Contemporary Art, Zagreb
       Gallery SC, Zagreb
1983   Gallery Koprivnica, Koprivnica

Selected group exhibitions
1981   *13th Salon of Young Artists*, Zagreb
       16th Zagreb Salon, Zagreb
       New painting, Gallery Loža, Koper
1982   *Young Yugoslav Art*, Lodz, Poznanj, Poland
       XVII Internationale Malerwochen in der Steirmark, Graz, Austria
       Young Croation Art, Gallery Rotovž, Maribor
1983   *Junge Maler aus Zagreb*, Rathaus, Mainz

Selected bibliography
Marijan susovski, *Breda Beban*, Studio of the Gallery of Contemporary Art, Zagreb 1982
Wilfried Skreiner, *XVII Malerwochen in der Stiermark*, Graz 1982

THE ANGEL OF MELANCHOLY, 1984
Oil on canvas
200 × 200

LITTLE DEATH, 1984
Oil on canvas
200 × 200

Courtesy of the artist

JOSEPH BEUYS

Born Krefeld, 1921
Lives in Dusseldorf

GESAMTKUNSTWERK (TOTAL ART WORK)
"Freie und Hansestadt Hamburg"

Description of project (in brief)

The planting of a tree by Joseph Beuys, a project for the Fifth Biennale of Sydney, is one of a series of ecological actions conceived by the artist. In *documenta 7* (1982), he undertook an action aimed at the planting of 7000 oak trees. Another ecological pilot project has been undertaken for the Hamburg Arts Council, *City-Nature-Sculpture*. This larger project is for one of the *Spuelfelder* (water fields) on the edge of the port of Hamburg under which the former district Altenwerder is buried.

In the middle of the field — a desolate deposit of highly polluted mud for the Elbe and the North Sea that is regularly dredged from the basin of the port, causing an ecological timebomb — is erected one of Beuy's basalt columns from the series *THEENDOFTHE20THCENTURY*. At the same time, to revitalise the area and to avoid the absorption of the poisonous substances into the subsoil, a native plant cover is spread using modern techniques. This death zone, designated an art zone, is marked by a ring of fast-growing trees such as willows and poplars. These will later be economically useful. The *Spuelfeld* assumes the character of a memorial — a sign of the end of a human epoch and a new start through the innovative impulse of art.

The main purpose of this project is the foundation of a research institute of the Free International University (FIU). Starting from the dilemma of the *Spuelfelder* which cannot be unravelled in isolation, it requires a whole range of more complex, alternative measures. All parties interested in the overall solution of the ecological crisis, are grouped together in a "cultural initiative" entitled *Gesamtkunstwerk "Freie und Hanestadt Hamburg"*. It is intended that this will develop new possibilities that will eventually transform the area into an ecological work area with new workplaces for many people.

The implications of this culture-model or extended art-concept reach beyond the borders of Hamburg. Working areas can be made fruitful for the renewal of society's organism in the sense of a "social sculpture".

With the establishment of a donation or people's bank, the ones who cause damage to the environment will be involved in its restoration.

An FIU office of planning and co-ordination will be established in the centre of Hamburg to provide public information and a discussion forum.

It is conceivable that through this example other interested circles — cultural, civic and industrial — will follow and thus cure the ecological disease afflicting the whole of society. The Freie und Hansestadt Hamburg is supporting this model project *Gesamtkunstwerk* (Total Art Project) and will profit itself, as well as being a signpost extending far beyond the borders of Hamburg.

Selected individual exhibitions

1967	Städtisches Museum, Mönchengladbach
1968	Van Abbemuseum, Eindhoven
1969	*Zeichnungen, Kleine Objekte*, Kunstmuseum Basel
1969-70	*Werke aus der Sammlung Karl Ströher*, Kunstmuseum Basel
1970	Sammlung Hans und Franz van der Grinten, Kranenburg, Galerie im Taxispalais, Innsbruck
1971	*Zeichnungen und Objekte 1937 bis 1970, aus der Sammlung van der Grinten*, Moderna Museet, Stockholm *Entwürfe, Partituren, Projekte, Zeichnungen*, Galerie René Block, Berlin *La Rivoluzione Siamo Noi — Partitura di Joseph Beuys*, Modern Art Agency, Neapel
1972	*Selbstporträts — Weekend*, Galerie René Block, Berlin *Zeichnungen von 1949 bis 1969*, Galerie Schmela, Düsseldorf
1974	*The Secret Block for a Secret Person in Ireland (Zeichnungen 1936 bis 1972)*, Museum of Modern Art, Oxford; National Gallery of Modern Art, Edinburgh; ICA, London; Municipal Gallery of Modern Art, Dublin; Arts Council Gallery, Belfast *Ziechnungen 1946-1971*, Museum Haus Lange, Krefeld
1975	*Joseph Beuys, Ziechnungen, Bilder, Plastiken, Objekte, Aktionsphotographien*, Kunstverein Freiburg
1977	*Richtkräfte*, Nationalgalerie Berlin Guggenheim Museum, New York
1980	*Zeichnungen*, Museum Boymans-van Beuningen, Rotterdam
1981	Anthony d'Offay, London

Selected group exhibitions

1964	*documenta 3*, Kassel
1965	*Kinetik und Objekte*, Staatsgalerie Stuttgart
1967	*Hommage à Lidice*, Galerie René Block, Berlin
1968	*documenta 4*, Kassel
1969	*Sammlung Karl Ströher*, Neue Nationalgalerie, Berlin *When Attitudes Become Form*, Kunsthalle Bern *Düsseldorfer Szene*, Kunstmuseum Lucerne
1970	*Jetzt, Künste in Deutschland Heute*, Kunsthalle Cologne *Kunst und Politik*, Badischer Kunstverein Karslruhe *Die Handzeichnungen der Gegenwart*, Staatsgalerie Stuttgart *Biennale d'Arte Contemporanea*, San Benedetto del Tronto
1971	*Happening & Fluxus*, Kölnischer Kunstverein *Prospect 71*, Kunsthalle Düsseldorf
1972	*documenta 5*, Kassel
1973	*Kunst im Politischen Kampf*, Kunstverein Hannover *Op Losse Schroeven*, Stedelijk Museum, Amsterdam
1974	*Art into Society, Society into Art*, ICA, London
1977	*documenta 6*, Kassel
1978	*Door Beeldhouwers Gemaakt*, Stedelijk Museum, Amsterdam
1981	*Westkunst*, Cologne
1982	*'60-'80*, Stedelijk Museum, Amsterdam *documenta 7*, Kassel

TREE-PLANTING, 1984
Art Gallery of New South Wales
for the Fifth Biennale of Sydney

Courtesy the artist and René Block, Berlin

Photography Ute Klophaus, Wuppertal

TONY BEVAN

Born in Bradford, England, 1951
Currently resident in London

In "Condition", a male figure hides his face with his hands and stares downward with a single eye. Is he the witness of a nuclear explosion, hot "radioactive" pigment burning him up, disintegrating the line that contains his form, or is the painting about something else? Bevan describes his figures as being "lit from within", suggesting a psychological reading. The colour is emotionally charged, the faces and hands are signs or emblems of private feelngs and states of mind made public.

A prophet is a revealer, and in the painting of the same name we see the only image in which the isolated figure is freed from anguish; his reflective gaze and tranquil expression suggesting a state of grace. Like the punks who displayed and celebrated society's rejection of them, "The Prophet" externalises his suffering, and perhaps, in accepting and revealing his condition (fear of emasculation?), a resolution occurs, and he is liberated from the shame and guilt expressed in the gestures of "Headache" and "Condition". "Natural Mystic" is the most recent painting and although more fluidly handled, again represents a fixed and immobile figure: the line has changed but the figure's feet are trapped in sand. This cross-eyed figure too, suggests a sexual/psychological interpretation : the shape contained bctween his hands could be a vagina or a lost penis.

Bevan's source material is often photographic — unposed photographs of real people taken from crime magazines and newspapers. Through successive drawings on paper and on canvas ("drawn" using dry pigment with the canvas on the floor), the images are re-interpreted and developed.

Once seen, Bevan's portraits are hard to forget. The images touch us somewhere deep in our psyches; we may not fully understand them, but in the moment of recognition they are known.

Brian Deighton
London 1983

Studied

1971-74 Goldsmiths College, London
1974-76 Slade School of Art,
University College, London

Selected individual exhibitions

1981 Matts Gallery, London
1982 Matts Gallery, London
1983 Galeria Akumulatory 2,
Poznan, Poland
1984 Gallery Wittenbrink,
Regensburg

Selected group exhibitions

1981 White Columns, New York
1981 Lisson Gallery, London
1982 *Before it Hits the Floor*, ICA,
London
1984 *Factory Show*,
Kunstlerwerkstatten, Munich
Museum Leerer Bevtel,
Regensburg
Bluecoat Gallery, Liverpool

Selected bibliography

Jean Fisher, "Tony Bevan", *Art Monthly*, October 1982

HEADACHE, 1980
Acrylic
44.5 × 67.3

THE PROPHET, 1982
Dry pigment on canvas
457.2 × 335.2

CONDITION, 1982
Pigment on Triwall
152.4 × 127

INTRUSION, 1982
Pigment on Triwall
40.6 × 94

NATURAL MYSTIC, 1983
Pigment on canvas
274.3 × 182.9

Courtesy of the artist

ANNETTE BEZOR

Born in Adelaide in 1950

Annette Bezor is a painter of startling pictures. They startle the contemporary viewer more accustomed to the crude and shaggy tail-end of neo-expressionism and the veiled hints of codified systems.

To me she is a latter day symbolist. Her work reminds me of the "Sacred Woods" of Puvis de Chavannes, the "Orpheus" of Moreau or, the "Sleeping Water" of Leon Frederic. Like those aesthetes of a century ago who dwelt with their androgynous friends, this modern equivalent uses extremely appealing imagery.

But Annette Bezor's figures are truly in the landscape or on the point of emerging, quietly masturbating, from their rocky couches. Often they flaunt their self satisfied charms in a landscape littered with the debris of our consumer society.

"Being realistic — almost photo realistic — her paintings can appeal at the gum tree level as well as at an ideological feminist level, and this makes them especially intriguing."(1)

Works such as these inevitably invite misunderstanding but one clear statement seems to be made by all her frontal and assertive figures ... this is the plea ..."not guilty".

In her epicene garden of Eden the apple tasted good and the snake was taken away by a passing eagle.

(1) Review, *Adelaide Advertiser*, 26 October 1983

Neville Weston
Adelaide
November 1983

Studied

1974-77 South Australia School of Art, Diploma of Fine Art (painting)

1978 Co-founder Round Space Artists' Collective
1981 Teacher of Design/Drawing, Centre for the Performing Arts, Adelaide

Selected individual exhibitions

1983 Round Space Gallery, Adelaide

Selected group exhibitions

1977 Young Artists Exhibition, Festival Centre, Adelaide
1978 Round Space Members, Union Gallery, University of Adelaide
1980 *Micro Show*, Contemporary Art Society, Adelaide

Tarot Card, Contemporary Art Society, Adelaide
The Real Thing, Contemporary Art Society, Adelaide
Maude Vizard Wholohan Art Prize Exhibition, Art Gallery of South Australia, Adelaide
1981 John McCaughey Exhibition, National Gallery of Victoria, Melbourne
1983 John McCaughey Exhibition, National Gallery of Victoria, Melbourne
Australian Perspecta, 1983, Art Gallery of New South Wales, Sydney

VENUS EMERGING, 1983
Oil on canvas
200 × 190

A BEDROOM PIECE I, 1983
Oil on linen
192.5 × 203.5

A BEDROOM PIECE II, 1984
Oil on linen
192 × 204

FALLEN ANGEL, 1984
Oil on canvas
199 × 211.5

Courtesy of the artist

FRANCOIS BOISROND

Born in 1959
Lives and works in Paris

Francois Boisrond is a genre artist, or something of the sort. Like Joseph Vernet, he paints storms; like Hubert Robert, catastrophes. The making of his painting is stiff and the subject succinct. Boisrond is one of those artists who has rediscovered some good manners in paintings thanks to *Figuration Libre* (free figuration). To paint is to expose sheaves of life. The "high style" of the preceding generation is not his strong point, nor "high taste"; of course, the taste he prefers is bad. Instead of painting history, he paints stories. He doesn't side with comic strips, he doesn't align himself with bad drawing; he opts for the role of a very good showman of images, a showman who knows how to cut and paste; like a crack cameraman he takes his shots, puts them together and tucks them into the composition. You can't call his elliptic scenario a narrative. It's up to the spectator to fill in the blank spaces. Boisrond always says just enough, for the real or for the figurative. Why develop when one simple image suffices?

Xavier Girard
Art Press
April 1982

Selected individual exhibitions

1981   Rivolta Gallery, Lausanne
1982   Farideh Cadot Gallery, Paris
1983   Annina Nosei Gallery, New York
1984   Farideh Cadot Gallery, Paris

Selected group exhibitions

1981   *Ateliers '81-'82*, ARC2, Musée d'Art Moderne de la Ville de Paris
        Finir en beaute, Paris
        Un regard autre, Farideh Cadot Gallery, Paris
1982   *Kunst unserer Zeit*, Groninger Museum, Netherlands
        Catherine Issert Gallery, Saint-Paul-de-Vence, France
        L'air du temps, Galerie d'Art Contemporain des Musées de Nice
1983   *Neue Bilder aux Frankreich*, Ursula Krinzinger Gallery, Innsbruck; Nachst-St-Stephan Gallery, Vienna; Grita Insam Gallery, Vienna
        New Art, The Tate Gallery, London
        Holtmann Gallery, Cologne
        Salon de Montrouge, France
        Biennale of Tours, France
        Groninger Museum, Netherlands
        Figures Imposées, ELAC, Lyon-Perrache, Lyon

Douceur de l'Avant-Garde, Association *C'est rien de le dire*, Rennes
1983-84   *New French Painting*, Riverside Studio, London; Museum of Modern Art, Oxford
1984   University Art Museum, University of California, Santa Barbara
        University Art Museum of Southern California, Los Angeles
        La Jolla Museum of Contemporary Art, La Jolla, California

Selected bibliography

Jean de Loisy, "New French Painting", *Flash Art*, No 110, January 1983
Catherine Strasser, *Art Press*, No 62, September 1982
Xavier Girard, "Jeunes Artistes", dossier, *Art Press*, No 58, April 1982
"Freie Figuration — Neue Bilder aus Frankreich", *Kunstforum International*, March 1983

Selected catalogues
L'air du Temps, Galerie d'Art Contemporain des Musees de Nice, June 1982
Ateliers '81-'82, ARC 2, Musée d'Art Moderne de la Ville de Paris
Kunst unserer Zeit, Musée de Groninger, Groninger, Netherlands, Summer 1982
Blanchard, Boisrond, Di Rosa, Combas, Musee de Groninger, Groninger, Netherlands, February 1983
Figures Imposées, ELAC, Lyon-Perrache, Winter 1983
La Douceur dans l'Avant-Garde, Association *C'est rien de le dire*, Rennes, January 1983

MASH, 1983
Acrylic on canvas
366 × 142

UNTITLED, 1982
Acrylic on canvas
Triptych, 215 × 360

UNTITLED, 1983
Acrylic on paper
Diptych, 260 × 238

UNTITLED, 1983
Acrylic on canvas
178 × 240

Courtesy Galerie Farideh Cadot, Paris

Photography Galerie Farideh Cadot

TONY CRAGG

Born in 1949
From 1977 living in Wuppertal, West Germany
From 1979 teaching at Düsseldorf Kunstakademie

The interests. Man's relationship to his environment and the objects, materials and images in that environment. The relationships between objects, materials and images. Obvious and immense areas; but apparently difficult areas for artists to work in without resorting to magic, alchemy or mystification. That could infer an objective approach, or, as I prefer to see it, a refusal to equate subjectivity with certain kinds of heavy-handed dramatics.

The objects. I am not interested in romanticising an epoch in the distant past when technology permitted men to make only few objects, tools etc. But, in contrast to today, I assume a materialistically simpler situation and a deeper understanding for the making processes, function and even metaphysical qualities of the objects they produced. The social organisations which have proved to be most successful are productive systems. The rate at which objects are produced increases; complementary to production is consumption. We consume, populating our environment with more and more objects. With no chance of understanding the making processes because we specialise, specialise in the production, but not in the consumption.

The materials. The use of various materials, stone, bronze, iron etc. has been used as indications of technological development. Our use of materials goes as far as radioactive elements and biochemical substances of the most complex nature. Particularly exploitable have proved to be the chemically stable polymers — plastics. Due to the long relationship between men and such materials as earth, water, wood, stone and certain metals they evoke a rich variety of emotional responses and images. The experience of these materials alters, however, as they appear increasingly in synthetic, industrial forms. What does it mean to us on a conscious, or, perhaps more important, unconscious level to live amongst these and many other completely new materials? Many materials/objects because of their function or chemical instability need a protective coating. It is often possible and then usually desirable to give materials/objects a colour.

The colours. It has not always been easy to produce colours and then they were frequently impermanent and limited. The colours of plants and animals are also limited and related to function. The possibilities for making the colours are unlimited and the choice should be too. But many decisions about the colours of objects in our environment are industrial, commercial or even administrative. A response to demand? A demand often created by the supplier. The choice is between a range of offers which already represent some kind of lowest common denominator. These colours only become interesting after they have led a life reacting to the atmosphere and light, touched by other materials.

The images. Celluloid wildlife, video landscapes, photographic wars, Polaroid families, offset politics, quick change, something new on all channels. Always a choice of second-hand images. Reality can hardly keep up with its marketing image. The need to know both objectively and subjectively more about the subtle fragile relationships between us, objects, images and essential natural processes and conditions is becoming critical. It is very important to have first order experiences — seeing, touching, smelling, hearing — with objects/images and to let that experience register.

Artist's statement
from *documenta 7*
catalogue 1982

Studied
1969-70 Gloucestershire College of Art and Design
1970-73 Wimbledon School of Art, London
1973-77 Royal College of Art, London

During studies at the Royal College, spent one year teaching in Metz at the invitation of the French Ministry of Culture.

Selected individual exhibitions
1979 Lisson Gallery, London (and '80,'82)
Lützowstrasse Situation, Berlin (and '80)
Kunsterlhaus Weidenallee, Hamburg
1980 Arnolfini Gallery, Bristol
Konrad Fischer, Düsseldorf (and '82)
Chantal Crousel, Paris (and '82)
Lucio Amelio, Naples (and '83)
Franco Toselli, Milan (and '83)
Saman Gallery, Genoa
1981 Schellmann and Klüser, Munich (and '82)
Musée d'Art et d'Industrie, St Etienne
Whitechapel Art Gallery, London
Nouveau Musée, Lyon (and '82)
Front Room, London
Von der Heydt Museum, Wuppertal
Vacuum, Düsseldorf
1982 Badischer Kunstverein, Karlsruhe
Kanransha Gallery, Tokyo
Nisshin Gallery, Tokyo
Marion Goodman, New York (and '83)
Buro Berlin
Kröller-Müller Museum, Otterlo
1983 Buchmann, St Gallen
Art & Project, Amsterdam
Kunsthalle, Berne
Thomas Cohn, Rio de Janeiro

Selected group exhibitions
1975 Brunel University, Uxbridge
1976 Ecole des Beaux Arts, Metz
1977 Lisson Gallery, London (and '79,'81)
Fine Arts Building, New York
RCA Degree Show, London
Silver Jubilee Sculpture Show, Battersea Park, London
1978 *Ja-Na-Pa III*, Paris
1979 *Europa — Kunst der 80er Jahre*, Stuttgart
1980 *Nuova Immagine*, XVI Triennale, Milan
A Perspective, Basel
Aperto '80, Venice Biennale
Kunst in Europa na '68, Museum van Hedendaagse Kunst, Ghent
1981 *Enciclopedia, il magico primario in Europa*, Modena
The Motor Show, Front Room, London
1982 *British Sculpture in the Twentieth Century*, Whitechapel Art Gallery, London
Aspects of British Art Today, Japan
Indian Triennale, New Delhi
De la Catastrophe, Geneva
Art and Architecture, ICA, London
Neue Skulptur, Galerie Nächst St Stephan, Vienna
documenta 7, Kassel
Englische Plastik
Heute/British Sculpture Now, Kunstmuseum, Lucerne
Leçons des choses, Berne, Chambery, Châlon-sur-Soane
Kunst im offentlichen Raum, Chambery
Objects and Figures, Fruitmarket Gallery, Edinburgh

1983   *Figures and Objects*, John
Hansard Gallery,
Southhampton
La Trottola di Sirio, Centro
d'Arte Contemporain,
Syracuse
*Truc et troc, Leçons des
choses*, ARC, Musée d'Art
Moderne de la Ville de Paris
*A Pierre et Marie, un
exposition en travaux*, rue
d'Ulm, Paris
The Sculpture Show,
Hayward and Serpentine
Galleries, London
Arcaico Contemporaneo,
Museo de Sannio,
Benevento
New Art, Tate Gallery,
London
British Section, XVII Bienal
de São Paulo (and tour)

Selected bibliography

Edward Phelps, "Joel Degen, Tony
Cragg, Bruce McLean, Arnolfini
Gallery, Bristol", *Art Review*, July
1980
Domus, No 611, November 1980
Lynne Cook, "Tony Cragg at the
Whitechapel", *Artscribe*, No 28,
March 1981
Germano Celant, "Tony Cragg and
Industrial Platonism", *Artforum*,
November 1981
documenta 7, catalogues 1 and 2,
1982
Michael Newman, "Tony Cragg:
Fragments and Emblems", catalogue
text, Kunstmuseum, Luzern 1982
Michael Newman, "New British
Sculpture", *Art in America*,
September 1982
Jean-Louis Mabuant,
"Découpage/Collage à propos de
Tony Cragg", *Cahiers du Cric*, NDLR
No. 4, 1982
Jean-Hubert Martin, "Interview mit
Tony Cragg", catalogue text,
Kunsthalle Bern 1982
Peter Winter, "Puzzlespiel und
Superzeichen", *Kunstforum*, Bd. 64,
June 1983
"Vous prenez quel apart?", *Actuel*,
No. 47, 1983

INSTALLATION, 1984
Designed especially for
the Fifth Biennale of Sydney
Courtesy the artist

Tendencies 5, Galerija Suvremene Umijetnosti, Zagreb
Expoprojecoa, Grife, São Paulo
International Triennal of Coloured Graphic Prints, Grenchen
Biennale de Paris
Films als Kunstwerk, Kunsthalle, Cologne

1974 *Art Systems in Latin America*, Institute of Contemporary Arts, London
Coloured Graphic Prints, Pratt Graphics Center, New York
Projekt 74, Kunsthalle, Cologne
Video Bander, Kunstverein, Cologne
Impact Video Art, Musée des Arts Decoratifs, Lausanne
Video Bander, Kunstverein, Cologne
International Biennale Exhibition of Prints, National Museum of Modern Art, Tokyo and Kyoto

1975 *Video Art*, Institute of Contemporary Art, Philadelphia and tour
Video Art, Palais des Beaux-Arts, Brussels
Small Press, Zona, Florence

1976 *The Museum of Drawers*, Museum der Stadt, Solothurn; International Cultureel Centrum, Antwerpen; Museum Schwabisch Gmund, Prediger

1977 *Sonora*, Calcografia Nazionale, Rome
Moving (Part II), Hal Bromm Gallery, New York
Libri Oggetto, Palazzo Vecchio, Florence
The Record as Artwork, The Fort Worth Art Museum, Texas

1978 *Arte & Cinema*, Biennale of Venice
Artisti e Cinema Negli Anni '70, Pinacoteca Comunale, Ravenna
Pittura Fatta col Cinema, Cineteca Italiana, Milano
Geometria Sensivel, Musu de Arte Moderna, Rio de Janeiro
The Museum of Drawers, The Museum of Art, New Orleans; Kunsthaus, Zurich

1979 *Das Schubladenmuseum*, Kunstmuseum, Bern
Cinema d'Artista e Cinema Sperimentale in Italia, Cinemathèque Française, Paris

1980 *Biennale of Venice*
Camere Incantate, Palazzo Reale, Milano
Quasi Cinema, Centro Internazionale di Brera, Milan

1981 *Kunstlerbucher*, Kunstverein, Frankfurt
Quase Cinema, Fundacao Nacional de Arte, Rio de Janeiro
Bienal of São Paulo Contemporary Latin American Art and Japan, National Museum of Art, Osaka

1982 *11 Italienische Kunstler in Munchen*, Kunstlerwerkstatten, Munich
Kunstler aus Lateinamerika, DAAD Galerie, Berlin
Contemporaneidade, Museu de Arte Moderna, Rio de Janeiro

1983 *Codici e Marchingegni 1482/1983*, Casa di Leonardo, Vinci
Cultura Contemporanea, Cultura Fisica, Club F. Conti, Milan

WORLD, HEAD, BODY, CHILD, 1980
Mixed media
4 units each 140 dia

Photography Thomas Con Arte Contemporanea, Rio de Janeiro

GONZALO DÍAZ

Born Santiago, Chile, in 1947
Lives and works in Santiago

In relation to the main lines in Chilean *avant-garde* art of the last decade — the irruption of photography in pictorial space, the displacement and extension of the concept of engraving beyond conventional techniques, the notion of extending the bearings of art as far as considering it as acting on the social body itself — the work of Gonzalo Díaz introduces a new dimension in the field of Chilean art; it capitalises on the weapons of a rhetoric snatched from the hands of an *avant-garde* no longer able to fulfill the demands of its own program. That is, it transfers back into the field of painting, a field that had been considered as dismantled, the models of sign production that would propose a new pictorial code, pulling painting away from axis pictorial tradition.

Let's see if you can run as fast as me is visual tautology and it builds itself up by articulating three rhetorical means: 1) by forcing the image, through repetition, into a denial — an irony — a perversion of the icon; 2) by forcing the image to state its own tautology — its own excess — by placing in the work not only the image, but the actual object depicted; 3) by forcing the image — the coloured image — to a recognition of the tautology of its colour, as seen against the brighter colour of a text in neon, as from the image. These operations point towards a visual (cultural) space seen as a "display window" in which the inventory of images proposed by the metropolis is disfigured, discoloured; it is acted upon.

Justo Mellado
Santiago, Chile
August 1983

Studied

1965-69 University of Chile, School of Art

1969-75 Instructor in Painting, School of Art, University of Chile

1977 Contemporary Art Institute founder and Lecturer in Painting

1979 Bachelor of Art, University of Chile

1975-83 Lecturer in Painting, School of Art, University of Chile

Selected individual exhibitions

1978 *Lost Paradise*, CEDLA Gallery, Santiago

1982 *Sentimental History of Chilean Painting*, SUR Gallery, Santiago
Luminist Catalogue, Centro Cultural Mapocho, Santiago

Selected group exhibitions

1978 IV Competition *CNV*, National Art Museum, Santiago

1979 XV Biennale of São Paulo, Brazil
IV Biennale of Valparaiso, Chile

1980 *Benson & Hedges Panorama of the New Latin American Painting*, National Art Museum, Buenos Aires
VI Competition *CNV*, National Art Museum, Santiago

1981 IV Biennale of Medellín, Colombia

1982 *Con-Textos*, SUR Gallery, Santiago

1983 *Arte & Textos*, SUR Gallery, Santiago

LET'S SEE IF YOU CAN RUN AS FAST AS ME, 1983
Silkscreen and enamel on plastic canvas
270 × 400
Courtesy of Dr and Mrs Díaz

EUGENIO DITTBORN

Born Santiago, Chile, in 1943
Lives and works in Santiago

Close looking

About looking

To find photographs, the photographs of long since forgotten figures, long since forgotten criminals (whose faces were printed for purposes of detection), long since forgotten prostitutes, long since forgotten victims of crimes: to find those photographs printed in the media, the Chilean media of many years ago — perhaps this would be the starting point for the work of Eugenio Dittborn, and perhaps this work might be described simply as an activity of close looking: and of trying to make explicit, by visual means, this act of close looking.

About working on those photographs

Visual means of making explicit this act of close looking: among them, giving those photographs a wholly different context and a wholly different physical dimension, thus forcing on them a way of looking to which they were alien; thus creating a space in which the gaze of the spectator is thrown back upon itself; in which the faces send none of the signs with which the spectator is familiar, but rather the signs of their own remoteness, their belonging to another order, previsual or nonvisual, prephotographic or nonphotographic, these forgotten people mostly pictured against their will for purposes of identification or detection, for the purposes of being fixed in their own sorry place within a society with no place for them; among these visual means, also, the act of superimposing on them the text of verbal clichés, sayings, lyrics of popular songs, whatever can be recognised as collective, "used" speech, and of doing so in the penmanship of someone who never quite learned to write, who still writes as if drawing, each letter a laborious design in pursuit of some ill-conceived perfection; among these visual means, the use of different techniques and materials for the printing of the photographs, thus bringing simultaneously into play the memory of the different occasions and times in which each of those techniques or materials is or was commonly used — establishing in the one place occupied by each work the coexistence of different historical times, of different social spaces, the discontinuity hidden behind each idea of a society taken as a continuum in space or in time.

About visual means, society, history

The work of Eugenio Dittborn seen from the viewpoint of its production within Chilean society, during these last years, a time in which the social tensions existing in an underdeveloped society have reached paroxysm, have seemingly left behind any possibility of expression or explanation based on previous ideological discourse; a baffled, incoherent time, whose lessons have not yet been learned, and have not yet even been expressed; a time in which history as it is written, ideas on society as they have been expressed, are evidently in tatters, and any possible understanding is based on an awareness of the *débris* in which thinking is at the moment immersed — this work rescues the evidence — the photographic trace, the physical imprint of what official history has left behind, the tangible evidence of bodies erased by written history, the visible proof of the gap, the lack that both invalidates official history and makes its writing possible; it exposes our notions of society and of history, and creates visible awareness of the discontinuity underlying them — and, from Chile, projects the notion of repressive society, of enforced unison, and exposes it, bringing into play the different strata forced into a pose — a gesture — that masks the open wound of their incompatability, their forced and contradictory existence.

Adriana Valdés
Santiago, Chile
1983

Studied

1962-65	Escuela de Bellas Artes de la Universidad de Chile, Painting, engraving and drawing
1965	Escuela de Fotomecanicac de Madrid, photoengraving
1966-69	Hochschule für Bildende Kunst, West Berlin, silkscreen and lithography
1968	Ecole des Beaux Arts de Paris, painting.
1972	Atelier Estudios Norte, Santiago, photosilkscreen

Selected individual exhibitions

1964	Galeria Marta Faz, Santiago, Chile
1965	Colegio Hispanoamericano, Madrid
1969	Galerie Eva Rosiner, West Berlin
1974	*Acontecimientos para Goya, pintor*, Museo Nacional de Bellas Artes, Santiago
1975	*Premios 1975*, Galeria Matta, Santiago
1976	*Delachilenapintura, Historia*, Galeria Epoca, Santiago
1977	*Final de Pista*, Galeria Epoca, Santiago
1978	Galeria San Diego, Bogota
1979	Galeria la Trinchera, Caracas
1980	Galeria Sur, Santiago
1983	Galeria Sur, Santiago

Selected group exhibitions

1968	Galerie des Beaux Arts, Paris
	Galerie de France, Paris
1979	Iglesia de San Francisco, Santiago
1980	*Visual works for a poet*, Galeria Cal, Santiago
	Fifth Norwegian International Print Biennale, Oslo
1981	*First French-Chilean Video Festival*, Instituto chileno frances de cultura, Santiago
	Bienal de Medellín
1982	*Writing and Reading*, Galeria Sur, Santiago
	Artists' books, Metronom, Barcelona
	Registro, Medellín
1983	*in-out*, WPA, Washington
	Artists' Books, Franklin Furnace, New York
	El Cayman Gallery, New York
	Textos infernos, The Festival of International Poetry: Latinoamerica, Galeria Venezuela, New York
1984	Intergraphyk, East Berlin

Selected bibliography

Nelly Richard, Ronald Kay, "v.i.s.u.a.l.", *Delachilenapintura, Historia*, Santiago 1976
Nelly Richard, *Una mirada sobre el arte en Chile*, 1981
Gonzalo Muñoz, "Tres notas sobre la obra de Eugenio Dittborn", text in catalogue of *in-out*, Washington Projects for the Arts, Washington 1983

By the artist
Estrategia y proyecciones de la plástica nacional sobre la decada del 80, 1979
With Ronald Kay, *Definitivamente transitorio*, 1979
Final de Pista, 1977, 1981
Fallo Fotografico, 1981

A WHOLE DAY OF MY LIFE, 1983
Photo silkscreen and painting on acrylic and masonite
Wall panel 240 × 400
Floor panel 77 × 400

Courtesy of the artist
Under the auspices of the Instituto Superior de Comunicación y Diseño
Santiago

Photography Jaime O'Ryan, Santiago

FELIX DROESE

Born in Singen/Htw, Düsseldorf, 1950

"Self redemption". "Condemned, to redeem ourselves . . ." Can one actually be more exact in deciding one's own horizon of faith? Who eliminates the curse, banishes divine pity; whatever they do, they do as condemned ones. They usually don't enquire further as to who condemned them; it suffices to know that this trial of condemnation is unjust and that it belongs to the emancipation of the new man, to declare this trial null and void, and this by the act of self-redemption.

Redemption from what? From economic misery? Today they know as well as their opponents that the forms of work organisation, which have developed through historic necessity in countries under Marxist administration, do not eradicate misery but generalise it. They do not supplant the world's curse, instead they consecrate work. Work is the single valid thing, even the ritual which outlasts this "death of God" (not to mention the various smaller twilights of the lesser deities), which facilitates the communication of people with the world (by now curseless), as they imagine, in religious forms. By this rite the redemption of the world is celebrated with a seriousness, a ferocious fervour, which creates the suspicion that, at that time in the rebellion against the bourgeois *Weltschmerz*, the pain itself was not really conquered but its bourgeois forms, and by the destruction of these forms — which like old fashioned phials had bound the poison in the vessel — the pain now is distributed with even less restraint into the air we breathe.

Walter Warnach
Extract from
"Die Welt des Schmerzes"
(The World of Pain), 1952
Statement for *dort 1981-83*
(there 1981-83)
Tape by the artist
Neske Verlag, Pfullingen, 1984

Studied

1970-72 Academy of Art, Düsseldorf, arts and crafts
1972-76 Academy of Art, Düsseldorf, social sculpture

Selected individual exhibitions

1980   *Schwarz auf Weiss*, Kunstsammlung, Museum Bochum
1983   *infelix lignum*, Kunstraum Muenchen, Munich

         dort 1981-83, Orangerie Schloss Augustusburg zu Bruehl; Kunstverein, Bruehl
1984   *Mangelmutanten ueberleben Kapitalismus*, Museum Hans Lange, Krefeld

Selected group exhibitions

1974   *Vietnam — Solidaritaetsausstellung*, Mensa of the University of Frankfurt
1977   *Gegen politische Unterdruekcung in der BRD und DDR*, Old Mensa of the University of Cologne
1981   *Westkunst*, Cologne
1982   *documenta 7*, Kassel

ELF — "WIR SIND KEINE AMERIKANISCHEN LAMPENSCHIRME", 1976-84
(We are not American lampshades)
11 processed cowskins

LENINISTISCHE FRIEDHOEFE, 1980
Drawings on paper

Courtesy of Galerie R. Zwirner, Cologne

Photography Oleski Galerie R. Zwirner

MARLENE DUMAS

Born in Cape Town, South Africa, in 1953

It is obvious that at such a pitch, it no longer matters whether the passion is genuine or not. What the public wants is the image of passion, not passion itself. There is no more a problem of truth in wrestling than in the theatre. In both, what is expected is the intelligible representation of moral situations which are usually private.

Roland Barthes
"The World of Wrestling"
Mythologies, 1957

Unsatisfied desire and the untrustworthy language of art

I   Some people die of their own passion. Some by the passion of others. And some simply die of illness or another natural cause. I am against it.
II   Art is not a mirror. Art is a translation of that which you do not know, but of which you want to convince others or rather, that which no-one knows, but by which everyone can be seduced to believe that although "it" is bad, "it" is good; it's good not to have what you desire most.
III   I'll continue to cry for the doomed: innocent brushstrokes, painterly trances, the exotic other, love-fictions ... To lipread and name the silence; to use the dream that torture will stop when the prisoner talks.

Marlene Dumas
January 1984

Studied

1972-75 B.A. Skone Kunsten, University of Cape Town
1976-78 Ateliers '63, Haarlem, Netherlands
1979-80 Psychologisch Instituut, University of Amsterdam

Selected individual exhibitions

1979 Galerie Annemarie de Kruijff, Paris
1980 Galerie Lambelet, Basel
1983 *Unsatisfied Desires*, Galerie Helen van der Meij, Amsterdam

Selected group exhibitions

1978 *Atelier 15*, Stedelijk Museum, Amsterdam
1980 *Ateliers '63, een keuze uit het werk van deelnemers 1975-1980*, Bonnefantenmuseum, Maastricht and Museum
Fodor, Amsterdam
The Critic Sees, Museum Fodor, Amsterdam
1981 *Lis '81*, Lisbon
Drawing Triennale, Wroclaw, Poland
1982 *Zeichnung Heute*, Kunsthalle, Nuremburg
Junge Kunst aus den Niederlanden, Sonderschau, Art 13 '82, Basel
Jonge Kunst uit Nederland, Haags Gemeentemuseum, The Hague
documenta 7, Kassel
1983 *Restrisiko*, Bonnefantenmuseum, Maastricht
IJsland/Amsterdam, Living Art Museum, Reykjavik
La Divina Comedia, Galerie 't Venster, Rotterdam
Veertien Kunstenaars uit Nederland, Museum Boymans-van Beuningen, Rotterdam
1984 *Het Persoonlijke = Politiek*, Dutch Art Foundation, Amsterdam

Selected bibliography

Jetteke Bolten, "Marlene Dumas", *Dutch Art* + Architecture Today (DA+AT), May 1984

LOVE VERSUS DEATH SERIES, 1980
Blueprint paper, paper, watercolour, pencil
4 units, 235 × 100
1 unit, 222 × 24
1 unit, 197 × 19

THE THREE CROWNS OF EXPRESSIONISM, 1982
Oil, canvas, photograph
2 units, 250 × 120

EXOTIC LINGERIE, 1983
Acrylic, canvas, crayon, ink
2 units, 130 × 110

MARTHA — SIGMUND'S WIFE -, 1984
Oil on canvas
130 × 110

MARTHA, 1984
Oil on canvas
130 × 110

Courtesy the artist and Paul Th. Andriesse, Amsterdam

Photography Paul Th. Andriesse

EDWARD DWURNIK

Born Radzymin, Poland, 1943
Lives in Warsaw

A short note inspired by the
Sportsmen Series

I was just about to start writing
exactly the way I should: clearly and
simply, without errors and without
praise, without too many generalities
and without too much detail, rather
cleverly, a bit on the lofty side,
altogether congenially... Suddenly I
thought: "Wouldn't it be better to go
out to the street and see what's
going on?"

I closed the door after myself and
entered *Dwurnik's Theatre*. "...Pace!
What rapid pace!" A sharp light
outlines silhouettes and things. It
builds plans for which the sky is the
limit. There is little air and very
much excitement. It is a sportsman's
recipe for life. The stage is crooked
and there is not enough room for the
crowd.

"... You, too, will be a hero
tomorrow ..." It is warm and
clammy. Cramped and grimy. Things
seem to be too close to one another.
"... Happy birthday to you! Happy
birthday to you! ..." An image of
agony and ecstasy or a narcotic
vision of the finale? A condensed
smell of the on-going life? A
photogenic face, a cheap detail, a
desperate gesture, a provincial joke.
A short skirt, a red nose, a slimy
smile, a boozed glance ...

Is there a heaven anywhere?
Anything for the soul? What about
you, head, you have reached as high
as the towers, you keep inhaling air
and laughter. You have grown as
stupidly inflated as a balloon and you
are proud to look down on the earth.
There is a jingle of shovels, chains,
pickaxes and bottles. Shoes are
singing in their rhythmic march;
there is a rattle of orders and tolling
of bells; overused beds creak, smoke
oozes and beer has a bracing effect.

"... Give me a kiss, love, dinner's
waiting, there is no work on
Saturdays, we are free tomorrow
..."

A trickle of blood is getting nearer,
zigzagging across the stage before it
finally soaks into the ground. A
lonely dog is cowering to sniff. He
seems to be reading words into
human blood. He has lit a pipe. He
watches and listens: "Count off: one,
two, three, four ..." A lingering five
is being brought into a straight line.

Dorota Gierzynska
Poland

Studied
1963-70 Academy of Fine Arts,
Warsaw

Selected individual exhibitions
1978 Ośrodek Propagandy Sztuki,
Łodz
1980 Gallery Sćiana Wschodnia,
Warsaw
Gallery BWA, Warsaw
1981 Gallery ON, Poznań
Gallery Sciana Wschodnia,
Warsaw
1982 Gallery BWA, Lublin
1983 Museum Alvar Aalto,
Jyväskyla, Finland
Gallery Depolma, Düsseldorf
Gallery BWA, Poznań
1983-84 Gallery Veritas, Warsaw

Selected group exhibitions
1978 *7th International Print
Biennale*, Cracow
*6th International Print
Biennale*, Florence
1979 *IV International Biennale of
Drawing*, Cleveland
*VI International Biennale of
Print*, Bradford
*1st International European
Biennale of Print*,
Heidelberg
Polsk Kunst, Copenhagen
Premio Biella 79
1980 *III World Print*, San
Francisco
*8th International Print
Biennale*, Cracow
*VIII International Biennale
of Posters*, Warsaw
1981 *One Year After the August*,
Gallery Pryzmat, Cracow
1982 *documenta 7*, Kassel
1982-83 *De Plastic Tas*, Rotterdam

Selected bibliography
Andrzej Oseka, "Der Polen Eigenes
Porträt", *Westermanns Monstshafte*,
August 1981
Paweł Kozłowski, *Edward Dwurnik —
Kuvia Puolasta*, catalogue,
Alvar-Aalto-Museo 1983
Stanisław Urbański, *documenta 7*,
Zdanie September 1982

By the artist
"Forum", *Projekt*, 14 January 1980

AFTER TRAINING, 1972
Oil on canvas
146 × 114

NEW AIRPORT, 1974
Oil on canvas
146 × 114

THEY ARE ALREADY TAKING HIM,
1974
Oil on canvas
146 × 114

SUNDAY MASS, 1983
Oil on canvas
146 × 114

Courtesy the artist and Muzeum
Sztuki, Łodz, Poland

MIMMO GERMANA

Born Catania, 1944
Lives in Milan

...It is no coincidence that some basic experiences of recent years refer to cultural movements of the past, like Romanticism, which, in their various expressionistic and abstract manifestations, the arts practiced without losing the joy of painting and the nobility of its role. In the post-technological age in which we live it is possible to grasp once more the personal, by avoiding the hyper-realistic levelling caused by massive usage of the mass media. The art of the last generation does not confuse the demise of political dogma with the demolition of critical consciousness, which cannot be abrogated in a work of art. In this area Mimmo Germanà operates. Art is also resistance against one's own present, if such a present wants to distort it until it loses its prospective value. The tension of art overtakes even the present and lands directly in the future. By this landing, the artist has rediscovered his own healthy and effective solitude, a feeling of inferiority, which leads him to identify the minority with his own self. The function of security in art reaches the point where the notion of minority — always in the social sense — is concentrated on the creative needs of the individual.

... (Germanà) works in this direction with plastic and relaxing feeling for decoration. Painting is the medium which materialises such a dimension, but without the exaggeration of individual elements that characterised Abstract Expressionism or non-representational art. The works of art, in which Germanà uses the myths of his Mediterranean soil, strive for a stronger pictorial rendering. They do not conserve the feeling of a distant, objective image. The painterly material becomes a support and means of expression which surpasses the classical fine art tradition. While classical fine art had the desire, from its Greco-Roman ancestry up to metaphysical times, to describe the natural and urban landscape figuratively, now the figures do not stand out clearly in front of the background — as in a performance without stage props — but are accelerated. At other times, Germanà creates figurative paintings and objects which represent, in an ironic way, domestic scenes, where the memory of the subject matter is abolished and the drawing or design of figures dominates. These figures are taken from traditions which derive from the connections between dream and ornament.

Achille Bonito Oliva
Extracts from
Mediterranean Painting
Translation Rudi Krausmann
and Don Maynard

Studied
1967　Istituto d'Arte, Catania
1967-70　Accademia di Belle Arti, Rome

Selected individual exhibitions
1970　Galleria l'Attico, Rome
1977　Galleria Toselli, Milan
1978　Galleria Pio Monti, Rome
1979　Galleria Toselli, Milan
　　　Galleria Persano, Turin
　　　Perspektive 79, Kunstmesse, Basel
1980　Galleria Mazzoli, Modena
　　　Studio Cavalieri, Bologna
　　　Galleria Toselli, Milan
1981　Galleria Mazzoli, Modena
1981-82　Advance, Agency for Modern Artists, Düsseldorf
1982　Galleria Ariadne, Vienna
　　　Studio Cavalieri, Bologna
1983　Galerie Antiope, Paris
　　　Galleria Ferrari, Verona
1984　Galerie Hans Barlach, Hamburg

Selected group exhibitions
1971　*Persona*, Belgrade
　　　Biennale de Paris
　　　Situation-concept, Innsbruck; Vienna
1973　*Contemporanea*, Parcheggio di Villa Borghese, Rome
　　　XV Triennale, Milan
1979　*Pittura-Ambiente*, Palazzo Reale, Milan
　　　Europa 79, Stuttgart
　　　Parigi, oh cara, Galerie Yvonne Lambert, Paris
1980　*Italiana Nuova Immagine*, Pinacoteca, Ravenna
　　　Aperto 80, Biennale of Venice
　　　Genius Loci, Acireale
1981　*Biennale Trigon*, Graz
　　　Talijanska Transavangarda, Zagreb
　　　Taormina Fin de Siècle, Taormina
　　　Ritratto, Galleria La Salita, Rome
1982　*Avventura*, Reggio Emilia
1983　*Il Nuovo Disegno Europea ed Americano*, Capodistria

Selected bibliography

Mimmo Germanà, catalogue, Galleria Persano, Turin 1979
L. Cherubini, "La Luce Come Protagonista", *L'Avanti*, Milan, 27 April 1980
A. Borgogelli, *Flash Art*, No 101, January-February 1981
L. Cherubini, "La Transavanguardia in Italia", *Transavantgarde International*, Achille Bonito Oliva, Giancarlo Politi Editore, Milan 1982
Achille Bonito Oliva, *Mediterrane Malerei*, catalogue, Galerie Ariadne, Vienna 1982

By the artist
"Si Sta Già Trasformando", *Domus*, Milan, October 1980
With I. Puliafito, *Domus*, Milan, May 1983

Details of works to be in the Biennale were not available at the time of publication.

GILBERT & GEORGE

Gilbert
Born Dolomites, Italy, 1943

George
Born Devon, England, 1942

The works (of Gilbert & George) . . . are exquisite and vigorous. I tend to see them as social emblems in that great English tradition that began with Hogarth.

Emblematic too is their formal structure, built on balances and symmetries which tighten the images into concise constructions of imagery and text. They scan the states of mind of modern man — but offer no advice nor consolation.

The prospects are bleak; and there is no reason to see the art of Gilbert & George as witty or frivolous. The subject is modern man seen from the dark and in the dark. His miserable state requires wit to sustain it; the basic tone, however, is a grim seriousness.

I admire this art. At times it may be almost mannerist in its formal elegance but that does not matter. I admire the beautiful attempt to capture and hold to view the sensibility of our time. They are our Baudelaire. They walk the streets and see the sadness and the hope, the poetry and beauty of our generation.

Rudi Fuchs
Gilbert & George 1968 to 1980
Eindhoven 1980

Studied

Gilbert
Wolkenstein School of Art
Hallein School of Art
Munich Academy of Art

George
Dartington Adult Education Centre
Dartington Hall College og Art
Oxford School of Art

Met and studied

St Martin's School of Art 1967
Live and work in London

Selected individual exhibitions

1968   *Snow Show*, St Martin's School of Art, London
1969   *The Singing Sculpture*, The Lyceum, London
Posing on Stairs, Stedelijk Museum, Amsterdam
1970   *George by Gilbert & Gilbert by George*, Fournier Street, London
The Pencil on Paper Descriptive Works, Konrad Fischer Gallery, Düsseldorf
To be with Art is all we ask, Nigel Greenwood Gallery, London
1971   *The Paintings*, Whitechapel Art Gallery, London
The General Jungle, Sonnabend Gallery, New York
1972   *The Bar*, Anthony d'Offay Gallery, London
1973   *The Shrubberies & Singing Sculpture*, John Kaldor Project, Art Gallery of New South Wales, Sydney
1974   *Dark Show*, Art & Project, Amsterdam
1975   *Post-Card Sculptures*, Sperone Westwater Fischer, New York
Dusty Corners, Art Agency, Tokyo
1976   *The Red Sculpture*, Sonnabend Gallery, New York
The General Jungle, Albright-Knox Art Gallery, Buffalo
1977   *New Photo-Pieces*, Konrad Fischer Gallery, Düsseldorf
1980   *New Photo-Pieces*, Karen & Jean Bernier, Athens
Modern Fears, Anthony d'Offay Gallery, London
Photo-Pieces 1971-80, Stedelijk Van Abbemuseum, Eindhoven
1981   *Photo-Pieces 1971-81*, Kunsthalle, Düsseldorf; Kunsthalle, Bern; Centre Georges Pompidou, Paris; Whitechapel Art Gallery, London
Photo-Pieces 1980-81, Chantal Crousel, Paris
1982   *Crusade (New Postcard Pieces)*, Anthony d'Offay Gallery, London
New Photo-Pieces, Gewad, Ghent
1983   *Modern Faith*, Sonnabend Gallery, New York
New Works, Crousel-Bussonet, Paris
1984   *New Photo-Pieces*, Anthony d'Offay Gallery, London
Gilbert & George 1974-1984, The Baltimore Museum of Art, Baltimore and tour: Contemporary Arts Museum, Houston; The Norton Gallery of Art, West Palm Beach, Florida (and The Solomon R. Guggenheim Museum, New York in 1985)

Selected group exhibitions

1969   *Conception*, Städtisches Museum, Leverkusen
1972   *The New Art*, Hayward Gallery, London 1972
1976   *Arte Inglese Oggi*, Palazzo Reale, Milan
1977   *Europe in the 70s*, The Art Institute, Chicago
1978   *documenta 6* , Kassel
1979   *Un Certain Art Anglais*, ARC, Musée d'Art Moderne de la Ville de Paris
1980   *Kunst in Europa na '68*, Museum Voor Hedendaagse Kunst, Ghent
1981   *Westkunst*, Cologne
1982   *Aspects of British Art Today*, Metropolitan Art Museum, Tokyo
documenta 7, Kassel
Zeitgeist, Berlin
1983   *New Art* Tate Gallery, London

Selected bibliography

Ger Van Elk, "We would honestly like to say how happy we are to be Sculptors", *Museumjournaal*, No 5, 1969
Anne Seymour, "An Interview", *The New Art*, catalogue, Arts Council of Great Britain, London 1972
Bruce Adams, "Gilbert & George for High Tea", *Sunday Telegraph*, Sydney, August 26 1973
Lynda Morris, "Gilbert & George", *Studio International*, Vol 188 No 968, London 1974
Rudi H. Fuchs, "Gilbert & George. Dark Shadow", *Art Monthly* , No 6, 1977
Richard Lorber, "Gilbert & George", *Artforum*, Vol 16 No 9, 1978
Carter Ratcliff, "Gilbert & George and Modern Life", *Gilbert & George 1968 to 1980*, catalogue, Van Abbemuseum Eindhoven, 1980
Stephen Walker, "Living with Fear and Gilbert & George", *Blitz*, Vol 1 No 4, London 1981
John Roberts, "Gilbert & George at Anthony d'Offay", *Artscribe*, No 27, London 1981
Gordon Burn, "The Perfect Couple", *Sunday Times Magazine*, London, October 18 1981
Alberto Moravia, "Ma che belle statuine", *L'Espresso, Rome, January 1 1982*
Roberta Smith, "*Gilbert & George's Modern Faith*", *Village Voice*, New York, May 17 1983
Brenda Richardson, "No Puzzle — Just Difficult Truth", *Gilbert & George 1974 to 1984*, catalogue, Baltimore Museum of Art 1984

DRUNK WITH GOD, 1983
Photo-piece
480 × 1100
Courtesy the artists and Anthony d'Offay Gallery, London

Photograph courtesy Anthony d'Offay Gallery, London

MIKE GLIER

Born Fort Thomas, Kentucky, in 1953
Lives and works in New York City

Mike Glier's art is an exercise of conscience. It is also irrepressibly American in that his habit of social criticism is translated into an act of positive sentiment. His drawings and paintings seem to more accurately relate to popular culture than high culture. If one were to place him in a creative tradition, the temptation would be to look toward a film heritage that includes such gentle activists as Frank Capra and Preston Sturges rather than a high art heritage where sentiment is suspect and conscience is a big stick. Glier's choice of serial subject matter (the murdered children of Atlanta, "white male power", Reaganomics, specifically stated "non-sexist" portraits of women) can sound suspiciously self-dramatising. Yet, his solutions are either engagingly delicate or seductively comedic. It's a tightrope-walker's strategy, similar to that which Charlie Chaplin exercised in The Great Dictator's ballet with the balloon of a globe.

Always in Glier's work, subject matter dominates style; yet style is of paramount importance. Nobody draws quite the way he does. There is a brusque illustrational flourish that insinuates urgency. There are very immediate gestural sparks that continue to ignite his drawings long after the chalk dust has settled. There is also, stylistically and compositionally, a wonderfully expressive link to the commercial graphics of a younger, more earnest America — an America that had never lost a battle or started a war (not a really big war, anyway).

Curiously, Glier's backward referencing is never used ironically and is only occasionally satiric. Rather, it is as if the almost naive boldness of his imagery was meant to serve both as an homage and a caution — an homage to the dream of a classless democracy and a caution against almost everything which stands in opposition to that dream. It is a simple and, often, knowingly simplistic program. And, if that program may occasionally appear clouded, I suspect it is due to the dust that is raised by passion.

Richard Flood
1983

Studied

1975 Rhode Island School of Design, Providence
1976 B.A., Williams College, Williamstown,
1979 M.A., Hunter College, New York City

Selected individual exhibitions

1980 *Training for Leisure: A Public Display of Collapsed Desire Designed for the Next World's Fair*, gallery installation, The Kitchen, New York City
1981 *White Male Power*, Annina Nosei Gallery, New York City
1982 *New Wall Drawings from the Exploding Refrigerator Series*, NAME Gallery, Chicago
1983 Annina Nosei Gallery, New York City

Selected group exhibitions

1979 CAGE Exhibition, Cincinnati Contemporary Art Center, Ohio
The Dog Show, Robin Winters, New York City
1980 Lisson Gallery, London
Annina Nosei Gallery, New York City
Stupid Victor Mural, Times Square Show, New York City
Vigilance: Strategies for Social Concern, a book exhibition, Franklin Furnace, New York City, co-organised with Lucy Lippard
Macho, Macho, Hot Cha Cha, window installation, Mason Gross School of the Arts, New Jersey
The Landlord Show, Delancy Street, New York City
1981 *Schemes/A Decade of Installation*, Elise Meyer Gallery, New York City
Consumerism, Group Material, New York City
Lisson Gallery Summer Group, London
Represent Representation Representative, Brooke Alexander Inc., New York City
Sexism and Racism, University of Massachusetts, Amherst and State University of New York at Binghampton
The Two Suitcase Show — An Exhibition of Great Economy, organised with Collaborative Projects Inc., And/Or, Seattle
The Anxious Figure, Semaphore Gallery, New York City
New York Black and White, Museum of Modern Art, New York City
1982 Young Hoffman Gallery, Chicago (and '83)
New New York, Florida State University at Tallahassee; travelling to Coral Gables, Florida and Phoenix, Arizona
New Figuration in America, Milwaukee Art Museum, Milwaukee
Anti-Nuke Show, Ben Shawn Gallery, William Patterson College, New Jersey
Reagan Show, Institute for Art and Urban Resources, PS1, Long Island City
Urban Kisses, Institute of Contemporary Arts, London
Banff Gallery, Banff, Canada
Face It, curated by William Olander, travelling in Ohio
1983 *Back to the USA*, Kunstmuseum, Lucerne; and Rheinisches Lanedesmuseum, Bonn; Wurttembergischer Kunstverein, Stuttgart
1983 Biennial, Whitney Museum of American Art, New York City
Art and Social Change, USA, Allen Memorial Art Museum, Oberlin, Ohio
Compassionate Images, Herron Gallery, Indianapolis
"The Revolutionary Power of Women's Laughter", Protetch-McNeil Gallery, New York City
Putting on the Ritz, Washington Project for the Arts, Washington DC

Selected bibliography

Jeffrey Deitch, "Report from Times Square", *Art in America*, September 1980
Lucy Lippard, "Sex and Death and Shock and Schlock", *Artforum*, October 1980
Flash Art, November 1980
Valerie Smith, review section, *Flash Art*, Summer 1981
Lisa Liebmann, *Art in America*, October 1981
Carter Ratcliff, "Art and Resentment", *Art in America*, Summer 1982
Sara McFadden, "The Expressionism Question", *Art in America*, December 1982

By the artist
"The 1979 Dime Store Figurine", *Artforum*, March 1980
"Patience, Observation and Investigation, Learning from Aubodon", *Artforum*, April 1982
"White Male Power", *The Paris Review*, Autumn 1982

INSTALLATION, 1984
Designed especially for the Fifth Biennale of Sydney
Courtesy of the artist and Barbara Gladstone Gallery, New York

Photography courtesy Barbara Gladstone Gallery

HANS HAACKE

Born Cologne 1936
Lives in New York

If art contributes to, among other things, the way we view the world and shape social relations then it does matter whose image of the world it promotes and whose interests it serves.

Studied

MFA Staat Werkakademie, Kassel
Atelier 17, Paris
Tyler School of Art, Philadelphia

Selected individual exhibitions

1965 Galerie Schmela, Düsseldorf
1966 Howard Wise Gallery, New York
1968 Howard Wise Gallery, New York
1969 Howard Wise Gallery, New York
1971 Paul Maenz Gallery, Cologne
1972 Francoise Lambert Gallery, Milan
Museum Haus Lange, Krefeld
1973 John Weber Gallery, New York
1974 Paul Maenz Gallery, Cologne
1975 John Weber Gallery, New York
1976 Françoise Lambert Gallery, Milan
Lisson Gallery, London
Max Protetch Gallery, Washington DC
1977 John Weber Gallery, New York
Durand-Dessert Gallery, Paris
1978 Durand-Dessert Gallery, Paris
Californian Institute of Technology, Pasadena
Museum of Modern Art, Oxford
1979 Stedelijk Van Abbemuseum, Eindhoven
Renaissance Society, University of Chicago
Gemeentelijke Culturale Dienst, Middleburg
Arnolfini Gallery, Bristol
Spectro Arts Workshop, Newcastle-upon-Tyne
New 57 Gallery, Edinburgh
South Hill Park, Bracknell
Midland Group, Nottingham
South Yorkshire Photographic Project, Sheffield
John Weber Gallery, New York
1980 Grabelija Suvremene Umjetnosti, Zagreb
Saman Gallery, Genoa

1981 John Weber Gallery, New York
Paul Maenz Gallery, Cologne
Banff Centre, Banff, Canada
1982 District 1199, New York
Southern Alberta Gallery, Lethbridge
University of Alberta, Edmonton
Mendel Art Gallery, Saskatoon, Saskatchewan
1983 Gallery France Morin, Montreal
John Weber Gallery, New York
1984 Tate Gallery, London

Selected group exhibitions

1968 *Machine as Seen at the End of the Mechanical Age*, Museum of Modern Art, New York
1969 *When Attitudes Become Form*, Kunsthalle, Bern
1970 *Biennial*, Tokyo
1972 *documenta 5*, Kassel
1973 *Contemporanea*, Rome
1976 *Biennale of Venice*
Kunstverein, Frankfurt
1977 Wadsworth Atheneum, Hartford, Connecticut
Social Criticism and Art Practice, San Francisco Art Institute
A View of a Decade, Museum of Contemporary Art, Chicago
1978 *Pop Art, Minimal Art, Koncept Kunst*, Kunstmuseum, Lucerne
Aspect Der 60er Jahre Aus Der Sammlung Reinhard Onnasch, Nationalgalerie, Berlin
1979 *Artist as Social Critic*, Municipal Art Gallery, Los Angeles
1980 *Forscher Sozialarbeiter?*, Kunsverein, Munich
1981 *Art Allemagne Aujourd'hui*, ARC, Musée d'Art Moderne de la Ville de Paris
Die Kehrseite Der Wünschdilder, Kunstverein, Bonn
International Cultureel Centrum, Antwerp
1982 *'60-'80 Attitudes, Concepts, Images*, Stedelijk Museum, Amsterdam
documenta 7, Kassel
1983 *Contra Media*, Alternative Museum, New York
Bonjour, Monsieur Manet, Centre Georges Pompidou, Paris
Master Works of Conceptual Art, Paul Maenz Gallery, Cologne
Photography in Contemporary Art: 1960s to 1980s, National Museum of Modern Art, Tokyo;

National Museum of Modern Art, Kyoto

Selected bibliography

Edward F. Fry, Hans Haacke, *Werkmonographie*, Cologne 1972
Jack Burnham, Howard S. Becker, John Walton, *Hans Haacke, Framing and Being Framed: 7 Works 1970-1975*, The Nova Scotia College of Art and Design Press New York, University Press, New York 1975
Hans Haacke, catalogue, Museum of Modern Art, Oxford; Van Abbemuseum, Eindhoven, 1978-79
Margaret Sheffield, "Hans Haacke" interview, *Studio International*, March-April 1976
Hans Haacke, "Arbeitsbedingungen", *Kunstforum*, Bd42, July 1980

WE BRING GOOD THINGS TO LIFE, 1983
Assistance from Max Hyder
Marbled wood pillar with fins, lettering, copper plate, gold leafed plaster bust and circular fluorescent tube
Overall height 279
Height of bust 68.5

In the 1950s, Ronald Reagan appeared on television in promotional campaigns for General Electric. The company is generally known for its consumer products, including light bulbs and fluorescent tubes. But it is also a defense contractor and performs major work on the nuclear warheads for the MX and other missiles. Mark 12A is the code name of these warheads. "We Bring Good Things to Life" is the slogan GE uses in its advertisements for electrical appliances. President Reagan favours the development of weapons for space warfare.

REAGANOMICS, 1982-83
Colour transparency in black wood frame
4 fixtures with fluorescent tubes
183 × 124.5
Photograph of President Reagan by Michael Evans, The White House

The *New York Post* of October 14 1982, carried a front page photograph of Ron Reagan, showing the 23 year old son of President Reagan on an unemployment line in Manhattan. He had been laid off from the Joffrey Ballet troupe, where he had worked as a dancer. Returning to his West 10th Street home in Greenwich Village, he was reported to have said: "I talked to my mother before I signed up and she said it was fine."

Courtesy the artist and John Weber Gallery, New York

Photography Fred Scruton, New York

PETER KENNEDY
with John Hughes

Peter Kennedy
Born Brisbane, 1945
Lives and works in Sydney
Currently Director of Sydney
University Art Workshop

It seems to me that the most
impressive contributions to current
progressive art, and not only in
Australia, are those which provide
not only a new image or even a new
form of language but delve down
and move out into social life itself
through long-term projects. These
works tend to be intricately stuctural,
the results of years of thought and
labour — not autonomous series for
exhibition, but on-going sequences of
learning, communication, integration,
and then relearning from the
responses of the chosen audience.
Such works concern themselves with
systems critically, from within, not
just as commentaries. Such artists
tend to be asked when they are
going to "start some new work",
because innovation in the
international art world is understood
as stylistic and *short-term*, geared to
the market. Artists aren't supposed to
go so far beneath the surface to
provoke change, but are merely
supposed to embellish, observe and
reflect the sights, sites, and systems
of the status quo. (This is also a
danger for much oppositional art
today — that its necessary
immediacy becomes reactive rather
than radically alternative in the long
run.)

On the one hand, Australian socialist
art is historically invisible, dependent
on institutions for visibility both
locally and abroad. On the other
hand, the weight of a repressive
dominant history is not so embedded
in this relatively young culture that
the possibility of change seems out of
reach. This generates a kind of
optimism that contrasts with the
situation of British activist artists who
are trapped in a formalisation of
earlier labour struggles and an
increasing pessimism. Content is
uppermost in many Australian artists'
minds, and their forms, if not "new"
in terms of the international avant-
garde, are integrated with and
specific to that content. The forms
themselves "have politics". Realism is
used as a tool rather than as a style,
often in formally interesting ways;
conceptual mediums are reversed
back to their own origins in dialogue,
away from the philosophical
obscurities of the once-powerful Art
& Language group. The "long-term"
artists tend to avoid the parochialism
of social art from the 1930s and 40s,
because their own experience is

rooted in the specifics of local
environments and campaigns and
placed within the general experience
of a country struggling like so many
others for freedom from cultural
imperialism.

Lucy R. Lippard
Extract from
"Out of Control: Australian Art on
the Left"
Village Voice
19 October 1982, New York

Selected individual exhibitions

1965	Johnstone Gallery, Brisbane
1970	*Neon-light Installations*, Gallery A, Sydney
1971	*But the Fierce Blackman*, Inhibodress Gallery, Sydney *Luminal Interferences*, Gallery A, Sydney
1976	*Introductions*, Institute of Contemporary Art, Sydney; Experimental Art Foundation, Adelaide
1980	*November Eleven*, Installation No. 1, Institute of Modern Art, Brisbane
1981	*November Eleven*, Installation No. 2, Institute of Modern Art, Brisbane *November Eleven*, Installation No. 2, Praxis, Fremantle *November Eleven*, Installation Nos 1 & 2, Ewing Gallery, Melbourne

Selected group exhibitions

1965	*Young Contemporaries*, Farmers' Blaxland Gallery, Sydney
1967	*Australian Young Contemporaries*, Argus Gallery, Melbourne
1970	*CAS Annual Exhibition*, Farmers' Blaxland Gallery, Sydney *Tim Johnson & Peter Kennedy*, Gallery A, Melbourne and Sydney
1971	*Twenty Australian Artists*, Bonython Gallery, Sydney *Activities*, Inhibodress Gallery, Sydney *Videotapes by Peter Kennedy & Mike Parr*, Inhibodress Gallery, Sydney
1972	*Trans Art 1 — Idea Demonstrations, Peter Kennedy & Mike Parr*, Inhibodress Gallery, Sydney *Peter Kennedy & Mike Parr*, A Space Gallery, Toronto; Nova Scotia College of Art & Design, Halifax *Notes and Scores for Sound*, Museum of Conceptual Art, San Francisco *Summer Festival Exhibition*, Reykjavik *Action Film Video*, Galerie Impact, Lausanne

1973	*Peter Kennedy & Mike Parr*, Gallerie Media, Neuchatel
1975	Performance, Documents, Film, Video, National Gallery of Victoria, Melbourne
1976	*Two Contemporary Artists: Peter Kennedy & John Nixon*, National Gallery of Victoria, Melbourne
1977	*Illusion & Reality*, Australian tour
1979	*Third Biennale of Sydney: European Dialogue*, Art Gallery of New South Wales
1980	*Video Mayfair*, Sydney Filmmakers' Co-op, Sydney *Videotapes from Australia*, Biennale of Venice
1981	*Australian Perspecta, 1981*, Art Gallery of New South Wales
1981-2	*Recent Australian Video Tapes*, Australian tour
1982	*¡Eureka! Artists from Australia*, Institute of Contemporary Arts, London *Australian Videotapes Touring Japan*, Japan
1983	*D'un Autre Continent: l'Australie. Le Rêve et le Réel.*, ARC, Musée d'Art Moderne de la Ville de Paris

Selected bibliography

Donald Brook, "Sydney Commentary:
New Art in Australia", *Studio
International*, London, February 1971
Lucy R. Lippard (ed), *Six Years*,
Studio Vista, London 1973
James Murray, "Australia", *Art and
Artists*, November 1972
Donald Brook, "Idea
Demonstrations . . .", *Studio
International*, London, June 1973
Noel Sheridan, *Data Magazine*, 1976
Geoffrey de Groen, "Conversations
with Australian Artists",
Quartet, 1978
Max Germaine, *Flash Art*, Milan,
June/July 1979
Sandy Kirby, "Direction in Australian
Radical Art: Affirmation and
Opposition", *Art Network*,
Sydney 1982
Lucy Lippard, "Out of Control:
Australian Art on the Left", *Village
Voice*, New York, October 1982
Peter Kennedy, "Inhibodress — Just
for the Record", *Art Network*,
Sydney 1982

JOHN HUGHES

Born Melbourne, 1948
Lives in Melbourne

Selected films

1971-72	*Nowhere Game*
1973-74	*A Film about the Kinetic Art of John Hanson*
1973	*Abortion: A Woman's Decision*
1977	*Menace*
1981	*Film Work*

1983   *Working to Live*

Selected videotapes

1972-73 Series on Contraception
1973   *American War Crimes in
        Vietnam*
1974   *Guardians in Australia
        CIA in Australia*
1979   *November Eleven*
1981   *November Eleven" — work
        in progress*
1982   *Gunara — the "Woomera
        Dancers" from Mornington
        Island*
1983   *Galiamble Half-Way House*

ON SACRED LAND,1983-84
Banner: oil paint on canvas
designed and painted by Peter
Kennedy
Videotape: colour, 3/4", mono
cassette
John Hughes and Peter Kennedy

Courtesy the artist

ANSELM KIEFER

Wood — (Cut) — Paths

Under the Title *Holzwege* (Paths Through the Woods), Martin Heidegger issued in 1950 a collection of philosophical essays prefaced by the following sentences: "Woods is an old name for a forest. In the woods are paths which mostly and suddenly entangle in wilderness. They are called paths in the woods. Each runs separately, yet in the same forest. Often they appear to be similar. Yet it only seems so. Timber getters and forest rangers know the paths. They know what it means to be off the beaten track."

In Anselm Kiefer's woodcuts, *Wege Der Weltweisheit: Die Hermannsschlacht* (Ways of World Wisdom — Hermann's Battle), the superimposition of different picture levels corresponds to different levels of reality, which point towards pathways of perception and ways of action. The lower stratum consists of single woodcuts which are put together in changing combinations. While raw woodblocks, by the pressure of their material structure, represent tree-trunks and forest, other plates are prepared by the artist. As timber getters hack paths into the forest, to cut the wood implies to clear it, in the literal as well as the metaphorical sense. The woodpath, on which sawn wood is transported, is a harvest path, but it also has the double meaning of being the wrong path. The productive artist who forsakes the conventional beaten track blazes a new path through the wilderness, and by so doing may yet lose his way. And that raises the first question: which new direction has Anselm Kiefer taken?

He uses the woodcut in a surprisingly fresh way. In modern art, this graphic technique reached its peak with the expressionist woodcuts of Edvard Munch and Ernst Ludwig Kirchner.

Since then, the vitality of the woodcut has been drained by decorative repetitions of expressionist forms. More by the interaction with photography, other print-graphic processes served the perfectionist concepts better. With Anselm Kiefer, the woodcut is not the image but its element, which is used by him as a prefabricated material for the image. The shaping of the woodcut is already completed when the actual image is created.

The woodblock is first printed "in the raw" for the reproduction of its grain, then it serves for the reproduction of the traditional images. The representation of the

heads is not an expressive art in the way that expressionist woodcut portraits are. But it is an historic quotation, a graphic transposition of old pictures, etchings or photographs of historic frames which Anselm Kiefer deals with by visualising the cutting of wood. The woodcuts comprise a layer of images which reflect nature and history.

The nature of wood points to its origins. The trunks together create a forest which has, apart from the actual, a symbolic meaning of growing and dying. Yet in Anselm Kiefer's perception, the observation of nature combines with his historical consciousness. The glimpse of the landscape sees in it, at the same time, the theatre of human history whose battles and storms — more devastating than natural catastrophies — passed over it and deprived it of its naturalness. The landscape having been changed, reshaped and destroyed by mankind, shows its traits. Hence, for Anselm Kiefer, the forest is no longer a natural forest. It is, rather, full of history. The fate of people and nations is interwoven with it. The forest, a place of decision about its rise and decline.

The Teuteburger Forest revives the memory of Hermann's Battle, which marks the beginnings of the German Empire, and the end of the Roman Empire. Like every historical event, Hermann's Battle is not only in the past but contains its effective impact; it can at any time again be transformed into present action. Klopstock and Kleist use the material of Hermann's Battle in their works in order to celebrate, in Hermann, a hero of liberation from foreign domination and to awaken nationalistic feeling. Heinrich von Kleist took his *Hermann's Battle* to be not so much an historical play as a work that falls at the centre of the early 19th century. Also in C.D. Friedrich's painting *Tombs of Old Heroes* (1812) Christian and political motifs combine into a patriotic image of the time, a call to rebellion against Napoleon. The ruined tomb bears the inscription: *"Arminius" (Herman)*.

If poets, philosophers and painters turned Hermann into a model for freedom and unity of the German people, then today the image has been overshadowed by its ideological use by the National Socialists who misused this symbol of freedom for suppression. Hermann's achievement is — like all historical facts — in every age differently assessed.

An historic event cannot be fixed as an objective happening. It can only be reflected, and it will be reflected differently, depending on the mirror which catches it. Belief in the oneness of truth and history —

testified by Friedrich Gottlieb Klobstock in the ode *The Memorial*: "Thou, Truth! and thou, History! If you are united the pen writes flames!" — disintegrated long ago. For Anselm Kiefer there is no historic truth which can be continued in a straight line towards a certain *Weltanschauung* (philosophical world view) or instruction for action. His perception is undogmatic and unheroic. The memorials collapse, when one recognises why they were erected. By making clear the subjectivity of the context, Anselm Kiefer relieves them of the impact which they make by appearing objective. By the sculptural treatment of his historic experience he freed the historical image of the accretion of layers of interpretation and ideological exploitation.

The setting of Hermann's Battle assembles the heads of poets, philosophers and field-marshals, but also Alfred Krupp and Albert Leo Schlageter (court-martialled and shot by the French in 1923) relating to the battle, or drawn by Anselm Kiefer into this context. What is important is the subjectivity of the selection. The artist does not write history, nor does he paint a picture of it. He conveys his bewilderment of events, reports about people present in his mind. The distance of centuries fades; everything is, at the time, in the here and now of perception. As the actual or imagined connection to Hermann's Battle unites the portraits thematically, so they are gathered formally round a central fire. Also, the picture of the burning logs has the ambivalent meaning of all-consuming and purifying fire, and as a symbol for spiritual fire which bestows soul on all portrayed.

With the ambiguity and the paradox of historical experience manifested in the pictures, the rare unity of art criticism is remarkable, with which Anselm Kiefer reproaches German sentimentality and National Socialist attitudes. The short glimpse of this criticism does not see the relativity of the mode of perception and recognises only an aspect of its own past, which it does not want to acknowledge. The intensity of damnation is a sign that Anselm Kiefer has touched, a complexity which has been taken as taboo and is carefully suppressed. Criticism as an act of repression, instead of following the artist in making it obvious and conscious.

Anselm Kiefer has — and perhaps art criticism is really frightened of it — rediscovered the mental image. If one thinks of his seasonal pictures, of the landscapes which represent thoughts on landscapes, of the mythological halls and chambers, then there can be no doubt that he connects with romantic tradition, and thus a further point of characterisation is achieved: Anselm Kiefer breaks with the predominance of abstract forms by providing a mental content of his pictures. Here exists a concordance with the artistic view of romanticism which places the content above its formal creation, as Thomas Gottfried Herder (*Letters for the Advancement of Humanity*) expressed it: "Form is much in art, but not all. The most beautiful forms in antiquity, a spirit, a great thought revives, which transmutes form into form and reveals its essence as in its body. Take the soul away, and the form is a ghoulish mask".

On top of the woodcuts is a coating of spontaneous painting. Traces of colour cut paths through the wilderness of the forest, appear as "annual rings", circumscribe particular heads and cut across others; painted flames ignite. Both the sufaces of the woodcuts and of the paintings bring the dialectic between past and future into the picture. The artist proves his freedom from the historical background which he has created himself. He releases the burgeoning foundations of the woodcut by his action; he is the one who acts, confronted by his memory. His action transforms — in the work as much as in life — the reconstructed subjective image of history. From the fact of the non-obective, historical context it follows that the decision of the present action forms not only the future but the past as well.

The title *Ways of World Wisdom* stands in dialectic relation to the picture. He provokes an expectation which the work refutes. The expectation is the one after an objective context of meaning in history, by a metaphysical, redemptive plan. As historical truth is a mirage, it is an error to assume that Hermann's Battle and the persons represented are necessarily connected by a coherence of meaning. Wisdom does not take actual or metaphysical paths; it is an attribute of individual people. Through the insight that there is no objective coherence of meaning, the artist establishes by the picture a subjective meaning. Now, according to Friedrich Nietsche, the highest form of art is to give life new meaning. In Anselm Kiefer's woodcut pictures the conceptual idea and the material realisation converge. Woodcut and painting combined create a work in which sensual power and content of ideas balance out.

Günther Gercken
West Germany, 1983
Translation by Rudi Krausmann and Don Maynard

DER RHEIN, 1982
Woodcut on paper on canvas
380 × 280

WEGE DER WELTWEISHEIT: DIE HERMANNSSCHLACHT, 1978-80
(Ways of World Wisdom — Hermann's Battle)
Woodcut on paper, oil on canvas
290 × 390

Courtesy of the artist

KAREN KNORR

Born in Frankfurt am Main, 1954
Lives and works in London

In *Gentlemen*, the club is considered as a theatrical site where His Story speaks through objects, paintings and a classical spatial order. Gentile men are frozen into parodies of Enlightenment. Erect, they stand, pledging allegiance to property and their ancestral fathers.
Representations already, they repeat a repertoire of gestures and rituals as if to reactivate their past history.

The work refers to a genre inextricably linked to the upper classes' formal portraiture. A portrait conventionally is the *mis en scène* of an individual (the proper name, whereby the importance of the portrait is proportioned to name and social position of the sitter). This work is non-portraiture to the extent that it doesn't focus on the individual, on the proper name but on a general stereotype of a class.

Statement by the artist

Studied

1980   Polytechnic of Central London, BA Hons Photographic Arts

Selected individual exhibitions

1980   *Belgravia*, La Remise du Parc, Paris
1983   *Gentlemen*, La Remise du Parc, Paris
1984   *Country Life*, Samia Saouma, Paris

Selected group exhibitions

1982   *GLAA Awards 80/81*, Kingston Musem and Art Gallery, London; Sunlounge Fairfield Halls, London
Cinq Photographes, ELAC, Lyons
Light Reading, B2 Gallery, London
Lichtbildnisse, Bonn
Phototextes, Musée d'Art et d'Histoire, Geneva
An Account, Nouvelle Galerie des Philosophes, Geneva
Strategies, The John Hansard Gallery, Southampton
1983   *The Expanded Media Show*, Sheffield City Polytechnic
Architecture: Sujet, Objet ou Pretexte?, Musée des Beaux Arts, Agen; Musée Bonna, Bayonne; Centre d'Art Plastique Contemporain, Bordeaux
New Beginnings, Pentonville Gallery, London
Beyond the Purloined Image, Riverside Studios, London
The Way We Live Now: Beyond Social Documentary, PS 1, New York
1984   Ravensbourne College of Art, London
The Way We Live Now: Beyond Social Documentary, Gallery 400, Chicago
Outopia: Milton and Keynes, Pentonville Gallery, London

Selected bibliography

Camerawork 12, 1979
British Journal Annual, 1980
About 70 Photographs, Arts Council of Great Britain, London 1980
"Swiss Account", *Creative Camera*, July 1981
Furor 4, Geneva 1981
European Photography, January 1982
Dumont Foto 4, 1982

GENTLEMEN, 1982-83
10 photographs from the series
Gentlemen
Each 48 × 58

BELGRAVIA, 1980
10 photographs from the series
Belgravia
Each 38 × 51

COUNTRY LIFE
4 photographs from the series
Country Life
Each 51 × 61

HIGH LIFE/LOW LIFE
2 photographs from the series
High Life/Low Life
Each 48 × 56

Courtesy the artist

BARBARA KRUGER

Born Newark, New Jersey
Lives in New York

Barbara Kruger propositions us with commonplaces, stereotypes. Juxtaposing figures and figures of speech — laconic texts superimposed on found images (Kruger does not compose these herself) — she works to expose what Roland Barthes called "the rhetoric of image": those tactics whereby photographs impose their messages upon us, hammer them home. It was Barthes who first proposed to replace the ideology of literary invention with an "ideolectology" whose operative concepts would be citation, reference, stereotype; and many artists today work within the regime of the stereotype, manipulating mass-cultural imagery so that hidden ideological agendas are exposed — or so it is supposed. But most of these artists treat the stereotype as something arbitrarily imposed upon the social field from without, and thus as something relatively easy to depose. Kruger, however, regards it as an integral part of social processes of incorporation, exclusion, incorporation and rule — that is, as a weapon, an instrument of power.

. . . An inventory of Kruger's montage techniques — she juxtaposes, superimposes, interposes images and texts — and of the ends to which these techniques are put — she exposes, opposes and deposes stereotypes and clichés — indicates the importance of a "Rhetoric of Pose" to all her work. Most of the photographs Kruger reuses were originally staged — posed — and she crops, enlarges and repositions them so that their theatricality is emphasised. She does not work with snapshots, in which the camera itself suspends animation, but with studio shots, in which it records an animation performed only to be suspended — a gesture, a pose.

Craig Owens
Extract from
*The Medusa Effect or,
The Spectacular Ruse*
New York

Selected individual exhibitions
1974   Artists' Space, New York
1975   Fischbach Gallery,
        New York
1976   John Doyle Gallery, Chicago
1979   Franklin Furnace, New York
        Printed Matter (window),
        New York
1980   PS 1, Long Island City,
        New York
1982   Larry Gagosian Gallery,
        Los Angeles
        CEPA/Hallwalls Gallery,
        Buffalo NY
1983   Annina Nosei Gallery,
        New York

Selected group exhibitions
1973   *Biennial*, Whitney Museum
        of American Art, New York
1976   John Doyle Gallery, Chicago
1977   *California Annual*,
        San Francisco Art Institute,
        San Francisco
1978   *False Face*, NAME Gallery,
        Chicago
1979   *Imitation of Life, University
        of Hartford, Connecticut
        Art and Comedy*, University
        of Chicago, Chicago
1980   *Four Different
        Photographers*, Padiglione
        Arte Contemporanea, Milan
1981   *Window, Room, Furniture*,
        Cooper Union, New York
        Moonlighting, Josef Gallery,
        New York
        19 Emergent Americans,
        Guggenheim Museum,
        New York
        Gender, Group Material,
        New York
        Pictures and Promises,
        The Kitchen, New York
        Love is Blind, Castelli
        Photography, New York
        Inespressionismo Americano,
        Genoa
        Biennale/Photography,
        Vienna
        Public Address, Annina
        Nosei Gallery, New York
1982   *The Atomic Salon*, Ronald
        Feldman Gallery, New York
        Public Vision, White
        Columns, New York
        Art and Politics, Randolph
        Street Gallery, Chicago
        Fatal Attractions,
        Renaissance Society,
        University of Chicago
        The American Exhibition,
        Art Institute of Chicago
        Resource Material, Bard
        College, Annendale-on-
        Hudson NY
        Frames of Reference,
        Whitney Museum of
        American Art, Downtown,
        New York
        Photographs In, Daniel Wolf
        Gallery, New York
        Image Scavengers, ICA,
        Philadelphia
        Biennale of Venice
        documenta 7, Kassel
1983   *Art and Social Change, USA*,
        Alen Memorial Art Museum,
        Oberlin Ohio
        Contra-Media, Alternative
        Museum, New York
        American Graffiti Gallery,
        Amsterdam
        *The Revolutionary Power of
        Women's Laughter*, Protetch
        McNeil, New York
        Young Hoffman Gallery,
        Chicago
        Kunsthalle, Basel
        Mary Boone Gallery,
        New York
        Biennial, Whitney Museum
        of American Art, New York
        *Critical Content:
        Contemporary Perspectives*,
        Long Beach Museum of Art,
        Long Beach
        *Photography used in
        Contemporary Art*, National
        Museum of Modern Art,
        Tokyo

Selected bibliography
Carrie Rickey, "Pictures and Promises", *Artforum*, April 1981
"Portraits" (conversation with B. Kruger et al), *Arforum*, May 1982
Annelie Pohlen, "The Dignity of the Thorn", *Artforum*, September 1982
Photographic portfolio –85, *Paris Review*, 1982
Hal Foster, "Window, Room Furniture", *Art in America*, 1982
Hal Foster, "Subversive Signs", *Art in America*, November 1982
Benjamin Buchloh, "Allegorical Procedures: Appropriation and Montage in Contemporary Art", *Artforum*, September 1982
Guy Bellevance, "Appropriation and Photography", *Parachute*, 1982
Roberta Smith, "Jack Goldstein's Flashes of Light", *Village Voice*, 30 March 1983
Grace Gluck, "Image Scavengers, ICA", *The New York Times*, 9 January 1983

UNTITLED (YOUR PLEASURE IS SPASMODIC AND SHORTLIVED), 1983
Black and white photograph
101.6 × 127

UNTITLED (YOU DO WHAT YOU CAN TO GET WHAT YOU WANT), 1983
Black and white photograph
182.88 × 121.9

UNTITLED (WE ARE NOT MADE FOR YOU), 1983
Black and white photograph
182.9 × 121.9

Courtesy the artist and Annina Nosei Gallery, New York

ROBERT LONGO

Born Brooklyn, New York, 1953
Lives in New York City

...Now for Longo to use old images like the statue — or elsewhere old mediums like the relief — is troublesome, but it hardly means he is celebratory of state power or *only* nostalgic for its representations (any more than with the "stock footage" of toppled monuments is he *merely* cynical about the revolutionary project of modernism). Rather, Longo is fascinated by the illusions at work in both discourses — fascinated by the confidence both of the state in its power (represented in the statue) and of the opposition in its truth (represented by the statue toppled). For in this regard the two sides are really of the same coin: they both invest in representation. To Longo, it seems, such investment is naive: in our world of diffuse subjection and delirious simulation, how can one hold to such models of power and truth?

The answer seems evident: in the authority of these representations is concealed a fear — about a lack of authority, a loss of reality. And this is what Longo explores in nearly all the new work: how, faced with this loss, our culture resurrects — morbidly, hysterically — archaic forms (here, the statue may stand for Presidential clichés about America, priestly adages about religion and family etc.) in order to recover at least the *image* of authority or a *sense* of the real. For "it is no longer a question of a false representation of reality (ideology), it is a question of concealing that the real is no longer the real, and thus of saving the principle of reality".

Hal Foster
Excerpt from
"The Art of Spectacle"
Art in America
April 1983

Studied

North Texas State University, Denton
Nassau Community College,
New York
State University College, Buffalo NY
(BFA)

Selected individual exhibitions

1976 *Artful Dodger/L'Espace Comme Fiction*, Hallwalls, Buffalo NY
The Water in the Bucket/The Cloud in the Sky, Visual Studies Workshop, Rochester NY (and performance)
Temptation to Exit/Things I Will Regret, Artists Space, New York (and performance)
Vehicule Art, Montreal (performance)

1978 *Sound Distance of a Good Man*, Franklin Furnace, New York (and performance)

1979 *An Evening of Performance and Film*, Fiorucci, New York
Surrender, The Kitchen, New York
Boys Slow Dance, The Kitchen, New York

1980 Studio Cannaviello, Milan
Surrender, Moderna Museet, Stockholm; Amerika Haus, West Berlin; American Center, Paris; Van Abbemuseum, Eindhoven (performance)

1981 Metro Pictures, New York (and '83)
Fine Arts Center, University of Rhode Island, Kingston
Empire: A Performance Triology, The Corcoran Gallery of Art, Washington DC
Larry Gagosian Gallery, Los Angeles

1982 Texas Gallery, Houston
Sound Distance, The Kitchen, New York (performance)

1983 Brooke Alexander Gallery, New York
Leo Castelli, New York

Selected group exhibitions

1975 *Working on Paper*, Hallwalls, Buffalo

1976 *Convergence and Dispersal*, Albright-Knox Art Gallery, Buffalo NY
Hallwalls Group Show, Artists Space, New York
Noise, Hallwalls, Buffalo NY

1977 *Noise II*, Hallwalls, Buffalo NY
In Western New York, Albright-Knox Art Gallery, Buffalo NY
Pictures, Artists Space, New York and tour

1978 NAME Gallery, Chicago

1979 Hal Bromm Gallery, New York
Re: Figuration, Max Protetch Gallery, New York
Hallwalls Five Years, Upton Gallery, State University College, Buffalo NY and tour

1980 *Illustration & Allegory*, Brooke Alexander Gallery, New York
A Matter of Choice: Selections by Critics, Artists and Collectors, Hal Bromm Gallery, New York
Opening Group Exhibition, Metro Pictures, New York
Drawings and Paintings on Paper, Annina Nosei

1981 *Il Gergo Inquieto*, Museo Sant'Agostino, Genoa
Picturealism — New York, Chantal Crousel Gallery, Paris
Westkunst: Heute, Museum der Stadt, Cologne
Metro Pictures, New York
On Location, Texas Gallery, Houston
Represent, Representation Representative, Brooke Alexander Gallery, New York
New Work in Black and White, Penthouse exhibition, The Museum of Modern Art, New York
Relief Sculpture, PS1, New York
Body Language: Figurative Aspects of Recent Art, Hayden Gallery, Massachusetts Institute of Technology, Cambridge and tour
US — Art Today, Nordiska Kompaniet, Stockholm
Figures: Forms and Expressions, Albright-Knox Art Gallery, Buffalo NY
35 Artists Return to Artists Space, Artists Space, New York

1982 *Flat and Figurative/20th Century Wall Sculpture*, Zabriskie Gallery, New York
A Few Good Men, Portland Center for the Visual Arts, Oregon
Dynamix, The Contemporary Arts Centre, Cincinnati, and tour
The Human Figure in Contemporary Art, Contemporary Arts Center, New Orleans
New New York, Florida State University Fine Arts Gallery, Tallahassee
Eight Artists: The Anxious Edge, The Walker Art Center, Minneapolis
Seven from Metro Pictures, Middendorf/Lane Gallery, Washington DC
Body Language: Current Issues in Figuration, University Art Gallery, San Diego State University
Focus on the Figure: Twenty Years, The Whitney Museum of American Art, New York
The New Reliefs, School of Visual Arts Museum, New York
documenta 7, Kassel
Neo-objective Sculpture, Dart Gallery, Chicago
Frames of Reference, The Whitney Museum, Downtown Branch, New York

Painting and Sculpture Today 1982, Indianapolis Museum of Art
Figurative Images: Aspects of Recent Art, Georgia State University Art Gallery
Metro Pictures, New York
New Figuration in America, Milwaukee Art Center
The Image Scavengers, Institute of Contemporary Art, Philadelphia
Art and Dance: Images from the Modern Dialogue 1890-1980, Institute of Contemporary Art, Boston and tour
Urban Kisses, Institute of Contemporary Arts, London

1983　*A Heritage Renewed: Representational Drawing Today*, University Art Museum, Santa Barbara and tour
An International Exhibition, Stiftelsen Karlsvik 10, Stockholm
Big American Figure Drawing, School of Visual Arts Museum, New York
Directions 1983, Hirshhorn Museum, Washington DC
1983 Biennial, Whitney Museum, New York

Selected bibliography

Thomas Lawson, "*Pictures* at Artists Space", *Art in America*, January/February 1978
Douglas Crimp, "About Pictures", *Flash Art*, March/April 1979
Thomas Lawson, "The Uses of Representation: Making Some Distinctions", *Flash Art*, March/April 1979
Carter Ratcliff, *Illustration & Allegory*, exhibition catalogue, Brooke Alexander Inc, New York 1980
Craig Owens, "The Allegorical Impulse: Toward a Theory of Postmodernism", *October* No 12, Spring 1980
Joan Simon, "Double Takes", *Art in America*, October 1980
Michael Shore, "Punk Rocks the Art World", *Art News*, November 1980
Carter Ratcliff, "Art Stars for the Eighties", *Saturday Review*, February 1981
Craig Owens, "Robert Longo at Metro Pictures", *Art in America*, March 1981
Kim Levin, "New York Reviews: Robert Longo, Metro Pictures", *Flash Art*, March/April 1981
Germano Celant, *Inespressionismo Americano*, Bonini Editore, Genoa 1981
Carter Ratcliff, "Robert Longo", *Flash Art*, Summer 1981
Jeanne Silverthorne, "Tableaux, Wave Hill", *Artforum*, September 1981

Carter Ratcliff, "The Distractions of Theme", *Art in America*, November 1981
Joan Casademont, "Represent Representation Representative", *Artforum*, December 1981
Helena Kontova, "From Performance to Painting", *Flash Art*, February/March 1982
Reagan Upshaw, "Figuratively Sculpting at PS 1", *Art in America*, March 1982
Flavio Caroli, *Magico Primario*, Gruppo Editoriale Fabbri, Milan 1982
Robert Hughes, "Lost Among the Figures", *Time Magazine*, 31 May 1982
Carter Ratcliff, "Contemporary American Art", *Flash Art*, Summer 1982
John Roberts, "The Art of Self-attention", *Artscribe*, No 36, London, August 1982
Carter Ratcliff, "Dali's Dreadful Relevance", *Artforum*, October 1982
Robert Berlind, "*Focus on the Figure: Twenty Years* at the Whitney", Art in America, October 1982
Rosetta Brooks, "New York's Heroic City", *Brand New York*, special issue of *The Literary Review*, London 1982
Robert Pincus-Witten, "Defenestrations: Robert Longo . . .", *Arts Magazine*, November 1982
Lynn Zelkevansky, "documenta: Art for Art's Sake", *Flash Art*, November 1982
"documenta 7 Ein Rundgang", *Kunstforum*, September/October 1982
"Empire: A Film by Robert Longo", *Museumjournal*, No 2, Amsterdam 1982
William Feaver, "The Shockers", *Observer*, London, 24 October 1982
Nena Dimitrijevic, "London, Urban Kisses, Institute of Contemporary Arts", *Flash Art*, January 1983
Grace Glueck, "Art: Works by Longo on View at Two Galleries", *New York Times*, 11 February 1983
Peter Schjeldahl, "Falling in Style, The New Art and Our Discontents", *Vanity Fair*, March 1983
Robert Hughes, "Three from the Image Machine", *Time Magazine*, 14 March 1983
Lucy R. Lippard, "Cross-Country Music", *Village Voice, New York*, 8 March 1983
Nives Ciardi, "Robert Longo", *Domus*, No 635, January 1983
Carter Ratcliff, "Robert Longo", *Interview Magazine*, April 1983

LOVE POLICE: ENGINES IN US (THE DOORS), 1982-83
Cast aluminium bonding
335.28 × 228.6 × 61

PURPLE KIDS (SOUND), 1983
Charcoal, graphite, acrylic on dyed paper
243.8 × 121.9

PURPLE KIDS (SOUND), 1983
Charcoal, graphite, acrylic on dyed paper
243.8 × 121.9

Courtesy the artist and Metro Pictures, New York

Photography courtesy Metro Pictures

COLIN McCAHON

Born Timaru, New Zealand, 1919

*My painting is almost entirely
autobiographical — it tells you where
I am at any given time, where I am
living and the direction I am pointing
in. In this present time it is very
difficult to paint for other people —
to paint beyond your own ends and
point directions as painters once did.
Once the painter was making signs
and symbols for people to live by;
now he makes things to hang on
walls at exhibitions.*

Colin McCahon, 1972

McCahon's paintings are neither
particularly private nor esoteric. If
words or symbols puzzle, the
pointers will prove to have been
implicit: learn a little Maori, check
out the Bible, look at some more
paintings. The desire to paint beyond
his own ends is inescapably there.
His subjects are often political. Cases
for what he calls "necessary
protection" abound: we need
protection from the menace of
nuclear holocaust, whales need it
from the threat of extinction. Land
may go under to the city, Maori
culture to European, the religious
impulse to a crude secularism.

McCahon is an artist of apocalypse,
of crisis. He forces the issue. And yet
there's this conservatism: the desire
to hang on to the good we seem
bent on destroying. And this: the
desire to hold together the life-work.
And this: the desire to retain all the
various and, some would argue,
mutually exclusive ways painters
have had of representing the world.
Hence his eclecticism. His
strangeness. As if everything's got to
be used and nothing is finally
adequate. Languages of art slipping
off, over, the world.

Wystan Curnow
Auckland, New Zealand

Studied

1933-35 Dunedin Technical College
Art School

Selected individual exhibitions

1948 Wellington Public Library
1958 The Gallery, Auckland
1959 Gallery 91, Christchurch
1961 Ikon Gallery, Auckland
(and '63)
1965 Barry Lett Galleries,
Auckland
1968 Bonython Art Gallery,
Sydney
Australian Galleries,
Melbourne
1969 Peter McLeavey Gallery,
Wellington (and '79)

1970 *Necessary Protection*, Barry
Lett Galleries, Auckland
1972 Retrospective, Auckland
City Art Gallery and tour
1974 *Jet Out from Muriwai*, Barry
Lett Galleries, Auckland
1975 *Jumps & Comets*, Barry Lett
Galleries, Auckland
"Religious" Works
1946-1952, retrospective,
Manawatu Art Gallery,
Palmerston North and tour
1977 *Angels & Bed*, Peter Webb
Galleries, Auckland
*McCahon's "Necessary
Protection"*, retrospective,
Govett-Brewster Art Gallery,
New Plymouth and tour
1980 Peter Webb Galleries,
Auckland
1983 Peter McLeavey Gallery,
Wellington

Selected group exhibitions

1954 *Object and Image*, Auckland
City Art Gallery
1961 *Painting from the Pacific:
Japan, America, Australia,
New Zealand*, Auckland City
Art Gallery
1964 *Contemporary New Zealand
Painting and Ceramics*, tour
of Japan, India and Malaysia
1965 *Eight New Zealand Artists*,
National Gallery of Victoria
and tour
1966 *Five Auckland Painters*,
Darlinghurst Galleries,
Sydney
1971 *Ten Big Paintings*, Auckland
City Art Gallery
1973 *Internationalem Markt fur
Aktuelle Kunst*, Dusseldorf
First Biennale of Sydney,
Sydney Opera House
1982 Opening exhibition,
Australian National Gallery,
Canberra

Selected bibliography

Charles Brasch, "A Note on the Work
of Colin McCahon", *Landfall*,
December 1950
Hamish Keith, "Colin McCahon",
Art & Australia, June 1968
Gordon H. Brown *With my Left
Hand I Write*: A Consideration of
Colin McCahon's Word Paintings",
Ascent, December 1969
Gordon H. Brown, Hamish Keith, *An
Introduction to New Zealand Painting
1839-1967*, London & Auckland 1969
Anthony Green, "Colin McCahon's
Paintings and Drawings at the Ikon
Gallery", *Bulletin of New Zealand Art
History*, No 2, 1974
John Caselberg, "Colin McCahon's
Shining Cuckoo", *Islands*, July 1977
Gordon H. Brown (ed), "Colin
McCahon: His Work Spanning Four
Decades", Art New Zealand No 8,
January 1978
Tony Green, "Colin McCahon's
Necessary Protection in Auckland",
Art New Zealand II, 1978

VICTORY OVER DEATH 2, 1970
Acrylic on canvas
207.5 × 597

Collection Australian National
Gallery, Canberra
Gift of the New Zealand Government
1978

Photography Australian National
Gallery

SYOKO MAEMOTO

Born Ishikawa Prefecture,
Japan, 1957
Lives in Yokahama city

The story of Syoko Maemoto's rejection of the Western mode of painting and conversion to the creation of *objets* in relief is typical of many of today's anti-formalist artists of the "free" style. From early on, Maemoto embraced extremely personal themes such as vague life anxieties, her desire to leave in solid form some evidence of her personal existence, and her complexes of not being loved by her parents. However, she was frustrated by her failure to express such themes using the oil painting techniques she learned at university.

This led her, after graduating from university in Kyoto, to travel five hundred kilometres to Yokohama to enter the private B Seminar School where she was allowed to choose freely whatever materials and creative methods she needed for the themes she wished to deal with. In fact, it was while she was at this school that she attracted so much attention by developing the uniquely exorcistic style that suits her very personal themes so perfectly.

Maemoto's art came into being when she began to emphasise content over form and became more faithful to the motivations of the ego than to group logic. This is not to say that Maemoto's works do no more than revel in the self. In her handmade *objets* humanity appears to be more magical than individualistic, and her constructs are always symmetrical, taking two-fold forms that mingle gentleness with outrage. These provocative and mysterious *objets* evidence a desire on her part to transcend the ego and chance to create an immortal objective reality. This attempt to portray the ego objectively is probably why she creates *objets* that are displayed on walls rather than an unlimited dispersing of works for floor display.

Studied
1980   Kyoto Seika Junior College
        (postgraduate course)
1982   B Seminar School,
        Yokohama

Selected individual exhibitions
1983   *Sweet Soul Party*, Kobayashi
        Gallery, Yokohama

Selected group exhibitions
1981   *New Painted Relief Part II*,
        G Art Gallery, Yokohama
        Children of the Sun,
        Muramatsu Gallery,
        Yokohama
        Place of Expression,
        Yokohama City Gallery
1982   *Gods of Category Mistake*,
        Group Y, Muramatsu
        Gallery, Yokohama
        To and From Form,
        Muramatsu Gallery,
        Yokohama
        Dynamite Exhibition,
        Group Y, Muramatsu
        Gallery, Yokohama
        *Artists Today, November
        Steps*, Yokohama City
        Gallery
        Girls made of Water, Gallery
        K, Yokohama
        *The Critical Point in Art
        1983*, Muramatsu Gallery,
        Yokohama

Selected bibliography
Akita Yuri, "Contemporary Art Now",
Sougetsu, February 1983
"New Style and New Generation of
Contemporary Art", *Bijutsu Techo*,
March 1983
"Art and Artists in the 1980s",
Ryukou Tsushin, March 1983
"Discussion by Three Women
Artists", *Informat Q*, June 1983
Mazar, October 1983
Ryukou Tsushin, October 1983
"Visiting the artist", *Bijutsu Techo*,
November 1983
"Art in the 1980s", *Ikebana Ryusei*,
November 1983
TRA No 4, 1983

WATER IN MY MIND, 1983
Mixed media
228 × 228

SOSHU YAKYOKU, 1983
Mixed media
228 × 228

Courtesy the artist

Photography Shigeo Anzai,
Yokohama

SANDRA MEIGS

Born Baltimore, Maryland, 1953
Canadian citizenship 1981
Lives and works in Canada

Sandra Meigs has made an important piece, a piece that's low-key with a vengeance because what's at stake in the low-keyness is a critique of the current exhortations in art towards fear and anxiety, towards the "...murder" and "collapse..." of her own soundtrack. Meigs has done a remarkable thing. She has taken a run at the prevailing sensibility by first depicting it and then withdrawing it from her depiction so that we get a new sense of distance on it.

I don't want to play up the polemics here of Meigs *vs* other 1980s art because the piece itself is smarter than that. There's no clear dividing line that says now I'm involved, now I'm not involved in 1980s anxiety, as if the sensibility was simply all wrong and that's that. With Meigs the cutting loose is cumulative and hard won. Let's not forget just what's involved here: one small picture after another illustrating boxers hitting each other, the heads and the gloves the same black shape so that sometimes they get mixed up — head or hand? hit or hitting? Captions to the drawings read: *Jab, Jab, Jab... After him even at rest... Up or Down...* By the time you get to the far end of the room, listening all the time to the shouted story of Delray's dream about a murder, and look at the two-minute film loop, every moment of the filmed boxers is imbued with a dark symbolism, a metaphysical hitting and being hit. If you want to stop here, you would have anxious art to rival the best anxious art.

This is why, when the pull-back comes, there's a degree of poignancy to it, almost as if she is not sure it's time to let go but she'll make the effort anyway. It's distance without detachment, like the voice that shouts from far off over the soundtrack, or that first long view with your ears full of noise, Meigs' critique keeps this ambivalence.

Richard Rhodes
Excerpt from review
"Semi Wind-Up Bout"
Parachute No 29
December-February 1982-83

Studied

1971-73   Rhode Island School of Design, Ceramics Major
1975   Nova Scotia College of Art & Design, BFA
1980   Dalhousie University, MA Philosophy

Selected individual exhibitions

1973   *Twenty Dresses*, Majestic Theater, Providence (performance)
1974   *Dogwatch 1* and *Dogwatch 2*, Nova Scotia College of Art & Design (performance)
1977   *A Dense Fog*, Eye Level Gallery, Halifax
Dogwatch 3, Nova Scotia College of Art & Design (performance)
1978   *A Dense Fog*, Vehicule Art, Montreal
The Pale Omnipresent Persistence, Franklin Furnace, New York; Saw Gallery, Ottawa; Eye Level Gallery, Halifax
1980   *The Maelstrom*, A Space, Toronto; 112 Workshop, New York; Anna Leonowens Gallery, Halifax
1981   *Purgatorio, A Drinkingbout*, Centre for Art Tapes, Halifax; The Ydessa Gallery, Toronto (1982)
Aphasia: Caught in the Act, Centre for Art Tapes, Halifax
1982   *Semi Wind-up Bout*, Main Exit Gallery, Vancouver; The Ydessa Gallery, Toronto
Purgatorio, A Drinkingbout, 49th Parallel, New York
1983   *Heavens to Betsy*, University of Lethbridge Art Gallery, Alberta
1984   *Temps Present/Critical Stage*, Museé des Beaux Arts, Montreal
Heavens to Betsy, The Ydessa Gallery, Toronto

Selected group exhibitions

1975   "Dogwatch Works", *Women's Bookworks*, travelling exhibition
1983   *Water/Colour*, Glendon Gallery, Toronto; Art Gallery of Northumberland, Cobourg, Ontario
O Canada, Berlin

Selected bibliography

Jennifer Oille, review, *Vanguard Magazine*, March 1982
Corinne Mandel, review, *Artmagazine* 58/59, May-July 1982
Douglas & McIntyre, *Visions: Contemporary Art in Canada*, Vancouver/Toronto 1983
Descant No 41, Summer 1983
Achille Bonito Oliva, *Trans Avant Garde International*, Milan 1983

By the artist
Dogwatch Works, with the assistance of Nova Scotia College of Art & Design, July 1975
Heavens to Betsy, University of Lethbridge Art Gallery, 1983

SEMI WIND-UP BOUT, 1982
Audio loop, sculpture/film loop
30 drawings
Each 50.8 × 66

Titles of drawings:

Round 6. Just about to get up.

Getting close to the outside option.

Up against the Ropes. Relentless.

Trying to Remember.

Round 6. He was just about to think.

Deadlock.*

Ha.

The Attendants.

Still on his feet. Just Rosey!

Coaching after the Buzzer Sounded.**

The Wrong Time to Say What He Thought.

The Referee Pulls Them Apart.

First Witness.

Round 2. Jab Jab Jab.

"I Don't Know".**

After Him Even At Rest.

Up or Down.

Maybe Things Behind Him Would Disappear.

Knockout. Speak Up!**

Jeez.

Round 3. One Minute to Go. Closing Off.

The Match Went on in One Way or Another.

A Punch out of the Kindness of His Heart.**

Purgatory.

Coached to Hold on to the Opponent.

Round 5. Wait a Minute!**

The Thing He Was at the Point of Saying.

Round 1. A Very Effective Evasion.

Going for his Kidneys.

Three Attendants Inside the Ring.

*   Collection Louis Grachos
** Collection Canada Council Art Bank

Courtesy the artist and The Ydessa Gallery, Toronto

Photography courtesy The Ydessa Gallery

CILDO MEIRELES

Born Rio de Janeiro, 1948
Lives in Rio de Janeiro

Clear Sphinx is a fragment of *Through* (1983). When I joined mashed cellophane paper and pieces of broken glass, I was not speaking of cellophane or glass but of a third and opaque subjacent thing — clear, clear sphinx: even so, it devours me.

Artist's statement
Brazil 1984

Selected individual exhibitions

1967   Museu de Arte Moderna, Bahia, Salvador
1975   *Eureka/blindhotland*, Museu de Arte Moderna, Rio de Janeiro
       Blindhotland/Gheto. Virtual Spaces: Corners, Galeria Luis Buarque de Holanda e Paulo Bittencourt, Rio de Janeiro
1977   *Sackfull Cases*, Museu de Arte e Cultura Popular, Cuiabá, Brazil
1978   *Cildo Meireles: Drawings*, Pinacoteca do Estado de São Paulo
1979   *The Sermon on the Mountain : Fiat Lux*, Centro Cultural Candido Mendes, Rio De Janeiro
       The Definite Articles, Galeria Saramenha, Rio de Janeiro
1981   Galeria Luisa Strina, São Paulo
1983   *Obscure Light*, Galeria Saramenha, Rio de Janeiro; Galeria Luisa Strina, São Paulo
       Eureka/Blindhotland, installation, Rio Arte Humaitá, Rio de Janeiro

Selected group exhibitions

1968   Museu de Arte Moderna, Rio de Janeiro
1970   *From Body to Earth*, Palacio das Artes, Belo Horizonte
       Agnus Dei, Petite Galerie, Rio de Janeiro
       Information, Museum of Modern Art, New York
1973   *Expo-projeção*, Galeria Grife, São Paulo
1976   *International Actuality*, Biennale of Venice
1979   *Excala: Aquila*, Nucleo de Arte Contemporanea, João Pessoa, Paraíba
1981   *The Sermon on the Mountain: Fiat Lux*, Museu de Arte Moderna, Rio
1982   *From Modern Art to Contemporary Art*, Gulbekian Foundation, Lisbon, Portugal
1983   *Bread in Meters*, Sul America, Rio de Janeiro

Discography

Mebs/Caraxia, independent production, 45 rpm, 1970
Salt without Meat, independent production, 33 rpm, 1977

CLEAR SPHINX, 1983
Cellophone paper, broken glass
16 m

Courtesy the artist

GIANNI MELOTTI

Born Florence, 1953
Lives in Florence

Carpet or image. The image of a
carpet. The carpet is an image. To
paint a picture like a carpet. Those
who enter the different rooms
(pattern, colour, design) decide to
leave their own house, their own
skin, their own nature. The carpet,
the picture changes continuously like
an art object, which fulfils itself in
the viewer's eye.

To sit on the carpet. The picture lies
on the floor. To prefer the horizontal
to the vertical. To invite shadow
conversations and not lyrical chit-
chat, as the artistic object is always
on the move to new shores. His
language is crass, upended, stands on
its head.

The viewer looks for a possible
anchorage and is thus already lost as
the art is always indeterminate in
colouring and surface contours; it
does not work by determining
substantial content but for change. So
it happens that the carpet assumes
constantly new forms until it
becomes an hallucinating vision of
itself.

Extract
The Carpet as an Art Object
Translation Rudi Krausmann and
Don Maynard

Studied

1968-70 Istituto d'Arte, Florence
1971-73 Magistero d'Arte, Florence

Selected individual exhibitions

1981   *Come As You Are/Jacket
       and Necktie*, Galerie
       Dioptre, Geneva; Centro
       Sixto Notes, Milan
1983   Galleria Alzaia, Rome
       Miraggi Solidi, Galerie
       Corinne Hummel, Basel
       Galerie Fina Bitterlin, Basel
1984   Galleria Franz Paludetto
       LP220, Turin

Selected group exhibitions

1975   Galleria Zona, Florence
1977   Galleria Schema, Florence
1978   Galleria Primo Piano, Rome
1979   *Il Desiderio e la
       Conoscenza*, Palazzo
       Pretorio, Certaldo
1980   Kunstlerhaus, Hamburg
1981   *Invasioni Spaziali*, Florence
       "Erweiterte Fotografie",
       *5.Internationale Biennale
       Weiner Secession*, Vienna
1982   *Sonorità Prospettiche*, Sala
       d'Arte Contemporanea,
       Rimini
       Scenario Informazione '82,
       Teatro Tordinona, Rome
1983   *Critica ad Arte*, Palazzo
       Lanfranchi, Pisa
       *Avant-Garde Photography in
       Italy*, Canon Gallery,
       Amsterdam
       Art 14'83, Galerie Corinne
       Hummel, Basel
       Kryptoniana, Galerija SKC,
       Belgrade
       Arco 84, Madrid; Galleria
       Fina Bitterlin, Basel

Selected video

1982   *Figurine*, 3/4", 26 min, Film
       & Tape Production,
       Florence
       Scanning, 3/4", 60 min,
       Film & Tape Production,
       Florence
1983   *Darkness (Enormous and
       Vacant)*, 3/4", 12 min,
       Obalne Galerije Piran and
       TV Koper-Capodistria,
       Yugoslavia

Selected bibliography

P.L. Tazzi, "Melotti Fotografo del
Tempo Fissa l'Attimo Che Trascorre",
Il Nuovo, 4 July 1975
C. Bertocci, "Un Mese", *Segno*,
January 1978
R. Bonfiglioli, *Gianni Melotti",*Flash
Art*, No 96-87, April-May 1980
C. Infante, "Esterno Notte", *Scena*,
September 1981
P. Balmas, "Roma, Scenario
Informazione", *Segno*, No 26, May-
June 1982
Ida Panicelli, *Alia Alieni ed Altro*,
catalogue, Galleria Alzaia 1983
F. Alinovi, "Avant-Garde
Photography in Italy", *Reflexions*,
No 8, 1983
R. Bonfiglioli, "E se la Critica Fosse
Pop", in *Modo*, No 60, June-July 1983
Ida Panicelli, *Kryptoniana*, catalogue,
Galerija SKC, Belgrade
R. Bonfiglioli, *Gianni Melotti*,
catalogue, Galerie Corinne Hummel,
Basel 1983
R. Bonfiglioli, *L'Immagine Corrotta*,
catalogue, Palazzo Lanfranchi, Pisa
1983

Details of works to be in the
Biennale were not available at the
time of publication.

MARISA MERZ

Born Turin, 1925
Lives in Turin

The inevitable dislocation between public and private not only affects artists but involves them more closely in the expression of their work. The sensitive fragments of Merz are often placed in two complementary but separate spaces: the openness of the gallery and the subterranean environment of a cellar (Ala, Milan 1977) or that of a space under a staircase (Biennale of Venice 1980). Both use the same knitted fabric made out of fine strands of copper, referring to the visible and the invisible. Everything is unfolded as in a diary where the structure is transparent, but fragmented and decentralised so as to almost create a continuous universe and an infinite potentiality able to be comprehended only in time. During a ten year period Marisa Merz gradually developed her work, forming a comprehensive mosaic. The exhibitions of Milan seem to be concerned with the complex interaction between her inner world and the expectation of the outside world.

...All her concerns tend towards the personal, where the work achieves a unified condition. There is no distinction between the intellectual and the physical, between the social and the private, since the states merge. Marisa Merz comes to the fore in mid-sixties when her work flourished. This was a time when the public threshold was crossed by a private one, when political art made way for dialogue.

Germano Celant
Extracts from
L'interno di Marisa
Translation Ambra Sancin

Selected individual exhibitions

1966 Galleria Sperone, Turin
1970 Galleria L'Attico-Esse Arte, Rome
1974 Galleria Toselli, Milan
1975 Galleria L'Attico, Rome
1977 Galleria Salvatore Ala, Milan
1978 Galleria Lucio Amelio, Naples
1980 Galleria Russo Tucci, Turin
      Biennale of Venice
1981 *Identite Italienne*, Centre Georges Pompidou, Paris
1982 Galerie Konrad Fischer, Dusseldorf
1984 *Il Modo Italiano*, Los Angeles Institute of Contemporary Art

Selected group exhibitions

1978 *Factura*, Palazzo Comunale, Acireale
1979-80 *Le Stanze*, Castello Colonna, Genazzano
1980 *Arte e Critica*, Galleria Nazionale d'Arte Moderna, Rome
      Biennale of Venice
1981 *Identite Italienne l'Art en Italie Depuis 1959*, Centre Georges Pompidou, Paris
      Mostra d'Arte, Acireale
      Trentanni d'Arte in Italia 1950-1980, Villa Manzoni, Lecco
1982 *documenta 7*, Kassel
      Avanguardia Transavanguardia, Mura Aureliane, Rome
      Art and Critics, Marshall Field, Chicago
1983 *Tema Celeste*, Gibellina

Selected bibliography

Tomasso Trini, "Marisa Merz", *Data*, No 16-17, June-August 1975
Germano Celant, "Una Scarpetta di Nylon Con Tanti Chiodini", *La Repubblica*, Rome, 4 December 1977
S. Sinisi, *Factura*, catalogue, Palazzo Comunale, Acireale 1978
L. Cherubini, "Le Stanzo", *Flash Art*, No 94-95, January-February 1980
L. Rogozinsky, *Flash Art*, No 98-99, 1980
Germano Celant, "L'Interno di Marisa", in *Arte e Critica 1980*, 1980
Catalogue, Galleria Nazionale d'Arte Moderna, Rome, July-September 1980
Ida Panicelli, *Art and Critics*, catalogue, Marshall Field, Chicago
documenta 7, catalogue, Kassel 1982
Achille Bonito Oliva, "Artisti Italiani Contemporanei dagli Anni '50 ad Oggi", *Flash Art*, No 113, April 1983
Germano Celant, *Il Modo Italiano*, Los Angeles 1984

ANNETTE MESSAGER

Born Berck-sur-Mer, France, 1943
Lives in Paris

. . . in the secret of her studio, Annette Messager has been devoting herself to terrifying hybridisations; she has been elaborating monsters. Annette Messager thrusts us into the blackest romanticism, the romanticism of howls bayed at the full moon, of awesome macabre emotions, the whole bathed in an atmosphere halfway between Hitchcock and Grand-Guignol.

After the images of happiness come images of terror. Clearly we are a long way from the tender ironic regard that she applied to the platitudes of our imagination. Today Annette Messager convokes dragons, witches, vampires, a whole fabulous bestiary mixed with the traditional emblems of terror: death's heads, moons, spiders, keys, scissors, knives . . . As exceptional as they may be these images effectively participate, from medieval apocalypses to the symbolism passing through fairy tales, in a heritage of the imaginary which is for all purposes quite ordinary.

. . . As a result of the manipulations carried out by Annette Messager, things are no longer in their places, the elements of the body become interchangeable, the organs undergo permutations, the rules of identity, of belonging and of resemblance can be seen to be systematically perturbed by terrifying claws. . .

. . . Now Annette Messager presses on with her art of cross-breeding and forces us to witness monstrous copulations between painting and photography.

Bernard Marcadé
Excerpt from text
Chimères
April 1983

Selected individual exhibitions

1973 Städtische Galerie im Lenbachhaus, Munich
Musée de Grenoble
Galerie Yellow Now, Liège
1974 Galleria Diagramma, Milan
Galerie Daner, Copenhagen
Galerie Saint Pétri, Lund, Sweden
Musée d'Art Moderne de la Ville de Paris
1975 Galerie 't Venster, Rotterdam
Galerie Ecart, Geneva
Galerie d'Art Contemporain, Zagreb
Galerie Space, Weisbaden
1976 Galerie Multimedia, Erbusce, Italy
Galerie Grafikmeyer, Karlsruhe
Modellbilder, Rheinisches Landesmuseum, Bonn
1977 Galerie Isy Brachot, Brussels
Galerie Seriaal, Amsterdam
1978 Holly Solomon Gallery, New York
Le Feuilleton, Rheinisches Landesmuseum, Bonn
Galerie Voksal, Warsaw
Galerie Gillespie Laage, Paris (and '80)
1980 St Louis Art Museum, St Louis
1981 Fine Arts Gallery, University of California, Irvine
San Francisco Museum of Modern Art
PS 1, New York
Hans Mayer Galerie, Düsseldorf
Artists Space, New York

Selected group exhibitions

1973 *Les Travaux de l'Atelier*, Musée Rude, Dijon
1974 *Ils Collectionnent*, Musée des Arts Décoratifs, Paris and Montreal
1975 *New Media*, Museum Malmö, Sweden
Je/Nous, Musée d'Ixelles, Brussels
1976 *Biennale of Venice*
La Photographie comme Art, l'Art comme Photographie, Chalons sur Saône and Kassel
1977 *Les Bôites*, ARC, Musée d'Art Moderne de la Ville de Paris
Maison de la Culture de Rennes
Identité/Identifications, CAPC, Bordeaux; PBA, Brussels
Selbstporträt, Kunsthaus, Stuttgart
Künstlerinnen International 1877-1977, Berlin
Festival en Juin, Museum Arnhem, Hollande
Frauen Machen Kunst, Galerie Magers, Bonn
Biennale de Paris
documenta 6, Kassel
Trois Villes — Trois Collections, Centre Georges Pompidou, Paris
Galerie Gillespie-Laage, Paris
Les Vacances, Centre d'Art et de Communication, Vaduz
1978 *Biennale de Paris*, Musée de Nice and Musée de Strasbourg
Matisse et les Artistes Contemporains, Musée de Gand, Belgium
Couples, PS1, New York
Les Artistes Français Contemporains, Serpentine Gallery, London
Third Biennale of Sydney: European Dialogue, Art Gallery of New South Wales, Sydney
Umrisse, Kunsthalle, Kiel
Artists' Books, Galerie Lydia Megert, Bern
Words, Museum Bochum
Photography as Art, West Germany
Trigon '79, Masculin/ Féminin, Kunstlerhaus Graz
Eremit? Forscher? Sozialarbeiter?, Kunstverein, Hamburg
1979-80 *Dix Ans d'Art en France*, ARC, Musée d'Art Moderne de la Ville de Paris
1980 *Zorn und Zärtlichkeit*, Galerie Maeght, Zurich
Works for Walls, Cincinnati Art Center
Biennale of Venice
FIAC 80, Paris
Ils Se Disent Peintres, Ils Se Disent Photographes, ARC, Musée d'Art Moderne de la Ville de Paris
1980-81 *Artist & Camera*, British Council tour
1981 *Från Frankrike (37 Artistes Contemporains)*, Liljevachs Konsthall, Stockholm
Art & Culture, Kunstverein Stuttgart
Toyama Now '81, Museum of Modern Art, Tokyo
Art Français, Toronto Art Fair

LES CHIMERES, 1983-84
Installation
Photographs and paint
8 units:

ARAIGNEE, NO 17
160 × 145

PAPILLONS
40 pieces each 20 × 30

LA LUNE-SEXE, NO 23
160 × 100

LE DRAGON 5 TETES, NO 42
250 × 300

L'ARBRE-LIANE, NO 51
280 × 290

LE MONSTRE-POISSON, NO 28
155 × 105

LA CLE ROUGE, NO 33
150 × 70

LA PLANETE, NO 39
80 × 100

Courtesy the artist

Photography André Morain, Paris

OLAF METZEL

Born Berlin, 1952
Lives in Berlin

Turkenwohnung Abstand 12.000 DM (VB) (Turk's Apartment Bond 12.000 DB VB) and *Tankstelle Landsbergerstrasse 193 (B2) (Petrol Station at 193 (B2) Landsberger Street)* belong to a three part series of space related works which were done between 1980 and 1982 in Berlin and Munich. To define these works is not so simple, because they distance themselves from the attendant usual terminology of contemporary art as much as from association with stylistic direction or movement. You can develop from these projects new sculptural categories, which go beyond the so called extended character of modern sculpture.

The space of these sculptures is neither (primarily) determined aesthetically, nor created artifically or artistically, with a definite externally closed volume. It is an already existing space with certain functions (as: factory, apartment, petrol station, etc.) — that is principally our total constructed environment — an endless continuum of spaces.

The notion of time which these sculptures contain, makes perhaps the most radical repudiation of the categories of permanence and eternal values of art: all works were soon destroyed after their creation, either by the artist himself or by the demolition of buildings in which they were made. The only thing that remained were documents like these photographs.

The swastika constituted the finale of *Turkenwohnung*. After the Turkish tenants had moved precipitately leaving behind all the furniture, Olaf Metzel rented the apartment. With the intention of destroying it totally, he moved in with a crowbar and other tools not usually used by sculptors. After an initial prelude of destruction and its synchronised documentation on video, the apartment was laid waste to create the space for the swastika.

This sculpture made clear that animosity towards foreigners, which today is particularly directed towards the Turks, stands in a direct historical and political line with fascism. To convert their apartment into a party room means to render the tendency of discrimination in visual terms. The monumentality gives the swastika a power which one cannot escape, and which forces an immediate and decisive stance.

The brutality finds its analogy in the colour of the floor: brilliant red which increases the terrible associations of blood and power, war and peace. The hastily added hook on the right wall suggests ironically that we like to see fascism as an already historically mastered past.

The idea which is behind the sculpture *Landsbergerstrasse 193 (B2)* was to give a significant expression to an object which was bound for demolition relating to the man in the street. The street is primarily public space, dominated by motor traffic and — for this we have the red star — political demonstrations.

While the swastika symbolises the regressive and reactionary tendencies of our society, the red star points to the East, but not only to the systems of socialism in practice. Far removed from the illusion of changing social conditions through art, here an image within the aesthetic domain was designed under the sign of the red star, through which conditions could be changed.

Swastika and red star represent cxtrcmc polcs of historical and social reality between which (political) everyday life moves. The majority of artists have retreated from this reality and prefer to produce harmless (and no less banal) "wildness". Since he never leaves this area, but searches always for on-the-spot confrontations and lets concrete daily experiences infuse his work, this gives unique importance to Metzel's sculptures.

Dr Luise C. Horn

INSTALLATION, 1984
Designed especially for
the Fifth Biennale of Sydney

Courtesy the artist

JOSEF FELIX MÜLLER

Born in Eggersriet, Switzerland, 1955
Lives in St Gallen

Opposition and Integration in Josef Felix Müller's Art

Müller's paintings are powerful, are intense. They either fascinate us, or make us turn away. Both responses indicate that something mysterious, dark and numinous is being evoked. Their power lies in their ability to lead us into something inexplicable, all-encompassing; something that is beyond our control, yet in which we all participate.

Müller says his paintings are about sexual energy. Indeed, his paintings vibrate with sexuality, and not merely due to the fact that most of his works are so obviously phallic in their content. Since sexuality is ultimately creative, it is not only logical, but necessary that the artist focus on this topic. This artist has made sexuality his central, his only topic up until now. But it is necessary for the viewer to avoid the delusion that sexuality is only sexuality. Sexuality is not just a harmless biological activity, rather it is a symbol for something that has to do with the meaning of life, with our striving and longing for the godly. A connection which has become almost lost for most of us.

In his paintings of 1981 and 1982, the artist depicted males in group situations in which sexual energy was being released (e.g. *Dance, Burning Heads*, and *Group with Head*). It is, in fact, the initiation ritual that is being depicted and not merely a form of group sex. The initiation ritual acknowledges the mysterious, acts out the mysterious in patterns of expression shared by the group's members, brings the participants into contact with the mysterious, the religious. Our culture, in contrast to ancient Greek culture, does not provide us with a god-image through which our instincts can be experienced. Our religious figures are wanting of all instincts, thus depriving us of examples for the initiation into sexual being. Thus we can easily become a victim of our own complexes.

It is the brutish aspect of sexuality which has been central in J.F. Müller's work. The brutish, dark side of sexuality has to be accepted as a uniquely human quality and not merely as something which man still has in common with lower animals. Sexuality is basically ambivalent: masculine and feminine, death and life, destruction and construction, demon and *daimon* (inner, cautionary spirit). The one-sidedness of Müller's depictions makes us aware how far removed human sexuality is from the integration of these opposites, without which there is neither self-transcendence nor emancipation; neither union between the sexes nor with the divine, of which sexuality is a symbol. . . .

Decapitation is a theme that appears throughout Müller's work. The artist himself understands this as an expression of his conviction that man is guided by his flesh and not by his mind; that the body is more important than the brain centres. This is true as long as the mind is out of touch with gut reactions. Without his head, perhaps man can feel more but he cannot act. Müller's figures are living corpses with eyes that can't see, mouths that can't speak, hands that can't reach out. Total disintegration. Man has to know what he feels, feel what he knows and do both simultaneously. For this he needs his head. Total integration, i.e. becoming totally human, requires that each individual overcome in himself the split between thought and feelings, between masculinity and femininity, by acknowledging that the dichotomy exists and that both polarities, and therefore both possibilities, are in us.

Müller achieves this integration artistically, in one of his most recent sculptures: a massive human figure carved out of wood, standing on its shoulders while balancing its severed head playfully on its up-ended feet. Its genitals are those of a hermaphrodite, with both penis and vulva; a symbolic expression of the male and female in every human being.

Carol Idone
St Gallen, Switzerland
December 1983

Selected individual exhibitions

1981   Galerie 't Venster, Rotterdam
1983   Raum fur Aktuelle Schweizer Kunst, Lucerne
      Kreuzfahrt durch die Wasserfälle, Filiale Basel
      Küss die Hand..., Kunsthaus Zurich
1984   *Biss*, Galerie Corinne Hummel, Basel
      Galerie Farideh Cadot, Paris

Selected group exhibitions

1980   Kunstlerbücher, Produzentengalerie, Munich
      Mein Weg aus der Höhle zum Fluss (performance)
1981   *Bilder*, Kunstmuseum Winterthur
      Prospekt 81 Raum für Aktuelle Schweizer Kunst, Lucerne
      FRI-ART, Fribourg
      "Fleisches Lust", Die Wiederkehr des Sinnlichen — Die Erotik in der Neuen Kunst, Galerie Paul Maenz, Cologne
1982   Kunsthalle Basel
      Swiss Avant-Guarde, Galerie Nouvelles Images, The Hague
      Galerie Farideh Cadot, Paris
      Gesichter, Galerie Corinne Hummel, Basel
      CH-OST, Kunstverein St Gallen
1983   *Drei Länder, Drei Künstler*, Bodenseemuseum Friedrichshafen
      Art 14, Galerie Corinne Hummel, Basel
      Kunst aus St Gallen, Museum Singen
      "Eros-Mythos-Ironie" Trigon 1983, Graz
      Zeichnungen, Galerie Stampa, Basel
      Sammlung Kunst Heute, Kunstmuseum Olten
1984   *Lebenszeichen*, Kunstverein, Munich

Selected bibliography

Jean-Christophe Ammann, "Übermalungen", *Kunstbulletin* No 5, Switzerland 1981
Patrick Frey, *Bilder*, catalogue text, Kunstmuseum Winterthur, 1981
Prospekt 81, catalogue, Raum für Aktuelle Schweizer Kunst, Lucerne 1981
Jean-Christophe Ammann, Bernhard Bürgi, Armin Wildermuth, catalogue text, *Katalog Kunsthalle Basel*, Basel 1982
FOTOPOST, Edition St Galerie, St Gallen 1982
Werner Jehle, *Tages-Anzeiger-Magazin*, No 11, 1982
Jean-Christophe Amman, *Art 82*, VNU Books International, Paris 1983
KREUZERNACHTIGALL, Vertrieb: Comedia, St Gallen 1983
"Situation Schweiz", *Kunstforum International*, Nos 63/64

TISCH, 1983
Dispersion on packing paper
290 × 400

ARSCH, 1983
Dispersion on packing paper
290 × 400

KOPF, 1983
Dispersion on packing paper
290 × 400

Courtesy the artist

Photography Fotoatelier Menzel St Gallen, Mühletreppe

CHRISTA NÄHER

Born 1947
Lives and works in Cologne

"Each serious examination of the occult, surrealist, phantasmagoric gifts and phenomena has as its assumption a dialectic twist, which a romantic head would never adopt. It helps not at all to emphasise pathetically or fanatically the mysterious side of the enigmatic: rather, we penetrate the mystery only to such a degree as we find it in every day life, by a dialectic insight which recognises the mundane as impenetrable, the impenetrable as mundane."

Walter Benjamin

Nature not as an idyll but as a notion of a deadly threat, as a crisis yardstick for the end of human civilisation. This is one side of the startled awareness of nature. On the other side, the material reality is not filled except by liberation of life from the shackles of rationalist planning and the extinction of living energies. Näher's pictures are aggressive, powerful — in their content component of bestial bodies, in their formal component of dark colourfulness, intensified by a piercing diffused light — in a raw expressive style. The aim of the aggression is not readily definable. An uncertain threat makes itself felt. Today it assumes for us a ghostly character. Then the struggle of the artist with the beast, the courtship, the taming, until the verging of a partnership reaching to the limit of self-respect. There is no evidence for the conclusion of such a tense relationship. It is energy itself that determines the process of painting.

The relationships between animal and human life are as clear as the vision of life itself. Not actual morality, but the vehemence of the imagination gives the pictures their fighting character.

As little as the pictures are copies, their form is more than style. Subjectivity and engagement, unconscious targeted provocation, irrationality and intellect, myth, reflection of the present and visions of the future work together in these pictures. Pathetic visions of redemption you will not find here: no recipes, but autonomous and expressive painting, which finally achieved its aim through controlled operation of means.

Annelie Pohlen
Bonn, 1983

Studied

1970-81 Academy of Fine Arts, Berlin

Selected exhibitions

1975 Kunstler vom Bodensee, Konstanz
1977 Schloss Meersburg
1980 *Finger für Deutschland*, Düsseldorf
1982 Galerie Arno Kohnen, Düsseldorf
1983 *Kutscherhaus*, Berlin

UNTITLED, 1983
Dispersion on canvas
250 × 200

UNTITLED, 1983
Dispersion on canvas
250 × 200

UNTITLED, 1983
Dispersion on canvas
250 × 200

Courtesy the artist

Translation Rudi Krausmann

ROBERT RANDALL & FRANK BENDINELLI

Both born Melbourne, Victoria, 1948
Live in Melbourne, Victoria and Pistoia, Italy

Boys meet Girls meet Boys in Randall & Bendinelli's video narratives *Love Stories*. These are stylish metaphors on the human condition using found imagery from Italian teenage photoromance magazines where, while love itself may be apolitical, universally understood images, language and gesture are taken in their sparest form, and show basic cultural meaning in human relationships. The simplicity of the romance *cliché* is woven into an elaborate visual montage with actors chroma keyed against paintings and drawings in bright linear patterns, to the beat of popular music. Out of the most basic fantasies of human posturing, the artists have created a private language through high technology.

With fluidity of presentation and effortless combinations of levels of meaning, the cliché of the Love Story becomes incongruous. By manipulation of images and technology, an instant view of different modern styles of art and gesture are read through historic conventions which have been built into computer synthesizers. The narrative progresses by electronic changes on the monitor, of pages turning and curtains opening and closing to signal resolution, while photographic panels installed either side of the monitor can be read like a fresco, or a photoromance comic. These panels are made up of images from the series of videos, for *Love Stories* is poised halfway between a film and a book, with a monitor screen that is also a canvas, and communicates in its own video language.

Jennifer Phipps
Melbourne 1982

Studied

Robert Randall
1965-67 Caulfield Institute of Technology, Melbourne (painting)
1969-72 National Theatre of Australia, Melbourne (drama)
1980 Alexander Mackie College of Advanced Education, Sydney (video)

Frank Bendinelli
1966-72 University of Melbourne (architecture)

1973-74 National Theatre of Australia, Melbourne (drama)

Selected individual exhibitions and screenings

1981 *Screens*, Reconnaissance Gallery, Melbourne
1982 Schema Gallery, Florence
Galleria Civica d'Arte Moderna, Ferrara
Sixto Notes, Milan
ICA Cinémathèque, London
Air Gallery, London
Video Bank, Amsterdam
Saw Gallery, Ottawa
Plug-In Gallery, Winnipeg
Norman Mackenzie Art Gallery, Regina, Canada
ARC Gallery, Toronto
Musée d'Art Contemporain, Cité du Havre, Montreal
1983 Ed Video Gallery, Guelph, Canada
Off Centre Centre, Calgary
Western Front, Vancouver
Alberta College of Art Gallery, Calgary
Communale Sala d'Arte, Monticantini Terme, Italy
Studentski Kulturni Centar, Belgrade
Novi Sad Kulturni Centar, Novi Sad, Yugoslavia

Selected group exhibitions

1978 *Art & Technology*, Education Department, National Gallery of Victoria, Melbourne
1979 *Video Plus 1*, Open Channel, Melbourne
1980 *Videotapes from Australia*, The Kitchen, New York; Los Angeles Institute of Contemporary Art; Video Inn, Vancouver
Project 30 — Some Recent Australian Videotapes, Art Gallery of New South Wales, Sydney
Videotapes Dall'Australia, Biennale of Venice
Biennale de Paris
1981 *The First Australian Sculpture Triennial*, La Trobe University, Melbourne
Video Plus 2, Festival of Sydney
Video Plus 3, Moomba Festival, Melbourne
International Video Art Festival, Kobe
Australian Perspecta 1981, Art Gallery of New South Wales, Sydney
Anzart Encounter, Christchurch, New Zealand
1982 *¡Eureka! — Artists from Australia*, Institute of Contemporary Arts, London

Fourth Biennale of Sydney: Vision in Disbelief, Art Gallery of New South Wales, Sydney
Biennale de Paris
Video Roma 82/83, Museo de Folklore Romano, Rome
Metropoles Festival for Video & Experimental Film, Alabama Halle, Munich
1983 *Australian Video*, tour of Japan
Art 14'83, International Art Fair, Basel
A.U.S.T.R.A.L.I.A., Zona Gallery, Florence
Continuum '83, Tokyo
D'un Autre Continent: l'Australie. Le Rêve et le Réel., ARC, Musée d'Art Moderne de la Ville de Paris
Video Cankarjev Dom '83, Ljubljana
Australian Video, Vereniging van Videokunstenaars, Amsterdam
Video/Culture Canada, Harbourfront Gallery, Toronto

Selected bibliography

Maria Kozic & Phillip Brophy, "Randelli", *New Music*, No 1, Melbourne 1981
Warren Burt, "Video in a Public Space", Cantrills Filmnotes, Nos 35/36, Melbourne 1981
Marina Vaizey, "Australia: Images for a New Generation", *The Sunday Times*, London, 4 April 1982
John Russell Taylor, "Commonwealth Aversion to Playing it Safe", *The Times*, London, 6 April 1982
Sarah Kent, "Eureka", *Time Out*, London, 2-8 April 1982
Stuart Morgan, "Kangaroo Court", *Art Network*, No 7, Sydney, Spring 1982
John Hutchinson, "Medium Hot — The New Face of Video", *In Dublin*, No 184, 1983

LOVE STORIES — TOWARDS A VIDEO NARRATIVE, 1984
Video installation

6 videotapes:
PART 1. BLIND DATE
PART 2. LOVE FEVER
PART 3. BRIEF ENCOUNTER
PART 4. FOR EVER YOURS
PART 5. FEMMES DE MODE
PART 6. A QUESTION OF STYLE
PAL, colour, stereo sound
4 photopanels, hand painted black and white photographs:

BLIND DATE
LOVE FEVER
BRIEF ENCOUNTER
FOR EVER YOURS
Each 274.3 × 243.8

Courtesy the artists

JYTTE REX

Born Copenhagen, 1942
Lives in Copenhagen

Looking backwards, the *nomad* —
and the *dreamer*, the *rebel*, the *dove*,
the *couple*, the *thinker*, the *beam*,
the *stream* stand out as essential
steps towards the picture in front of
me today. Only the words are but an
atmosphere for some motives that
have become structures in the
picture.

The structure arises, merges into
something else to disappear once
again. Exactly like the colour in an
opera. The picture started one day
and it will only end a long time from
now. An opera in slow-motion. The
colour flows like a river in the opera
just like the structures in the
everlasting picture. The picture is
also like the door, tangible, the
borderline between open and closed.
Either-or. Catch, let go, leave. What
if the door was closed? A barbarian
door. My hand bleeds into the lines.
My earlier pictures flow like invisible
structures into my work of today,
although without interfering with
what I am trying to express at the
moment. Because it is constantly
shifting just like history. So in a way,
all the earlier pictures are sketches
for the present one.

Some pictures emerge so clearly
already before I start working that a
feeling of inner certainty leads me —
a certainty referring mostly to a
specific structure where no one
specific motive is the "right one", but
where different motives are
juxtaposed. But the motives, the
picture unavoidably springs up from
the senses, from thinking in pictures
as something inevitable, through the
hand as a necessary structure. And
the structure is *vast* and always
contains its own metamorphosis — as
opposite to consciously aiming at the
use of symbols, which in my opinion
limits, constricts, excludes equally
important significations. The
equilibrium of the structure lies
between abundance and the
wilderness.

Artist's statement
Copenhagen
January 1984

Selected exhibitions

1973   *The Gallery Operetta:*
       Reconstruction of the
       Dancers
1974   *Love is like the Proletariat*
       and the Anarchy a Public
       Secret
       The Dream and the Furious
       Laughter
1980   *Crossroads and Meeting*
       Places
1982   *Night Walks*

Selected films

1977   *Veronica's Veil*
1979   *The Achilles' Heel is my*
       Weapon
1981   *Belladonna*
1982   *The Sleeping Beauty* (with
       Kirsten Justesen)

Selected bibliography

By the artist
Book of Women, 1972
Bitches in Denmark (with Inge
Eriksen), 1978
I Didn't Close an Eye, 1978
The Balk in the Eye — 80 Drawings,
1982

FIGURE, 1983
Watercolour on paper
10 units
140 × 100

UNTITLED I, 1984
Tempera/acrylic on cardboard
140 × 100

UNTITLED II, 1984
Tempera/acrylic on cardboard
140 × 100

UNTITLED III, 1984
Tempera/acrylic on cardboard
140 × 100

VERONICA'S VEIL, 1977
16 mm film

BELLADONNA, 1981
35 mm film

Courtesy of the artist

GEORGES ROUSSE

Born Paris, 1947
Lives in Paris

The art of Georges Rousse is based on a simple principle. He introduces himself into a site that is destined to be demolished: an old building, an abandoned factory, a warehouse. On the walls, the ceilings, the floorboards, he paints monumental figures (usually characters), then he takes a photograph of the entire work. The apartment, the factory, the warehouse, will be destroyed. The painting will disintegrate along with it. What remains is the photograph and that is the work of art.

Thus the art of Georges Rousse is an art of synthesis: between the *figuration libre* (free figuration) from which it is obviously derived, as we can see by its manner, by the subjects, by a sort of unselfconscious *fa presto*, and the use of the photo as it was practised by a certain number of artists in the 1920s, especially in Land art. Which is to say that he places himself in the tradition while also participating in the flourishing of bad-painting with its multi-media practices.

Michel Nuridsany
"Georges Rousse, un Baroque Flamboyant"
Le Figaro
Paris
19 January 1983

Selected individual exhibitions

1982   Bibliothèque Nationale, Paris
1983   Zabriskie Gallery, New York
        Nicola Jacobs Gallery, London
        Farideh Cadot Gallery, Paris
        CAPC, Entrepôt Lainé, Bordeaux

Selected group exhibitions

1981   Galerie de France, Paris
1982   *Biennale de Paris*
        Un Regard Autre II, Galerie Farideh Cadot, Paris
        L'Air du Temps, Galerie d'Art Contemporain des Musées de Nice
1983   Ursula Krinzinger Gallery, Innsbruck
        Galerie Nächst St Stephan, Vienna
        Grita Insam Gallery, Vienna
        Peindre et Photographier, Espace Niçois d'Art Contemporain, Nice
        Réseau Art 83, Art-Prospect, France
        Salon de Montrouge, Montrouge
        Musée des Augustins, Toulouse

Biennale de Tours
Marseille Art Présent, Galerie Athanor, Marseille
Figures Imposées, ELAC, Lyon-Perrache, Lyon
1983-84 *New French Painting*, Riverside Studio, London; Museum of Modern Art, Oxford
1984   University Art Museum, University of California, Santa Barbara
        School of Fine Arts, University of Southern California, Los Angeles
        Museum of Contemporary Art, La Jolla, California
1984-85 *Tenth Anniversary Exhibition*, Hirshhorn Museum, Washington DC

Selected bibliography

Laurent Pesanti, Patrice Bloch, "Georges Rousse", *Artistes No 11*
Michel Nuridsany, "Georges Rousse, un Baroque Flamboyant", *Le Figaro*, Paris, 19 January 1983
Maiten Bouisset, "Une Photographie pour un Instant de Peinture", *Le Matin de Paris*, Paris, 28 January 1983
Geneviève Breerette, "Georges Rousse, Figures de l'Ephémère", *Le Monde*, February 1983
W. Januszczak, *Arts Guardian*, 8 February 1983
Télérama, 26 January 1983
Artline, No 4, February 1983
"Une Fin de Siècle Difficile", *Télérama*, 2 March 1983
Figures Imposées, catalogue, Lyon-Perrache 1983
L'Air du Temps, catalogue, Galerie d'Art Contemporain des Musées de Nice 1982

UNTITLED, 1982
Photograph of installation
127 × 156

UNTITLED, 1982
Photograph of installation
127 × 156

UNTITLED, 1982
Photograph of installation
127 × 156

UNTITLED, 1982
Photograph of installation
127 × 156

UNTITLED, 1982
Photograh of installation
127 × 156

UNTITLED, 1983
Photograph of installation
127 × 156

UNTITLED, 1983
Photograph of installation
127 × 156

UNTITLED, 1983
Photograph of installation
127 × 254

UNTITLED, 1984
Photograph of installation especially executed for the Fifth Biennale of Sydney

Courtesy the artist and Galerie Farideh Cadot, Paris

Photography Galerie Farideh Cadot

KLAUDIA SCHIFFERLE

Born 1955
Lives in Zürich

"Strange" is the word: Crystal Nose

About the paintings of Klaudia Schifferle

The painting is a stage for bold poses and suggestive glances; the painting is an island seen from the air on which demons of imaginative performance and demons of disguise throng, embrace and wound themselves (the demons understood as individually changed beings and the metamorphosis of people who cannot be separated). Each and every one/thing drives his/its fellow without knowing precisely what he intends doing, while the glances of the principal actors aim straight at the viewer, who stands in front of the painting floats above the island and says to himself, "Perhaps they, too, all want something from me" and, "This appears strange, what is happening? Strangely real and, most of all, alive. Also, without doubt, unbelievably peculiar..."

The open eyes develop a hypnotic energy; faces fix the viewer, forcing him to perceive what they carry within themselves: the more genuine pain, undivided from pure lust; ambivalences like 3 Wuensche (3 Wishes), the coquettish attitudinising of the lascivious, thin-linked being, leaning one-eyed against the black bar stool which changes in the upper part into a huge black cactus-like organisim. What the eye is saying is not the same as what the legs are doing.

In the paintings of Klaudia Schifferle experiences are shown, not feelings. There are also experiences from those hallucinatory buffer-zones of everyday life, so real as to have actually been lived through. And yet the reality to which they refer is of a quite different kind: visual inventions as a treatment of very real encounters with the unusual which is everywhere. In the spikes of the cactus the births of new beings seem to announce themselves, still nearly invisible, animated like the eyes and the mouth in the leaves of the plant from which the figure of the frog develops.

In Schifferle's paintings, visions from and memories of a knowledge expand, the origin of which is suspected rather than known. Her paintings are magic carpets, magic theatres in which everything seen on the surface of the external world wants to be changed into something different, into something of one's very own. One's own view of the world is real.

Klaudia Schifferle knows what her crystal paintings are all about. The crystal in the middle of the face in the self-portrait is believable and it's not only alive because of its nose.

Patrick Frey
Switzerland
December 1983
Translation Rudi Krausmann
and Don Maynard

Studied

1971-73 Lehre als Verkäuferin
1973-76 Schule für Experimentelle Gestaltung, Zurich

Selected exhibitions

1976 Biennale of Venice
1977 Galerie AK, Zurich
1978 Zürcher Künstler in Wien, Vienna
1979 Zürcher Fotografen, Strauhof, Zurich
1980 12 Junge Schweizer Künstler, Galerie InK, Zürich
1980 Saus und Braus, Strauhof, Zurich
      Maison de la Culture, Le Havre
1981 Galerie Appartement, Geneva
      Schweizer Maler, Kunsthaus Winterthur
      Galerie 't Venster, Rotterdam
      Aljofre Barocca, Syracuse
      Galerie Gugu Ernesto, Cologne
      30 Schweizer Künstler, Innsbruck, Frankfurt, Vienna, Zug
      Phoenix, Frankfurt
      Galerie Konrad Fischer, Zurich
1982 2.Internationale Jugendtriennale der Zeichnung, Kunsthalle Nürnberg
      documenta 7, Kassel
      Galerie Toni Gerber, Bern
1983 Übersicht, Aargauer Kunsthaus, Aarau
      Galerie d'Art Contemporain, Basel
      Aktuell '83, Städtische Galerie im Lenbachhaus, Munich

Music & theatre

1978 Established music group Kleenex, later LiLiput
1979-83 Produced for Rough Trade (England) 4 single and 2 long playing records
1981 Bulu (with Astrid Spirig), Wolfenschiessen
1983 Hundeschwindel von Moskau, musical
      Cabaret Götterspass (with Astrid Spirig)
      Elfenreigen, Zurich

Selected bibliography

Dieter Hall, Dokumentation 7, InK, Zurich 1980
Bice Curiger, "New Painting in Switzerland, Flash Art, No 102, Milan 1981
Schweizerisches Institut für Kunstwissenschaft: Lexicon der Zeitgenössischen Schweizer Künstler, Verlag Huber, Frauenfeld 1981
Caroline Kesser, "Ein Subversives Lachen", Archithese, I, 1982
Siegmar Gassert, "Umso Kesser Desto Besser", Basler Magazin, No 45, 1981
"Situation Schweiz", Kunstforum, No 63/64, July-August 1983
Hans-Joachim Müller, "Aktuell 83", Die Zeit No 41, 1983

By the artist
Um des Reimes Willen Könnt ich Einen Killen, Eigenverlag, Zurich 1979
Nachbar der Welt, Verlag Dieter Hall & Martin Disler, Zurich 1980

INSEL (ISLAND), 1983
Lacquer on canvas
2 units, dia 400

3 WÜNSCHE (3 WISHES), 1983
Lacquer on canvas
210 × 297

SELBSTPORTRAIT (SELFPORTRAIT), 1983
Lacquer on canvas
Dia 200

Courtesy the artist and Elisabeth Kaufmann, Zürich

Photography Livio Piatti, Zürich

HUBERT SCHMALIX

Born Graz, 1952
Lives in Vienna

Hubert Schmalix's development is impressively logical. His use of subject, colour and composition are very flexible, although the compositions which employ a characteristic basic pattern are the most accessible. What at first sight appears to be a wide variety of colour, subject and composition, proves in retrospect to be part of a logical development, evident only when everything is seen together. The artist's constant readiness to employ new subjects and compositions, to come to terms with the art of the recent and rather more distant past, in a seemingly playful way, is characteristic of his idea of art. He is searching for areas in which a dialogue can take place; and he does so in an obviously masterful way because in a dialogue his own independent self can confront a wealth of intellectual, formal, thematic and colouristic associations. What remains constant in his work is the painterly handling, the formal reduction, the preference for colour triads and an open, often rhythmical pictorial structure.

. . . The colours are earthy, like those of vegetation. They have substance, are condensed into brilliant contrasts, are alienated and brought into an artificial system, are purified, disembodied. They playfully allude to the art of the past. The compositions and the introduction of figurative elements in the nudes reveal a decorative tension, reminiscent of Jugendstil in their strict emphasis on the flat plane. In the pictures of the still-life type, a loose arrangement of rows and division of the plane, consciously alluding to the decorative, is held together by means of the differentiated ground and the skull motifs which are developed from double to treble layers. It is precisely here that the artist's cunning intention becomes clear: to communicate a meaning beyond that of the objects themselves. This meaning is employed in an intellectual, playful and ambiguous way, just as are the formal and colouristic allusions to symbolism and the formal variations of the skeleton motif. Hubert Schmalix's methodical development should not be disparagingly described as eclecticism. In the multiplicity of quotation and association it presents us with a masterly dialogue which (Schmalix), indebted to the Mediterranean tradition, conducts so convincingly.

Wilfried Skreiner
Excerpt from
Hubert Schmalix
Thirteen paintings 1983
Gouaches on Paper 1982
London 1983

Studied

1971-76 Akademie der Bildenden Künste, Vienna

Selected individual exhibitions

1976 Künstlerhaus, Vienna
1977 Pressehausgalerie, Vienna
1978 Galerie Ariadne, Vienna
Joanneum-Ecksaal, Graz
1980 Galerie Krinzinger
1981 Galerie Droschl, Graz
Galerie Nächt St Stephan, Vienna
Galerie Krinzinger, Innsbruck
1982 Galerie Camomille, Brussels
Galerie Buchmann, St Gallen
Galerie Mazzoli, Modena
Galerie 't Venster, Rotterdam
Galerie Krinzinger, Innsbruck
Galerie Nächt St Stephan, Vienna
Galerie Bitterlin, Basel
1983 Galerie Ariadne, Vienna
Funkhaus-Galerie im ORF-Studio, Graz
Galerie Friedrich, Munich
Galerie Nächt St Stephan, Vienna
Galerie Heinrich Erhardt, Madrid
Fischer Fine Arts, London
Galerie Bleich-Rossi, Graz
Galerija Grada Zagreba, Zagreb
Holly Solomon Gallery, New York

Selected group exhibitions

1977 *XII Internationale Malerwochen*, Neue Galerie, Graz
Murgalerie, Leoben
Galerie Ariadne, Vienna
1978 *Aspekte Zeitgenössischer Österreichischer Kunst*, Museum Zeitgenössischer Kunst, Skopje
Zeitgenössische Kunst aus der Steiermark, Landesgalerie, Eisenstadt
1979 *Europa '79*, Stuttgart
Positionen, Modern Art Galerie, Vienna
1980 *Biennale of Venice*
Galerie Ariadne, Vienna
1981 *Neue Malerei in Österreich I*, Neue Galerie, Graz
Westkunst — Heute, Cologne
Galerie Ariadne, Vienna
Phönixausstellung in der Alten Opera, Frankfurt am Main
Trigon '81, Kunstlerhaus, Neue Galerie, Graz

1982 Galerie Friedrich, Munich
Galerie Buchmann, St Gallen
Junge Künstler aus Österreich, Kunstmuseum, Lucerne; Rheinisches Landesmuseum, Bonn
Augenzeugen, Galerie Gmyrek, Düsseldorf
Galerie Ariadne, Vienna
Österreichische Figuration, Galerie Friedrich, Munich
1983 Galerie bei den Minoriten, Graz
Einfach gute Malerei, Museum Moderner Kunst, Vienna
Sommeraustellung, Galerie Bleich-Rossi, Graz
Aktuell '83, Städtische Galerie im Lenbachhaus, Munich
New Art, Tate Gallery, London
Neue Malerei in Österreich '83, Neue Galerie der Stadt Linz, Linz
Zeitschnitt Österreich, Galerie Thaddaus J. Ropac, Salzburg, Linz

KOSMISCHE TRAUME I, 1983
Oil on canvas
240 × 200

KOSMISCHE TRAUME II, 1983
Oil on canvas
240 × 200

KOSMISCHE TRAUME III, 1983-84
Oil on canvas
240 × 200

Courtesy the artist

CINDY SHERMAN

Born Glen Ridge, New Jersey, 1954
Lives in New York City

Part of what's prepossessing about these pictures is what they aren't: narcissistic or exhibitionistic, for instance. Much in and about them suggests both syndromes, but all of it mediated through the work's stylistic intelligence. Sherman the performer is wholly obedient to Sherman the director...

Like Hitchcock or Kubrick, Sherman appears to understand that the success of a technological art, after the stage of conception, is largely a technical affair: realising the idea to the practical limits of the medium. Her special insight is that this rule applies even to would-be deconstructors, unless they are content merely to signal their ideological probity to each other. Her special gift is to have a profound subject — selfhood, identity — that gives to her rivalling (and implicit criticism) of state-of-the-art movie-making a sharp emotional focus. This is serious art because it is about something serious.

Very much *unlike* Hitchcock or Kubrick, Sherman takes the movie fiction of a character observed in vulnerable solitude as the departure point for an exploration, in depth, of vulnerability itself. (In the movies, it's usually a narrative set-up, as with Hitchcock's excruciatingly oblivious females: the trustingness of Teresa Wright or Janet Leigh or Tippi Hedren like a soft bulls-eye for violence). To say that Sherman "gets inside" her characters is to state the simple truth. In each case, the "outside" — costume, wig, makeup, props — is a concise set of informational cues for a performance that is interior, the dream of a whole specific life registering in a bodily and facial expression so right and eloquent — albeit "blank", "vacant", and "absent-minded" — as to trigger a shock of deep recognition.

Peter Schjeldahl
Excerpt from
"Shermanettes"
Art in America
March 1982

Selected individual exhibitions
1976   Hallwalls, Buffalo NY (and '77,'79)
1977   Visual Studies Workshop, Rochester NY
1980   Contemporary Arts Museum, Houston
        The Kitchen, New York
        Metro Pictures, New York (and '81,'82,'83)
1981   Saman Gallery, Genoa
        Young/Hoffman Gallery, Chicago
1982   Texas Gallery, Houston
        Chantal Crousel Gallery, Paris
        Larry Gagosian Gallery, Los Angeles
        Carl Solway Gallery, Cincinatti
        The Stedelijk Museum, Amsterdam, and tour
1983   Fay Gold Gallery, Atlanta
        The St Louis Art Museum
        Galerie Schellmann & Kluser, Munich
        Fine Arts Center Gallery, State University of New York at Stony Brook; Zilka Gallery, Wesleyan University

Selected group exhibitions
1975   Albright-Knox Art Gallery, Buffalo NY (and '76,'77)
1976   *Hallwalls*, Artists Space, New York
1978   *Four Artists*, Artists Space, New York
1979   *Re-figuration*, Max Protetch Gallery, New York
        Hallwalls Five Years, Upton Gallery, State University College, Buffalo NY and tour
1980   *Remembrances for Tomorrow*, New 57 Gallery, Edinburgh
        Likely Stories, Castelli Graphics, New York
        Opening Group Exhibition, Metro Pictures, New York
        Ils se Disent Peintres, Ils se Disent Photographes, ARC, Musée d'Art Moderne de la Ville de Paris
        An International Exhibition of Fourteen New Artists, Lisson Gallery, London
1981   *Il Gergo Inquieto*, Museo Sant'Agostino, Genoa
        Love is Blind, Castelli Graphics, New York
        On Location, Texas Gallery, Houston
        Photos, Metro Pictures, New York
        Autoportraits, Centre Georges Pompidou, Paris
        Body Language: Figurative Aspects of Recent Art, Hayden Gallery, Massachusetts Institute of Technology, Cambridge, and tour
        "Erweiterte Fotografie", *5.Wiener Internationale Biennale, Weiner Secession*, Vienna
1982   *Lichtbildnisse: The Portrait in Photography*, Rheinisches Landesmuseum, Bonn
        New New York, Florida State University, Tallahassee; Metropolitan Museum of Art, Carol Gables, Florida
        Art and the Media, The Renaissance Society at the University of Chicago
        Frames of Reference, The Whitney Museum, Downtown Branch, New York
        Beyond Photography: The Fabricated Image, Delahunty Gallery, New York
        Biennale of Venice
        documenta 7, Kassel
        Face It, The Contemporary Arts Center, Cincinnati, and tour
        Recent Colour, San Francisco Museum of Modern Art
        Staged Photo Events, Lijnbaancentrum, Rotterdam and tour
        New Figuration in America, Milwaukee Art Museum
        Urban Kisses, Institute of Contemporary Arts, London
        The Image Scavengers: Photography, Institute of Contemporary Art, Philadelphia
        20th Century Photographs from the Museum of Modern Art, Seibu Museum of Art, Tokyo; University of Hawaii Art Gallery, Honolulu
1983   *Photographs*, Young Hoffman Gallery, Chicago
        Directions 1983, Hirshhorn Museum, Washington DC
        1983 Biennial, Whitney Museum of American Art, New York
        Reallegory, Chrysler Museum, Norfolk, Virginia
        Big Pictures by Contemporary Photographers, Museum of Modern Art, New York
        Back to the USA, Kunstmuseum, Lucerne, and tour
        New Art, Tate Gallery, London
        Douceur de Vivre, Rennes

Selected bibliography
"Cindy Sherman: Recent Pictures", *Sun & Moon*, Fall 1979
Valentine Tatransky, "Cindy Sherman", *Arts Magazine*, June 1980
Richard Flood, "Reviews New York City — Cindy Sherman, Metro Pictures", *Artforum*, March 1981
Lynn Zelavansky, "Cindy Sherman, Metro Pictures", *Flash Art*, March/April 1981
Germano Celant, *Inespressionismo Americano*, Bonini Editore, Milan 1981
Thomas Lawson, "Last Exit: Painting", *Artforum*, October 1981

Ronny H. Cohen, "Love is Blind",
Artforum, October 1981
Jamey Gambrell, "Cindy Sherman,
Metro Pictures", *Artforum*, February
1982
Carter Ratcliff, "Contemporary
American Art", *Flash Art*, Milan,
Summer 1982
John Roberts, "The Art of Self-
Attention", *Artscribe*, No 36, London,
August 1982
Richard Rhodes, "Cindy Sherman's
Film Stills", *Parachute*,
September/October 1982
Lynn Zelavansky, "Documenta: Art
for Art's Sake", *Flash Art*, November
1982
Klaus Honnef, "Das Bild — Das
Image — under der Mensch",
Kunstforum, August 1982
William Feaver, "The Shockers",
Observer, London, 24 October 1982
Hal Foster, "The Expressionist
Fallacy", *Art in America*, January
1983
Susan Hapgood, "Cindy
Sherman/Metro Pictures", *Flash Art,*
January 1983
John Roberts, "Masks and Mirrors",
Art Monthly, London, February 1983
Klaus Honnef, "Cindy Sherman",
Kunstforum, Cologne, April 1983
Douglas Davis, "Big Pix", *Newsweek*,
2 May 1983
"Scene Stealers", *Life Magazine*, May
1983
Pepe Karmel, "Photography: Looking
at the Big Pictures", *Art in America*,
September 1983
Lisbet Nilsen, "Q & A: Cindy
Sherman", *American Photographer,
September 1983
Jeanne Silverthorne, "Directions 1983,
Hirshhorn Museum", Artforum,*
October 1983
Ronny H. Cohen, "Star Quality",
Portfolio, September/October 1983

UNTITLED, 1983
Colour photograph
205.1 × 144.2

Private collection, New York

UNTITLED, 1983
Colour photograph
88.3 × 41.9

UNTITLED, 1983
Colour photograph
85.1 × 61

UNTITLED, 1983
Colour photograph
113 × 213.4

UNTITLED, 1983
Colour photograph
87.6 × 57.2

Courtesy the artist and Metro
Pictures, New York

PETER TAYLOR

Born Sydney, 1927
Lives in Huonville, Tasmania

Peter Taylor lives some kilometres out of Hobart in an area, the Huon, redolent with a European history which goes back to pre-settlement. During the past decade he has produced a substantial body of woodcarved figurative sculpture (more recently polychromed), the formidable coherence of which is now beginning to emerge.

His works range from "mythological heroes" like *Phil Helm*, 1981 (world champion woodchopper and native of Huonville), to poignantly emotional, often self-reflexive portraits like the Janus figure *For the Term of a Natural Life*, 1981, which carries with it all of the attendant attributes of that God — motifs which run through Taylor's work. A central concern has been a series of sculptures which address themselves to the way in which Aboriginal Tasmanians conducted themselves towards others and towards the landscape. Frequently based upon early factual accounts of contact between Aborigines and Europeans, works like *Two Figures Exchanging Birds*, 1980, (dealing with the first shy and generous encounter in 1801 between an Aboriginal Tasmanian woman and the French explorer, François Peron, at the mouth of the Huon River) are paradigmatic. Also, the polychrome wood sculpture *Return to Fraser Cave*, 1982, is itself exemplary (of the broad meaning of this body of sculpture and of the formal devices he uses). It deals with the Fraser Cave episode referred to at the outset, exemplified in the haunting observation of Mike Mansell at the threshold of the cave (they were the first descendants, it is thought, to have re-entered the cave in 19,000 years):

> You can sense the spirit here . . . This is the sort of stuff we need to get the dreaming back. We have been cut off from our past. (*The Age*, 23 December 1982)

The finial, a stark, frontal and anthropomorphic form which here expresses the spirit of the cave, in other works serves to represent the figure and its easy merging into a wooded landscpe. The gesturing hand, used here as a collective entreaty, is always used economically but with the certain knowledge of art historical precedents. And the symbolic use of colour, the envelope of expressionist brush painting, which at once camouflages as it describes,

is common to much of the recent *oeuvre*.

Jonathan Holmes
Hobart, 1983

Studied
1943-44 East Sydney Technical College

Selected individual exhibitions
1978 *Sculpture and Mythical Imagery*, Watters Gallery, Sydney
1981 *Mythical Figures*, Standfield Gallery, Melbourne
1982 *Figures in a Landscape*, Ray Hughes Gallery, Brisbane

Selected group exhibitions
1970-76 Tasmanian Art Gallery Annual Exhibitions
1975 *Six Sculptors*, Fine Arts Gallery, University of Tasmania, Hobart
1976 *Sculpture Triennal*, Mildura
1979 Watters Gallery, Sydney (with Kevin Perkins)
1980 *Some Contemporary Australian Sculpture*, Newcastle Regional Gallery
1981 *Relics and Rituals*, National Gallery of Victoria, Melbourne
Art and Animism, RMIT Gallery, Melbourne
Craft Expo, Sydney
Australian Perspecta 1981, Art Gallery of New South Wales, Sydney
First Australian Sculpture Triennial, Melbourne

Selected bibliography
N. Borlase, *Sydney Morning Herald*, Sydney, 4 November 1978
Nancy Borlase, *Sydney Morning Herald*, Sydney, 22 September 1979
Sandra McGrath, *The Australian*, Sydney, 29 September 1979
Ken Scarlett, *Australian Sculptors*, Melbourne 1980
Arthur McIntyre, *Craft Australia*, Autumn 1980
P.W. White, "Coming or Going — Eight Tasmanian Artists", *Tasmanian Review*, No 3, 1980
Suzi Gablik, *Art in America*, January 1981 (reprinted *Art & Australia*, Autumn 1981)
Jonathan Holmes, review, *Mercury*, October 1981
Bernice Murphy, *Australian Perspecta 1981*, catalogue, Art Gallery of New South Wales 1981
Jonathan Holmes, *Australian Art Review*, Sydney 1982
Nick Waterlow, *Australian Art Review*, Sydney 1982
Bernice Murphy, *Australian Art Review*, Sydney 1982
L. Nordness, *The Council House*, 1982

By the artist
Art View, Hobart, Autumn 1977
"Contemporary Tasmanian Drawing", *Tasmanian Review*, No 2, Summer 1979
Review, *Mercury*, Hobart, 27 November 1981
"Kevin Perkins", *Craft Australia*, Autumn 1979

MUTE FIGURE WITH SHADOW, 1982
Polychromed wood, metal
200.7 × 139.7 × 147.3

FIGURE WITH SHADOW IN LANDSCAPE, 1983
Polychromed wood
81 × 121.9 × 195.6

LANDSCAPE FIGURE NO 1, 1983
Polychromed wood
213.4 × 50.8 × 50.8

FIGURE IN LANDSCAPE NO 2, 1983
Polychromed wood
233.7 × 91.4 × 91.4

LANDSCAPE FIGURE WITH SHADOW, 1984
Polychromed wood
182.88 × 101.6 × 76.2

Courtesy Ray Hughes Gallery, Brisbane

Photography Uffe Schultz, Hobart

VINCENT TANGREDI

Born Compobasso, Italy, 1950
Lives in Toronto

The Rite of Sinfulness

The works in themselves, the sculptures and frescos, are in search of an expression of a divine harmony, to be of a concrete and material expression, an architecture, a plan, mysteriously inspired.

The fresco *Three Living — Three Dead* is one of such expression. Shown are three monks (from the order of Friars Minor), one riding naked on a horse, two weighed down by heavy bags, symbolically carrying their own mortal remains. Death laughs in the background.

The Devil's Pigs, another fresco, portrays a child paying homage or welcoming the pleasures of vice — a struggle based on the Catholic theory of sinfulness between man's aspiration toward goodness. The wild boar receives the crown, its disposition an attribute of lust personified as passivity, receiving such pleasure. This historical relationship is the basis for the architecture or plan.

Vincent Tangredi
Toronto 1984

Studied

1970-73 Ontario College of Art, Toronto

Selected individual exhibitions

1973 Ontario College of Art, Toronto
1974 A-Space Gallery, Toronto
1975-76 Carmen Lamanna Gallery, Toronto
1976 "Beautiful Blud", *The Attractive Male, Part A*, Carmen Lamanna Gallery, Toronto
1976-77 "Transitions", *The Attractive Male, Part B*, Carmen Lamanna Gallery, Toronto
1978 *C-3 Breaking a New Record*, Carmen Lamanna Gallery, Toronto
1978-79 *The Whole Course of Art History as Menu*, Carmen Lamanna Gallery, Toronto
1980 Carmen Lamanna Gallery, Toronto
1982 *Of the Four Considerations*, Carmen Lamanna Gallery, Toronto
1983 Carmen Lamanna Gallery, Toronto
1984 49th Parallel, Centre for Contemporary Canadian Art, New York
PS 1, Institute for Art &

Urban Resources, Long Island City NY

Selected Group Exhibitions

1972 *Common Sense*, A-Space Gallery, Toronto
1973 *Information and Perception*, Art Gallery of Ontario, Toronto
1974 Carmen Lamanna Gallery, Toronto
Scan Exhibition, Vancouver Art Gallery
1974-75 Carmen Lamanna Gallery, Toronto
1975 *Open Studio*, Canadian Cultural Centre, Paris; Glenbow Alberta Art Gallery, Glenbow, Alberta Carmen Lamanna Gallery, Toronto
1976 *Ontario Now: A Survey of Contemporary Art*, Kitchener-Waterloo Gallery; Art Gallery of Hamilton, Canada Carmen Lamanna Gallery, Toronto
1977 *Transparent Things*, Vancouver Art Gallery
1978 *Kanadische Künstler*, Kunsthalle Basel Carmen Lamanna Gallery, Toronto
1979 Galerie Marielle Mailhot, Montreal Carmen Lamanna Gallery, Toronto
1980 Carmen Lamanna Gallery, Toronto (two exhibitions)
1981 Carmen Lamanna Gallery, Toronto (two exhibitions)
Moving Pictures, 16mm film Rome
1982 Carmen Lamanna Gallery, Toronto
1983-84 *The Hand Holding the Brush: Self-Portraits by Canadian Artists*, London Regional Art Gallery, London, Canada and tour
1984 *Toronto Painting*, Art Gallery of Ontario, Toronto

Selected bibliography

Eric Cameron, "Vincent Tangredi, Un Pygmalion A Rebours", *Vie des Arts*, Vol XXII No 88, Autumn 1977
Andy Patton, review, *Artists Review*, Vol 2 No 2, 13 October 1978
Jean-Christophe Ammann, Eric Cameron, *Kanadische Künstler: 11 June-16 July 1978*, catalogue text, Kunsthalle Basel, June 1978
Ian Carr-Harris, "Vincent Tangredi: The Whole Course of Art History as Menu", *Artists Review*, January 1979
Philip Monk, "Arresting Figures Vincent Tangredi", *Vanguard*, Vol 11 No 2, March 1982
John Bentley Mays, "Of the Four Considerations", *Vanguard*, Vol 12 No 2, March 1983
Ian Carr-Harris, review, *Parachute*, March-May 1983
Paul Milliken, review, *Artmagazine*, Vol 14 No 62, Sring 1983
Ron Gillespie, review, *Slip Magazine*, No 14, December 1983

By the artist
Canadian Artists in Exhibition: 1972-73, Roundstone Council, Toronto, April 1974
Canadian Artists in Exhibition: 1973-74, Roundstone Council, Toronto, December 1974
Impulse, April 1976
Queen Street Magazine, Winter-Spring Issue 1976-77
Impulse, Vol 5 No 3, Winter 1977
Impulse, Vol 9 No 1, Spring 1981
Il Cobold — Rivista di Spazi Creativi, Vol 3 Nos 8/9, January-June 1983
Impulse, Vol 10 No 3, Spring 1983

THE DEVIL'S PIG, 1983
Fresco on canvas, mounted on aluminium honeycomb panel
213.4 × 182.9

GATHERING ACORNS FOR PIGS, 1983
Fresco on canvas, mounted on aluminium honeycomb panels, polychrome wood, carved skull
Three panels, overall 213.4 × 548.6

Both courtesy of the artist and Carman Lamanna Gallery, Toronto

THREE LIVING — THREE DEAD, 1983
Fresco on canvas, mounted on aluminium honeycomb panel
213.4 × 182.9
Collection of the Canada Council Art Bank

Photography The Carman Lamanna Gallery

DRAGOLJUB RAŠA TODOSIJEVIĆ

Born Belgrade, 1945
Lives in Belgrade

Dragoljub Raša Todosijević's *Schlafflage* reflects the same line of interest that can be observed in his works such as *Was ist Kunst* and *Vive la France — Vive la Tyrannie*. In all three works, the artist shows the relationship between ethical, moral and political questions, using his favourite art form — that of performance or installation.

The performances *Was ist Kunst* and *Vive la France — Vive la Tyrannie* illustrate the manifestion of oppression, tyranny and coercion in the modern world. With its title and execution, *Schlafflage* arouses a number of associations. *Schlafflage* is a play on words and meanings with the same connotation as the abovementioned performances. It is a word coined from German *schlafen* — sleep — and *flagge* — flag; it reminds us of "sleeping flags" in the same way as *schlafwagen* (sleeping car). It is unnecessary to explain the symbolism of flags which, though sleeping, are ready to be raised especially in the context of the present world political situation.

The installation has been formed in such a way as to evoke associations of many totalitarian symbols of the past and is therefore both a sign of threat and of warning; it sublimates various symbols which, under certain circumstances, may take on an oppressive meaning.

Schlafflage causes our conditioned reflexes without alluding to anyone or anything in particular, but warning us all.

Marijan Susovski
Zagreb, 1983

Studied
1964-69 Academy of Visual Arts, Belgrade

Selected individual exhibitions
1966 Gallery Dom Omladine, Belgrade
1971 Gallery Tribina Mladih, Novi Sad
1972 Gallery SKC, Belgrade
1973 Melville College, Edinburgh
     Gallery SKC, Belgrade
1974 Gallery Kulturni Centar, Belgrade
1975 Happy New Art Gallery, Belgrade
     Gallery of Contemporary Art, Zagreb
     Gallery of Museum of Modern Art, Belgrade
1976 Art/Tape 22, Florence
1977 Studio 16e, Turin
     Galleria Civica, Modena
     Galerie Farideh Cadot, Paris
1978 Podroom, Zagreb
1980 Gallery SKC, Belgrade
1981 Gallery SKC, Belgrade
     Gallery PM, Zagreb
1982 Gallery of Museum of Modern Art, Belgrade
     Gallery of Contemporary Art, Zagreb
1983 Gallery SKC, Belgrade
     Gallery SKC, Ljubljana
     Gallery PM, Zagreb

Selected group exhibitions
1970 Gallery Kolarčev Narodni Univerzitet, Belgrade
1971 Museum of Contemporary Art, Belgrade
     Galerie Zwarte Panter, Antwerp
1972 Museum of Contemporary Art, Belgrade
     Gallery of Contemporary Art, Zagreb
1973 *Post-object Trends in Yugoslav Art 1968-73*, Gallery of Museum of Contemporary Art, Belgrade
     Eight Yugoslav Artists, Edinburgh Festival, Richard Demarco Gallery
1974 Galleria Schema, Florence
     Couples in Art and *Primary Paintings*, Gallery SKC, Belgrade
1975 *Contemporary Yugoslav Art*, Richard Demarco Gallery, Edinburgh
     Ten Contemporary European Artists, Hillyer Gallery, Smith College, Northampton MA
1976 *Yugoslav Avant-garde Art*, Galeria Wspolczesna, Warsaw
     Contemporary Yugoslav Art, tour, Britain
1977 *03-23-03*, National Museums of Canada, Montreal and Ottawa
     Happy New Art Gallery, Belgrade
     10e Biennale de Paris
1978 *Tendenze in der Jugoslawischen Kunst*, Dortmund, Berlin, Nuremburg
1979 *Tendances de l'Art Actuel en Yougoslavie*, Rome, Geneva, Brussels, Luxembourg
     Third Biennale of Sydney: European Dialogue, Art Gallery of New South Wales
     International Festival: Words and Works, De Appel, Amsterdam
1980 Museum of Contemporary Art, Belgrade
     Camera Incantate, Palazzo Reale, Milan
1981 Yugoslav Modern Art, Helsinki; Warsaw
1982 *XVI Bienal de São Paulo*, Brazil
     Museo Nacional de Arte, La Paz, Bolivia
     Artists' Photographs, Crown Point Gallery, Oakland, California
     Artists' Books, Franklin Furnace, New York
     Primary and Analytical Paintings in Yugoslavia 1974-80, Art Gallery, Osjek; Museum of Koprivnica
1983 *New Art in Serbia 1970-1980*, Museum of Contemporary Art, Belgrade

Selected performances
1971 *Marinela*, Gallery SKC, Belgrade
1972 *Place, Sculpture, Sign*, Belgrade
1973 *Decision as Art*, Gallery SKC, Belgrade
1974 *Drinking of Water*, April meeting, Belgrade
     Washing of Feet, Gallery of Belgrade Cultural Centre
1975 *Art and Memory*, Gallery SKC, Belgrade
1976-81 *Was ist Kunst?*, Yugoslavia, France, Italy, Austria, Poland, Netherlands
1977 *Condolence Book*, Gallery SKC, Belgrade
1979 *Vive la France/Vive la Tyrannie*, De Appel, Amsterdam; AKI Enschede, Art Academy, Arnhem, Netherlands

Selected bibliography
Ješa Denegri, "La Situazione Jugoslava", *Data*, No 27, Milan 1977
Jasna Tijardović, "Raša Todosijević", *The New Art Practice in Yugoslavia, 1966-1978*, Marijan Susovski (ed), Gallery of Contemporary Art, Zagreb 1978
Ješa Denegri, "Art in the Past Decade", *The New Art Practice in Yugoslavia 1966-1978*, Marijan Susovski (ed), Gallery of Contemporary Art, Zagreb 1978
Ješa Denegri, *Raša Todosijević*, Gallery of Contemporary Art, Zagreb 1982

MY NAME IS PABLO PICASSO from THE PICASSO SERIES, 1981-83
50 drawings and texts
Each 24.5 × 19

SCHLAFFLAGE, 1980-83
Mixed media
200 × 300

VIVE LA FRANCE — VIVE LA TYRANNIE, 1984
Performance

Courtesy the artist

Photography Goranka Matic

VICKI VARVARESSOS

Born Sydney, 1949
Lives in Sydney

...Varvaressos handles paint with such expressive power that it both charges and underscores the image. It is hard to think of another young Australian artist who handles with such assurance the gap between painterly abstraction and figuration: there are loose, luscious sweeps of abstraction pulsating the background of all her paintings and the forms appear from this rich welter of brush-strokes, growing in strength and intensity because of the expressionist strokes, not weakened by them.

This combination of painterly virtuosity and tough, critical image-making is unusual. An art of explicit social comment either suggests a particular form — such as murals, posters or performance — that often seeks a venue and an audience outside that of the commercial gallery or it ignores the potential of the medium at the expense of the messsage. Varvaressos does neither: she is an easel painter developing a language of form and content from a political conscience as alert and as sensitive as her aesthetic sense.

Janine Burke
Excerpt from
"Vicki Varvaressos"
Art & Australia
Vol 19 No 4
Sydney, 1982

Studied

1970-73 National Art School

Selected individual exhibitions

1975	Watters Gallery, Sydney
1976	Watters Gallery, Sydney
1977	Watters Gallery, Sydney
1978	Watters Gallery, Sydney
1980	Watters Gallery, Sydney
	Stuart Gerstman Galleries, Melbourne
1981	Stuart Gerstman Galleries, Melbourne
1982	Watters Gallery, Sydney
1983	Watters Gallery, Sydney

Selected group exhibitions

1975	*Woman in Art*, WAIT, Perth
	Watters Gallery, Sydney
1976	*East Coast Drawing: Towards Some Definitions*, Institute of Modern Art, Brisbane
1977	*Recent Women's Images of Women*, Watters Gallery, Sydney
1978	*Australian Women Artists*, CAS exhibition, Paddington Town Hall, Sydney
	Lost and Found, Ewing Gallery, University of Melbourne
1979	*Drawing '78*, Stuart Gerstman Galleries, Melbourne
	Watters Gallery, Sydney
1980	Watters Gallery, Sydney
1981	*Australian Perspecta 1981*, Art Gallery of New South Wales, Sydney
1982	*Australian Painting & Sculpture 1956-1981: Survey from the Collection*, Art Gallery of New South Wales, Sydney
	Five Contemporary Australian Painters, Tasmanian School of Art, Hobart; Queen Victoria Museum and Art Gallery, Launceston
1983	*6x6*, Orange Festival, Orange
	Classicism and Romanticism in Contemporary Australian Painting, Geelong Art Gallery

Selected bibliography

Gary Catalano, "Watters at Pinacotheca: A Partisan Review", *Arts Melbourne*, Vol 2 No 1, 1977
Margaret Plant, "Quattrocento Melbourne: Aspects of Finish 1973-77", *Studies in Australian Art*, Department of Fine Arts, University of Melbourne (1977?)
Bernice Murphy, *Australian Perspecta 1981*, catalogue, Art Gallery of New South Wales, Sydney 1981
Janine Burke, "Art for the End of the World", *Meanjin*, No 3, 1981
Janine Burke, "Vicki Varvaressos", *Art and Australia*, Vol 19 No 4, 1982

WITH HIS CHIC RED CARRERA QUAD CAM SPEEDSTER, 1982
Acrylic on canvas
216 × 104

WHY, DR PAGET . . ., 1983
Acrylic on canvas
126 × 174

CLAIRE EXPLAINS . . ., 1983
Acrylic on canvas
154 × 142

I CAN'T EXACTLY . . ., 1983
Acrylic on canvas
127 × 154

Courtesy of the artist

Photography Jill Crossley, Sydney

JENNY WATSON

Born Melbourne, 1951
Lives in Melbourne

In her new work, Jenny Watson participates in the process of personal mythmaking, utilising individual experiences, cathected imagery and private symbols to metaphorically refer to human passions and instincts. Accordingly, the style and content of her work result from the psychological connotations and emotional reactions to her subject matter. Her new work is distinctive for its uncensoring directness of response to each figure; her rendering is perceptive and deliberately abrupt. Technical refinement is rejected and artistic liberationism becomes a primary concern. The conventional stretched canvas is relinquished and unprimed, and unstretched fabrics become practical supporting materials for the "soaked" and "stained" effects, thereby physically placing her work in a workaday context which socially concerns itself with the fundamental motivations of human life.

Her paintings are translations of actual experiences, posing as an intuitive development of personal imagery — whether it be a dream image as in *Transport* or a personal hardship as in *The Horse Hospital*. The recurring horse image, which now has become a token of Watson's work, functions as a metaphor for the passions of each person. The horse is a ruling preoccupation of Watson's *milieu*, symbolising a harnessing of archetypal psychic energy which refers to the "animal" vitality in each person: either the body with its instinctive desires, or the sub-human and "bestial" impulses of the subconscious. Watson's work makes explicit the counteracting passions in each person — the compelling drive which constitutes the positive and negative side of human nature. That is, a person on one hand can be driven by love and freedom (life instinct), by dreams to transcend reality and merely life-sustaining existence, or be driven by the passion for destruction and cruelty, the malignant aggression in all of us (death instinct). In *Transport*, the artist depicts Everyman's plight out of the banality of everyday living and a striving for freedom and escape. Simultaneously, the individual can be compelled by a lust for sadism, a necrophilic streak in each of us underlying a deep-rooted desire for life to turn against itself, as represented in The Horse Hospital — a scene of carnage and butchery.

The epidermal effects of these paintings are commanding — the large scale, the expressionistic use of colour, the economy of detail, the sheer potency of linear assertiveness, the broadly painterly and vigorous handling of brushwork, the flat and frontal approach to confrontation and the pristine manner of presentation — all ways of bludgeoning the viewer to share her experience. The supreme simplistic authority of these paintings exudes an atmosphere of sensuality and brutality, of strong-mindedness and unguarded enthusiasm. Thus, Jenny Watson's paintings make an assaultive statement about human nature: a person can be driven by the desire to be free and to love, or by the passion to destroy and to torture; in each case an existential need is satisfied: the need in each of us to "effect" or to move something.

Lorena Mazzocco
Melbourne, 1984

Studied

1972   National Gallery of Victoria Art School, Melbourne
1973   State College of Victoria at Melbourne

Selected individual exhibitions

1973   Chapman Powell Street Gallery, Melbourne
1974   Powell Street Gallery, Melbourne
1975   Abraxas Gallery, Canberra
       Powell Street Gallery, Melbourne
       Ray Hughes Gallery, Brisbane
1977   Powell Street Gallery, Melbourne
1978   Powell Street Gallery, Melbourne
1980   Ray Hughes Gallery, Brisbane
       Institute of Modern Art, Brisbane
       Q Space Annex, Brisbane
       Axiom Gallery, Melbourne
       David Reid Gallery, Sydney
1981   Q Space Annex, Brisbane
       Art Projects, Melbourne
1982   Art Projects, Melbourne
1983   Roslyn Oxley 9, Sydney
       Art Projects, Melbourne

Selected group exhibitions

1974   *The Supernatural Natural Image*, Geelong, McLelland and Ballarat Galleries, Victoria
1975   *Illusion and Reality*, tour of Australian State Galleries
1978   *Still Life, Eight Women Realists*, Victorian College of the Arts Gallery, Melbourne
       Powell Street Artists at Cuningham-Ward, New York
1979   *Still Life Still Lives*, tour, Australia

Works on Paper, Watters Gallery, Sydney
1980   *On Paper, Survey 14*, National Gallery of Victoria, Melbourne
       Self Portrait/Self Image, Victorian College of the Arts Gallery, Melbourne
1981   *Real Super Real*, Albury Art Gallery
       New Realism, National Gallery of Victoria, Melbourne, tour
       The Beacon, N Space, Sydney
       Australian Perspecta 1981, Art Gallery of New South Wales, Sydney
1982   *Fourth Biennale of Sydney: Vision in Disbelief*, Art Gallery of New South Wales, Sydney
       Painting/Painting, Art Projects, Melbourne
       New Painting, Roslyn Oxley 9, Sydney
       Popism, National Gallery of Victoria, Melbourne
       The Temple of the Winds, N Space, Melbourne
       Australian Art of the Seventies — The Phillip Morris Collection, Australian National Gallery, Canberra
       The Seventies, The National Bank Collection, National Gallery of Victoria, Melbourne
1983   Art Projects, Melbourne
       A Melbourne Mood: Cool Contemporary Art, Australian National Gallery, Canberra
       Minimalism, Institute of Modern Art, Brisbane
       A.U.S.T.R.A.L.I.A., Zona, Florence
       Drawing from the Face and Figure, Heide Park and Art Gallery, Melbourne
       D'un Autre Continent: l'Australie. Le Rêve et le Réel., ARC, Musée d'Art Moderne de la Ville de Paris
       Recent Australian Painting: A Survey of the 1970s and 1980s, Art Gallery of South Australia, Adelaide
       Image-Form-Sign, Art Gallery of Western Australia, Perth
       Vox-Pop — Into the 80s, National Gallery of Victoria, Melbourne
       Mattara Exhibition, Newcastle Region Art Gallery

Selected bibliography

Paul Taylor, "Jenny Watson's *Modernism*", *Art International*, January 1981
Paul Taylor, "Australian New Wave and the Second Degree", *Art & Text*, No 1 1981

Interview, *The Virgin Press*, February 1982

John Nixon, "From a Dream", *Notes on Art Practice*, Art Projects 1982

Ashley Crawford, interview, *The Virgin Press*, November 1982

Maggie Gilchrist, "Biennale of Sydney", *Art Network*, No 6 1982

"What is this thing called Pop?", *Australian Vogue*, January 1983

"Young Blood", *Notes on Art Practice*, Art Projects 1983

Richard Dunn, "A Strategy of Parts", *Art & Text*, No 3 1981

Joanna Mendelsson, "Exhibitions — Jenny Watson", *Art Network*, No 10 1983

Frances Lindsay, "A Melbourne Mood", *Art & Text*, No 11 1983

Art Press, Paris, October 1983

Bernice Murphy, "Painting", *Australian Art Review*, Sydney 1982

Bernice Murphy, "Recent Painting in Australia", *Flash Art*, Milan, January 1983

Paul Taylor, "Popism: The Art of White Aborigines", *On the Beach*, No 1 1983 and *Flash Art*, Milan, May 1983

Paul Taylor, "Popism", *Real Life Magazine*, New York 1983

THE HORSE HOSPITAL (STUDY), 1983
Gouache on watercolour paper
121.9 × 152.4

THE HORSE HOSPITAL, 1983
Oil, acrylic, pastel, charcoal and glass beads on cotton duck
274.3 × 304.8

TRANSPORT (STUDY), 1983
Pastel, charcoal, Conté on watercolour paper
121.9 × 152.4

TRANSPORT, 1983
Acrylic, oil, ink, charcoal, pastel and cord on hessian
274.3 × 304.8

Courtesy Art Projects, Melbourne and Roslyn Oxley 9, Sydney

Photography the artist and John O'Neill, Melbourne

MICHIKO YANO

Born Tokyo, 1956
Lives in Tokyo

Michiko Yano's best known work is a complex of various objects and painting: a vessel set on the floor and filled with water that evokes images of rivers or lakes. In the background some indeterminate single-leaf screens that remind one of a stage set, are decorated with tropical plants and breaking waves. This South Pacific scene, to Japanese the essence of the romantic setting, sums up best the psychological climate of this artist. The plants, water and trees of Asian nature, and the inseparable images they invoke, provide evidence of Yano's attempts to distance herself from the influence of Western European art and demonstrate Asia's own individual artistic roots.

But with this insight we must not forget the ubiquitous central presence of human figures in her works, beckoning to the surrounding nature and distant settings. A good example is the anthropomorphic water tank she made while at university. While this human figure is a generalisation of the human being, it is also a manifestation of the human figure as seen through Yano's eyes and sensitivities. Through this central human figure, it seems, she is tryng to enfold and envelop nature, geography, and even history in a new vision.

Needless to say her central use of the human form is not anthropocentric. The human figure standing before these captivating scenes, these waves with their powerful undertow, is always a diminutive figure. It may shout and assert its presence with all its might, yet in the end it must stand humbly before nature. And although this figure represents Yano's own vision and sensibilities, it assiduously avoids depicting any particular individual and becomes a generalised human figure. It is for this reason that it is coated in bronze.

Toshaki Minemura
Japan 1983

Studied

1981   Tokyo Zokei Daigaku, BFA

Selected individual exhibitions

1981   Gallery Parergon, Tokyo
         Gallery White Art, Tokyo
1982   Gallery Te, Tokyo
1983   Kaneko Art G1, Tokyo

Selected group exhibitions

1980   Gallery Yo, Tokyo
1981   *Relation*, Shinjuku Bunka Centre
         Fifteen Women's Exhibition, Kanagawa Kenmin Hall Gallery
1982   Ginzado Gallery
         From Her Field, Kanagawa Kenmin Hall Gallery
         To and From Form, Muramatsu Gallery, Tokyo
         Photo Express from Tokyo, 1982, Space WA, New York
         Artists Today, November Steps, Yokohama City Gallery, Yokohama
1983   *Photo Express from Tokyo, 1983*, Galerie Micro, Oosterhout, Netherlands
         The Critical Point in Art 1983, Muramatsu Gallery, Tokyo
         Second Asian Art Biennale, Dacca, Bangladesh
1984   Kaneko Art G1, Tokyo
         Gallery Yo

Selected bibliography

"Pick up the Works", *Art Vision*, February 1982
Yasuhiro Yurugi, Tadashi Akatsu, "Comment on the Exhibitions", *Bijutsu Techo*, March 1982
"Art", *Calendar*, May 1982 and July 1982
"Comment on the Exhibitions, *Atelier*, August 1983
"Art", *Calendar*, 1982
Takahiko Okada, "New Stars in Art", *Asahi Journal*, 14 January 1983
Seiichi Tsukada, "Art Random", *Calendar*, January-February 1983
"Art and Artists in the 80s", *Ryuko Tsushin*, March 1983
"New Generation and New Style of Contemporary Art", *Bijutsu Techo*, March 1983
Hideki Nakamura, "Vivid Pieces", *The Ikebana Ryusei*, April 1983
Kojin Tanaka, "Exhibition", *Mainichi Newspaper*, 28 July 1983
Yuri Akita, "Art at Present", *Ikebana Sogetsu*, August 1983
Yasuhiro Yurugi, *Mizue*, Autumn 1983
Tadashi Akatsu, "Art", *Ryuko Tsushin*, October 1983
Seiichi Tsukada, "Art of the 80s", *The Ikebana Ryusei*, October 1983
Shiroyasu Suzuki, Michiko Yano, "In Correspondence", *Gendaishi Techo*, October 1983
Koichi Yasunaga, *Second Asian Art Biennale*, Bangladesh 1983

JUKO, TABLE BLUE — KILLZY, 1982
Bronze, wood, clay, acrylic, lacquer
240 × 600 × 350

Courtesy the artist

Photography Shigeo Anzai, Tokyo

EVA MAN-WAH YUEN

Born Hong Kong, 1952
Lives in Hong Kong

Eva Man-Wah Yuen, a Chinese artist from Hong Kong, began working in the mid 1970s in the mainstreams of western avant-garde art (minimalism, conceptualism, environmental projects). Her works were often temporary arrangements of on-site materials (pebbles, twigs) which, in their careful ordering, suggested primitive rituals. These gentle if rather mysterious manipulations of the outdoor environment were a record of the artist's experience in nature, a reminder of her transient human presence and a witness to her romantic strain which accompanied the more cerebral conceptual framework of her art. She has only recently sought a more private, autobiographical expression exploring her own Chinese cultural heritage.

Such concerns began to appear in her project *Growing* (1979), an installation which documented in photographs, video tape, printed interviews and a constructed garden of seedlings, her study of an overseas Chinese family transplanted to New Zealand. In *Two Faces* (1980), Yuen moved to a more specifically autobiographical format, using her own photographic portraits to express the socio/political polarities of life in China and Hong Kong, and showing how each environment inevitably conditions and transforms the individual

In *The Third Face*, the photographic portraits of Two Faces reappear on a vastly enlarged scale and serve as an introduction to a startling environment of Chinese paper heads. One — the Third Face — is fashioned in the artist's own image. These standard paper constructions, traditionally used by Chinese craftsmen for the folk art figures in Chinese festivals and funeral rites, are here radically altered and wrenched from their normal context (without, however, losing their weighty cultural content, both festive and funereal) to serve as fetishistic references to the archetypal Chinese Woman, past and present, in China and out. (Note Yuen's depiction of exaggerated historical and contemporary hair styles with their whimsical abstract additions.)

Yet in this post-modernist work in which the artist displays her knowledge of traditional Chinese crafts, one still sees her modernist formal concerns: the grid-like arrangement of the heads on a regular bamboo sub-structure attests to her origins in conceptual art; the ready-made character of the heads (though substantially transformed by the artist) recalls her earlier use and subtle re-ordering of found natural objects. But in the sheer number of heads included, her romantic strain also resurfaces, calling up thoughts on the individual in the crowd, one Chinese woman among countless Chinese women (past and present), one face (Yuen's) among many faces. In attempting to come to grips with the artist's own Chinese society, heritage and crafts, Yuen has not dismissed universal concerns. Her private discourse is rich in public meaning.

Kathryn Moore Heleniak
Hong Kong
December 1983

Study

1970-74 Colombus College of Art & Design, Ohio US
1975-77 University of Case Western Reserve, Ohio

Selected individual exhibitions

1977 University of Case Western Reserve, Ohio
1978 Wellington Settlement Gallery, Wellington NZ
1979 Sculpture Centre, Sydney Experimental Art Foundation, Adelaide Queen Elizabeth Walk, Singapore
1980 Star Ferry, Hong Kong Hong Kong Arts Centre
1982 Swire Hall, University of Hong Kong

Selected group exhibitions

1978 *Small Works*, City Art Gallery, Auckland NZ
Project Programme, City Art Gallery, Auckland NZ
Work: Documentation by Five Wellington Artists, New Zealand Academy of Fine Art, Wellington
1979 *Propositions*, National Art Gallery, Wellington
1982 *Contemporary Hong Kong Artists Invitational 1982*, Tangeman Fine Arts Gallery, Cincinnati
1983 *Works by Artists Educated in the US*, American Library, Hong Kong

Selected performances

1978 *Sonic Five — Birth*, Radio New Zealand, Wellington
1979 *Colour, Smell & Taste*, Experimental Art Foundation, Adelaide
1979-80 *Two Faces*, Nanking, China and Hong Kong
1980 *MTR Districts in My Eyes*, Mass Transit Railway, Hong Kong
1982 *Nam Shan Estate Wall Mural Project*, Sham Shui Po District, Hong Kong

Selected bibliography

"Of Cabbages and String", *NZ Listener*, May 1978
"The Artists' Co-op", *Art New Zealand*, Winter 1978
"Plants, Earth and Rocks", *The Advertiser*, Adelaide, June 1979
"Nature Reinstalled", *The Nation*, Singapore, September 1979

By the artist
Kapiti Island Experiences, Auckland City Art Gallery, Auckland 1978
A Day with Michael Chan, Experimental Art Foundation, Adelaide 1979
Two Faces, Hong Kong 1980

THE THIRD FACE, 1984
Paper heads, 200 units each 20.3
Photographs, 3 units each
182.9 × 121.9

The materials for this project have been generously sponsored by Mr Y.K. Mok, Director of Art Pulse Contemporary Arts and Research Ltd, Hong Kong

Courtesy the artist

Photography Ng Hon-Lam, Hong Kong